The Politics of Arabic in Israel

The Politics of Arabic in Israel

A Sociolinguistic Analysis

Camelia Suleiman

EDINBURGH
University Press

Edinburgh University Press is one of the leading university presses in the UK. We publish academic books and journals in our selected subject areas across the humanities and social sciences, combining cutting-edge scholarship with high editorial and production values to produce academic works of lasting importance. For more information visit our website: edinburghuniversitypress.com

Edinburgh University Press Ltd
The Tun – Holyrood Road
12 (2f) Jackson's Entry
Edinburgh EH8 8PJ

Typeset in 11/15 Adobe Garamond Pro by
Manila Typesetting Company

A CIP record for this book is available from the British Library

ISBN 978 1 4744 2086 0 (hardback)
ISBN 978 1 4744 2087 7 (webready PDF)
ISBN 978 1 4744 2088 4 (epub)

Contents

Figures

Acknowledgements

This book is the product of a lifetime of engagement with the question of language, legal status and political and social space for the Palestinian citizens of Israel. It would have been inconceivable, however, without dialectic involvement in recent scholarship dealing with the question of the Palestinians in Israel. A dialogue with three works provide the scholarly background of this study. I am indebted to Gil Eyal (2006), Yonatan Mendel (2014a and 2014b) and Ahmad Saʿdi (2014). Last but not least, this book would not have been written without the intellectual rigour combined with humanistic enrichment which Ilan Pappé's scholarship has provided to the study of the conflict. I am indebted to him.

Conversations and correspondence with many people have also enriched this book indescribably. My thanks go to: Amir Abu Jabal, Mahmoud Abu Rajab, Zuhair Bahloul, Ibrahim Bassal, Rayeq Bawardi, Zvi Bekerman, Jawdat Eid, Hunaida Ghanim , Amir Hallol, Hanna Jubran, Zohar Kampf, Khaloub Kawar, Siba Khatib, Usama Khatib, Amnon Levi, Maroun Maalouf, Samih Maʿāytah, Raja Marjiyeh, Haseeb Shehadeh, Yehouda Shenhav, Roger Tabor, Ibrahim Ṭāha, Ruba Warwar, Ali Watad and Iman Younis. If there are names I have missed, I apologise. I also thank Ifat Maoz and Menachem Blondheim. I am also indebted to the late Shoshana Blum-Kulka.

I also thank the Muslim Studies Program, the Delia Koo fund at the Asian Studies Center, and the College of Arts and Letters, at Michigan State

University for travel and research funding which allowed me to conduct this research. I also thank Muslim Studies for a course release which helped me finish the book, but above all, for creating a safe haven for discussing ideas with faculty members from different academic and cultural backgrounds. The Harry S. Truman Institute for the Advancement for Peace at the Hebrew University of Jerusalem provided a research grant which helped me conduct the research for this book. I am thankful to all.

Special thanks go to Mohammad Alhawary, an old colleague whose advice is much valued. My special thanks also go to Bernard Spolsky who keenly reviewed the book, in its entirety, and who gave me valuable feedback. I also thank the wonderful team at the University of Edinburgh Press for making this book happen. I thank Nicola Ramsey, Ellie Bush, Rebecca Mackenzie, Eddie Clark; and last but not least, Christine Barton for the copy-editing. Thanks also go to Daniel C. O'Connell and Barbara Hicks for their friendship. At Michigan State University I would like to thank Bilqes Al-Barrak, Isis Alam, Anas Attal, Marc Bernstein, Waseem El-Rayes, Sonja Fritzsche, Kenneth Harrow, Salah Hassan, Najib Hourani, Sadam Issa, Mohammad Khalil, Christopher Long, Ayman Mohamed, Brady Ryan, Jyotsna Singh, Marianne Triponi and Suzanne Wagner. I thank Leila Monaghan for organising a conference on 'language, history and culture' at the University of Wyoming and for setting me to think seriously about writing a book on language issues in Israel. I also thank Michael Silverstein, whose intellectual rigour set a high standard for me, which I aspire to reach. I am also in debt to the late Father Solomon Sara at Georgetown University.

I am indebted to my family for supporting my academic endeavour for all of these years: my parents and my siblings who never doubted me, and my husband and children for providing a space for me to write.

I dedicate this book to the memory of Ali Faraj (1941–2016), a humanist, fighter and language lover.

والأرض تورَثُ كاللغة

'Land is inherited, like language'
Mahmoud Darwish (1942–2008)

Introduction

Palestinian poet laureate, Mahmoud Darwish writes that land is inherited like language. Most accounts of Arabs in Israel focus on the lost inheritance of Arab lands. This book investigates the problematic place of the Arabic language in Israel. While Arabic is an official language of Israel, according to a law which goes back to the year 1922, during the British Mandate, it is at the same time the language of the 'Arab' enemies surrounding and infiltrating Israel, the language of the Palestinians who remained in Israel after 1948 and who constitute today about 20 per cent of the total population, and also the language of the Palestinians in the West Bank and Gaza Strip. It is, moreover, the language of a dwindling number of speakers from the Mizrachi Jewish community. How are these seemingly contradictory positions of Arabic resolved, and what space is given to Arabic in the state? That is what this book is trying to answer.

Arabic is the language of instruction in Arab schools in Israel. These students also learn Hebrew starting from the second or third grade, and English starting from the third or fourth grade. They are expected to fully function in Hebrew when they get to university level, creating an academic disadvantage for them, according to Elana Shohamy (2007: 3). As for Jewish students, the language of instruction in their schools is Hebrew, and they learn English in school as a second language. They outperform Arab students in national tests, as a result of their proficiency in English (Shohamy 2007: 3, see also

Brosh-Vaitz 2005). Arabic is compulsory in Jewish schools between grades 7–9, but Jews do not see much value in learning it. Minimal levels of proficiency in Arabic are achieved in these schools and many schools ignore this policy altogether (Shohamy 2007: 3). However, in October 2015, the Israeli Knesset passed a bill in its first reading with a majority vote making the teaching of Arabic in Jewish schools compulsory from age six.[1] What is it that compels a right-wing government in Israel to support a law to make the teaching of Arabic compulsory in Jewish schools? I hope this book will provide some answers to this seeming contradiction as well.

Recently, much has been written on the status of Arabic in Israel in both the Israeli media and academia alike. The range of research varies from the sociolinguistic (Amara 2013, Spolsky 2014, Shohamy et al., 2010), to the legal (Saban and Amara 2002) to the socio-political (Mendel 2014a and 2014b), and the sociological-poetic (Somekh 2007). This project brings all of this literature together and adds another element, no less important, to the questions raised by the above researchers, namely, the ethnographic element – considering that the majority of Arabs in Israel today are speakers of Hebrew (with varying degrees of proficiency). Many of them are also proficient in English. Is there a contradiction between their identity as 'Arab' and their relationship to Hebrew, and to a lesser extent, English? The ethnographic fieldwork took place in the summers of 2013–15 and included informal meetings as well as interviews with writers, journalists, broadcasters and students. I also investigated printed journalistic, literary and academic works on the Arabic language as well as Arabic's relation to Hebrew. Finally, I explored the Linguistic Landscape (LL) of Arabic, i.e., its presence in public places such as in signage. Fieldwork was also conducted in Jordan and the West Bank during the same time.

Geographically speaking, the Arabs in Israel are located in three main areas: the Galilee, with Nazareth as the largest town; the Triangle, which is in the centre of Israel between the Mediterranean coast and the West Bank mountains; and lastly, the Negev desert where most of the Bedouin live, in settled villages. The Galilee area is the most diverse in terms of lifestyle and religious affiliation. Arab habitations constitute villages, towns and mixed cities such as Akka and Haifa. The Galilee is also home to some settled Bedouin tribes. In terms of religion, the Galilee is home to (Sunni) Muslims, different

Christian denominations, and Druze. In comparison, the Triangle is (Sunni) Muslim and constitutes villages redefined as towns in the nineties, as a result of their growing population, while the Negev is mostly Bedouin. All Bedouin follow (Sunni) Islam. Some Arabs of various backgrounds also live in the mixed cities of Akka, Haifa, Yaffa, Lod and Ramla (see Figure I.1).

Names of the Arab population in Israel vary from: the Arabs of '48, to the Arabs of the Interior (of Israel), to Israeli Arab, to Palestinian Arabs. While these names indicate their precarious place in the modern history of Palestine, as they are the remainders of the Palestinian community after the dispossession of 1948 who were given Israeli citizenship, I will be using any of these names throughout the book, interchangeably. This book will discuss the contours of Arab identity in Israel, as well as the contours of the Arabic language. Where does Arabic end and Hebrew begin, and where does Palestinian Arab identity end and Israeli identity begin? And what is the grey area in the middle, and who occupies it? Much of the existence of these contours and grey areas has been shaped by the conflict throughout most of the twentieth century and well into the first two decades of the twenty-first, with no seeming end in sight for both peoples. But let us not forget the problematic nature of the nation-state, in the first place:

> At some time, mainly since the end of the nineteenth century, the inhabitants of this state [the nation-state] have been identified with an 'imagined community' bonded together, as it were laterally, by such things as language, culture, ethnicity, and the like. The ideal of such state is represented by an ethnically, culturally and linguistically homogenous population. We now know that this standing invitation to 'ethnic cleansing' is dangerous and completely unrealistic, for out of the most 200 states today only about a dozen correspond to this program [one nation-one state]. (Hobsbawm 1996: 1066)

Thus, Israel as a state is not unique in its dilemmas regarding national minorities. Nor is it unique in its insistence on defining itself as Jewish on the one hand, and as democratic on the other hand, seemingly ignoring the presence of a substantial indigenous population of Palestinians, recognised as citizens. At the same time, Arabic is an official language, along with Hebrew, but with a primacy for the Hebrew language, if not by law, definitely by practice.

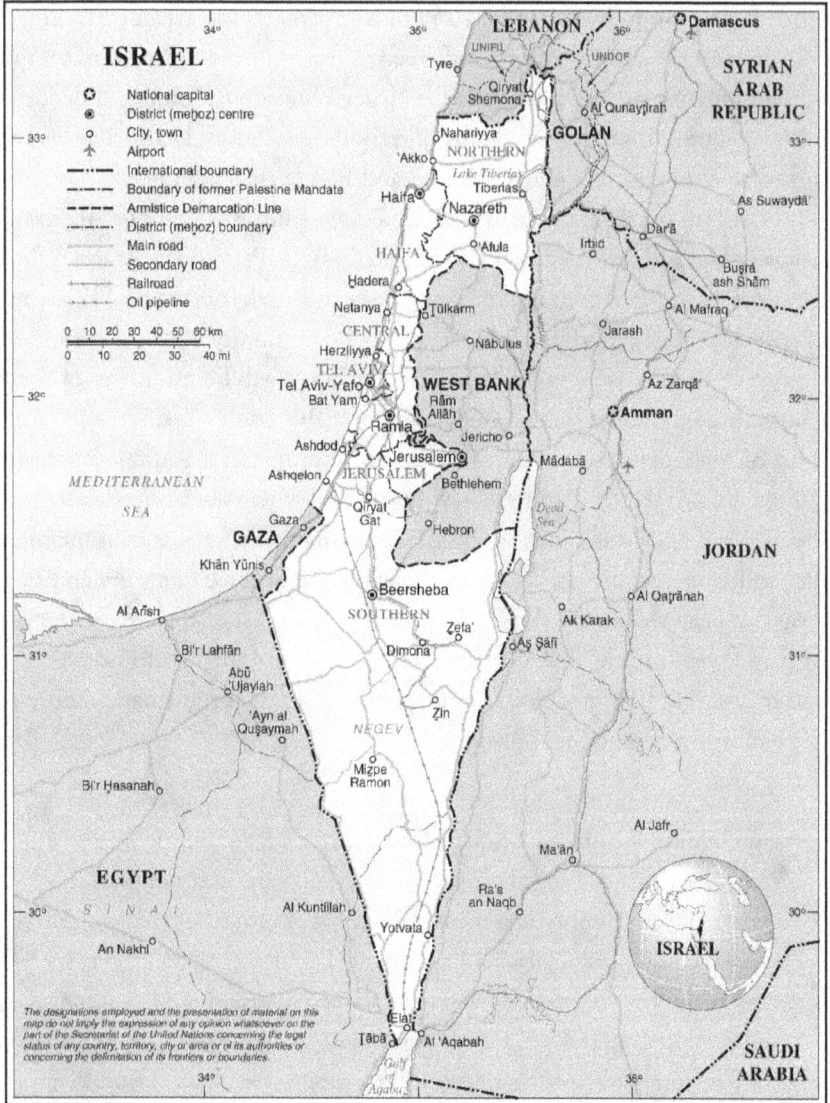

Figure I.1 A map of the geographic areas of Israel. Note that the Triangle as a name does not appear on any recent maps after 1948. However, it is the area roughly between the Carmel Mountain in the north, the Mediterranean Sea in the west and the mountainous West Bank in the east. (Source: Department of Peacekeeping Operations, Cartographic Section, United Nations, 2004)

Aiding me in analysing the Arabic language situation in Israel and the state of its Arab minority is the work of Gil Eyal (2006) on the boundary created between 'What is an Arab? And what is a Jew?' – a question which preoccupied Zionist activists from the beginning of the encounter with the Palestinian community, and a question which continues to preoccupy, if not haunt the Israeli policymakers and the Israeli public alike. Eyal's (2006) project can be summed up as follows:

> in this book, I try to trace the process of disintegration of this Orient and show how the contemporary experience of encounter was created out of its ruins. This experience is mostly a desperate attempt to affirm a separate Western identity. Desperate and futile, because the Arab keep resurfacing as the phantom presence. (Eyal 2006: 2)

In many ways, I see my work picking up where Eyal left off. Eyal (2006) emphasises the 'seamline' between what is Arab and what is Jewish in Israeli discourse. This seamline, while volatile and unstable, is far from being void. Rather it is occupied with three groups whose identity does not fall neatly into one or another category. These groups are: the Israeli Arabs, the Arab Jews or Mizrachim, and the Arabists who constitute various experts on the Arabs, and who may include, at some point or another, the 'Mista῾ravim' or people who model their behaviour after the Arabs in the service of the Israeli intelligence. Eyal (2006) convincingly argues:

> *Mizrahanut* is not merely a form of expertise but a core component of Israeli culture, of the way public discourse is conducted in Israel, of the way Israelis perceive the world around them, and of the manner in which they relate to themselves and define their own identity. In the same way that the linguistic codes of Israeli culture mandate speaking directly without beating around the bush (speaking *dugri*), they also include a certain Orientalist function – an authoritative mode of speech that encompasses attitudes, opinions, tropes and other discursive devices that can be used in ordinary conversation or in a political polemic and that position the speaker as someone who is observing from the outside (from the West), from a position of impartiality, and superiority, what goes on in the Middle East or how Arabs behave. (Eyal 2006: 3)

In other words, Eyal sees the discourse of Mizrahanut as so pervasive it has penetrated all levels of Israeli discursive practices. Further, the perception of the Jews in Israel of who they are in relation to the Arabs, particularly those who live among them as citizens of the state, has been shaped not only by the political events of the past century, but also by the evolution of Zionist political thought. It was not uncommon for some of the early Zionists, including David Ben-Gurion, the first prime minister of Israel, to believe that the Palestinians are the indigenous Jews who have forgotten their religion and their tongue, but who still adhere to some of the ancient Jewish traditions and customs of the land of Israel. As for the discourse on the period between the establishment of the state in 1948 and the occupation of the West Bank and Gaza strip in 1967 (before the domination of all of historic Palestine), many Jews in Israel today, particularly on the left, perceive this period as the age of innocence when Israel was not 'occupying' or 'colonising'; rather they tend to view themselves as a people who fought for their right to exist as a nation. In the 1990s, many Jews opposed the occupation of the West Bank and the Gaza Strip, and tended to yearn for the age of 'innocence' which preceded the occupation of the Palestinians. This period in the 1990s, according to Ilan Pappé (2014) was a period of unprecedented self-examination and openness. It was the time for creative thinking and reaching out for the Palestinians, including the Palestinians inside Israel. It is also the time when the global economic order hit Israel. Israel liberalised its economy (even though the process started in the 1970s), and more inclusion of Israeli Arabs in its new economic order was allowed. This also opened the door for mobility for other disadvantaged groups such as the Mizrachim (see Shafir and Peled 2002). Pappé (2014) states that this very special time in Israel's history came to an end with the advent of the second intifada in 2000. The discourse on Arabs in relation to Jews closed onto itself again.

Chapter 1 discusses the historical background to the study. It starts with a brief overview of the political events which shaped the conflict in the past century, and the inhabitants' awareness of their identity. It then discusses, also in brief, the Arab intellectual thought of the past century in the Levant and in Egypt, a time period dubbed the 'Arab Nahḍa' or 'Renaissance'. As the Ottoman Empire was disintegrating, the Arab East witnessed competing ideas of modern citizenship, and became preoccupied with how to reconcile these ideas with its own tradition. Three major strands of thought emerged: Islamic, local-nationalist and Pan-Arabist. All three strands emphasised the centrality of the Arabic language to the 'new' emerging nations. At the same time, the Zionist movement was taking shape, first in Eastern Europe, and later in Palestine emphasising the uniqueness of the Jews as a people, and the necessity of creating a homeland for them. Two major strands of Zionism dominated the political scene for much of the past century: the Labour movement, with its emphasis on republican socialist values, and the Revisionist movement with its emphasis on expansionism, with the Likud as its strongest manifestation since the 1970s. Today, the Labour movement is much weakened and in its place we find ethno-religious parties aligned with the Likud, who call for the expulsion of the remainder of the Arabs. We also find the remainders of the Labour movement, with the emphasis on a two-state solution and on giving equal rights to the Palestinian citizens of Israel. Lastly, we find an even smaller group calling for a single democratic state for its citizens (whether bi-national or multi-ethnic in character). The last group is exemplified by Ilan Pappé, a Middle Eastern historian of Ashkenazi origins, on the one hand, and Azmi Bishara and his Arab nationalist project, on the other. Lastly, this chapter also sets the tone for the following chapters on the question of boundaries between Arabness and Jewishness. It highlights three works: Gil Eyal (2006), Ahmad Saʿdi (2014) and Yonatan Mendel (2014a and 2014b). Eyal (2006) discusses the problem of setting the boundary between what is Arab and what is Jewish, as a state-building project. As mentioned earlier, he focuses on the 'seamline' and what it includes and excludes. Saʿdi (2014) on the other hand, discusses the methods of surveillance the state of Israel has used, in order to control its Arab population. He states that turning the Arab citizens into clients was unavoidable, but it prevented the state from focusing on turning the Arabs into citizens in the full meaning of the word in a democracy. The political system was set up in a way to encourage the clientele relationship as the only acceptable method of political participation, on the part of the Arab citizens. It also encouraged fractured politics of identity by emphasising the religious (Muslim, Christian, Druze), geographic (urban, rural, Bedouin), family (Ḥamula) and tribal fracturing of the Arab population. Mendel (2014a and 2014b), takes up the challenge of deconstructing the extent of the security concerns related to the status of Arabic in the country, and its teaching to the Jewish population, with the goal of training experts on the Arabs in the service of the security of the state. Lastly, Chapter 1 also discusses the boundaries of Palestinian Arabic today.

Chapter 2 takes up Eyal's (2006) argument further to show the extent of 'Orientalising' the Arabic language and in effect the Arabs in the public discourse in Israel and in academia. Three generations of scholars of Arabic and of Semitic languages (Hebrew, Aramaic, Samaritan) are identified. The first generation was mostly German-educated and is credited for building the departments of Arabic and of Hebrew studies at universities such as the Hebrew University in Jerusalem. This generation shared many European ideas about the East, but at the same time, was part of the Zionist ideas of Jewish nation-building in Palestine. Their research can be identified as examining the relationship between Arabs and Jews from ancient history to the Islamic Golden Age in, for example, Andalusia, to the modern-time Arab and Jewish rise after colonialism. They generally saw the Jewish people as the bridge between the rising East and the declining West. They also sought to find traces of ancient Jewish life in the customs, costumes and language of the Palestinian Arabs. The second generation was trained mostly in Israel, by the first generation. This generation seems to have been preoccupied with the positivistic scientific tools of its time period, on the one hand, and with the Orientalist spirit of its predecessors, on the other hand. The geographic boundaries of this generation's research was bound to the borders of 1948–67. The third generation is characterised by incorporating, to some extent, critical theory in the research, but at the same time, by opening the boundaries of the research subject to include Palestinians (both as researchers and as subjects of inquiry) in the post-1967 era. This chapter also discusses the language choice of Arabic departments in the major Israeli universities. It also discusses the Arabic of MK Ahmad Tibi from Taybeh in the Triangle, who has been in the Knesset since 1999 and who has a following in regard to his speeches in the Knesset, among Arabs and Jews alike. Tibi, while speaking in Hebrew, peppers his language with Arabic, mostly of Palestinian idiom as an affective persuasive technique in his speeches. Lastly, this chapter also discusses some of the interviews conducted with Arabic media personalities, academics and students about the status of Arabic.

Chapter 3 uses Linguistic Landscape (LL) as a tool for understanding the presence (or lack) of Arabic in public spaces in Israel. One of the strengths of LL is that it always has to be dealt with from within an ethnographic outlook (Blommaert 2013: 14). According to Jan Blommaert:

> physical space is also social, cultural and political space: a space that offers, enables, triggers, invites, prescribes, proscribes, polices or enforces certain patterns of social behavior; a space that is never no-man's-land, but always, *somebody's* space; a *historical* space, therefore, full of codes, expectations, norms and traditions; and a space of *power* controlled by, as well as controlling, people. (Blommaert 2013: 3)

The chapter links the legal status of Arabic in Israel to the status of the Arab citizens as a minority in Israel, before it discusses the LL of Arabic in the country. It identifies the following techniques in the process of marginalising Arabic in public signage: (1) Arabic is a transliteration of Hebrew on road signs, appearing always below Hebrew, (2) it is written carelessly with many mistakes, (3) many signs in Jerusalem appear with Arabic crossed over with black paint, as acts of vandalism, (4) in the main street of East Jerusalem, Saladin Street, one can notice an act of defiance to the occupation, (5) in Nazareth, a commercial hub for Israeli Arabs, Hebrew and English constructs are seen in Arabic letters advertising a local supermarket, and last, (6) in Jerusalem, a walk between the two major gates of the Old City can reveal the complex status of the Arab presence there, as the visual aspect of the signs in that very small quarter demonstrates how languages are politically negotiated. All of these observations combined can give an impression of the marginalised status of Arabic.

Chapter 4 discusses the effects of modernisation and globalisation on Israeli society in general and on the Arab population in particular. It discusses the political career and project of former MK, Azmi Bishara, from Nazareth, and the continuity of his project after his self-imposed exile in Qatar. The chapter also discusses the political changes in Israel, the legal meaning of an official language, Hebrew, as the national language, the role of language academies, bilingual schools, and the state of the Aramaic language in Israel today – a language long extinct in the country – and efforts to revive it among some Christian groups.

Chapter 5 compares the sociolinguistic language choices of Hebrew for three Arabic-speaking writers: Sasson Somekh, who grew up in Iraq and came to the country in the 1950s, becoming an international authority on Arabic literature; Anton Shammas, who was born in the 1950s in a village in Galilee, and who wrote an autobiographical novel in Hebrew in the 1980s, and lastly; Sayed Kashua, who was born in the 1970s in Tira in the Triangle, and writes in Hebrew for *Ha'aretz* newspaper, as well as novels. All three can write in Arabic, but choose to write in Hebrew. The chapter discusses their meeting points and their points of departure from each other. It concludes with an account on the writing and creative work of some Jews originating from Arab countries.

Chapter 6 discusses the status of Arabic in today's Jordan and Palestine (West Bank and Gaza). It starts with a brief discussion of the encounter between Palestinian and Jordanian nationalism earlier in the twentieth century, and the effect of globalisation on nationalism in both places. The chapter also discusses a 2007 debate between the American anthropologist Andrew Shryock and the political scientist of Palestinian-Jordanian origins, Joseph Massad, in regard to who can better represent the Jordanian 'Other' in academic writing: the 'impartial American', or the 'partial Palestinian'? In addition, the chapter discusses the uneasy relationship between Jordanian and Palestinian nationalism and its effect on language use as well as the production of scholarship on Arabic. Finally, it also discusses the effect of globalisation and the new economic order in both Jordan and Palestine, on language use.

The book poses open questions in regard to the utility of current research analytical tools such as 'superdiversity' (Blommaert 2013), 'enregisterment' (Agha 2007), 'first and second order indexicalities' (Silverstein 1979) 'crossing' (Rampton 2006), and 'translingualism' (Canagarajah 2015), the umbrella framework which may enable all of these analytical tools to be incorporated for a research project on Arabic in Israel or on Arabic in general. Superdiversity means 'diversity within diversity, a tremendous increase in the texture of diversity in societies such as ours [Western societies] (Vertovec, 2007, 2010)' (Blommaert 2013: 4). Blommaert (2013: 4–5, see also Rampton et al., 2015), following Vertovec, identifies two forces which have caused superdiversity: the end of the Cold War and its aftermath of border movement among people in Europe, and the popularity of online communication. The interaction of the two compels citizens in these superdiverse contexts to ask:

Who is the Other? And who are We? The Other is now a category in constant flux, a moving target about whom very little can be presupposed; and as for the We, ourselves, our own lives have become vastly more complex and are now very differently organized, distributed over online as well as offline sites and involving worlds of knowledge, information and communication that were simply unthinkable two decades ago. (Blommaert 2013: 5–6)

Blommaert overemphasises the utility of this term to European societies by focusing on movement and migration and how such movements have transformed these societies by creating more systems of complexity. To him superdiversity is driven by three forces: mobility, complexity and unpredictability (Blommaert 2013: 6). By destabilising terms such as 'multilingualism', 'languaging' and 'crossing' in his own society he seems oblivious to non-European societies and the vast changes they had to go through during the totality of the twentieth century (and not only the end of it), starting with World War I. Blommaert's assertions do not do justice to societies outside of what is considered 'Western', but at the same time, one cannot help but wonder about the (in)adequacy of academic tools of bygone times which were used to investigate very complex phenomena. In other words, social phenomena of the past century have been greatly complex, but perhaps the strict positivist tools of the past were not able to capture or comprehend them adequately. Blommaert (and others) while justly attempting to escape the strict norms of positivism, run into the other problem of perceiving every aspect of language existence as constructed, even the very presence of naming a language such as English, French or Swahili (Blommaert 2005: 390). However, my informants do seem to wish to demarcate the boundaries between Arabic and Hebrew (Chapter 2), as is the case of minority languages in other contexts (see May 2005, Skutnabb-Kangas 2009). On the other hand, research conducted in Jordan seems to be preoccupied with demarcating what is Jordanian and what is Palestinian Arabic, and how these two modes of speaking are negotiated in the language use of Ammani people (Chapter 6). Language as an identity marker is still resilient, as most people still live in a nation-state (May 2005).

In addition, it seems that research on Arabic in Israel/Palestine and in Jordan is also confined to the project of nation-building, as Chapters 2 and

6 demonstrate. This is not to say that the researcher is not equipped with the scientific tools and the knowledge to conduct such research. In all of this research, the opposite is true. Nonetheless, some recent research is more critical of the state of the reproduction of knowledge. One important point which this book touches on is the mobility of the researcher and the type of access she can have towards her informants. It is particularly true of the time of the military rule over the Arabs of Israel (1948–66), when a foreign researcher probably had more access than native researchers. It is also true in the 1990s in a place like Jordan, where the Palestinian identity of the researcher might have denied her sufficient access. Due to the complexity of twentieth-century politics, it has been also close to impossible for an ethnically Arab researcher to move around freely in the areas of Syria, Lebanon, Jordan, Israel and Palestine, where the various Arabic dialects form a continuum.

At the same time, I want to suggest that we should not confine superdiversity to Western centres of power. In Blommaert's words (2013: 8), in superdiverse contexts people seem to take the huge semiotic resources available to them and blend them together. 'Contemporary repertoires are tremendously complex, dynamic and unstable', to the point where it is hard to determine where the 'stuff' is coming from, how it is acquired, and how it is blended with other stuff, making it hard to analyse. Thus, terms such as 'code-switching', and 'multilingualism' exhaust their utility as analytical tools (see also Blommaert and Varis 2015). Arab societies have gone through upheavals, dislocations and forced immigration, with the Arab Spring in 2011 being the latest in a series of unfortunate events which could be traced back to at least World War I. Moreover, with the recent increased availability of the internet in those societies, many people were able to continue to be connected to the outside world as they were documenting their collective traumas. How can a term such as 'superdiversity' help analyse these tremendous changes? I may not have the answer to this question in this book, but rather, my hope is to open up a discussion about Arabic as I discuss the challenges this language faces in Israel.

Other terms which might be informative if adopted as tools are: 'enregisterment', which refers to 'processes whereby distinct forms of speech come to be socially recognised (or enregistered) as indexical of speaker attributes by the population of the language speakers' (Agha 2007: 38) and 'second order indexicality', when a first order linguistic referent becomes ideological. Both 'enregisterment' and 'second order indexicality' allow recursiveness, reiteration and reinterpretation of these processes, thus allowing for a 'third order indexicality' (Doughan 2010). As for 'crossing', it is defined as the polycentric spaces where mixing, styling and crossing are routine everyday practices (Rampton 2015: 3). Rampton applies the term 'crossing' to the British ethnic mixes and the complexity and fluidity of their language creations, whereby the old Labovian tools of mapping social categories to language variables do not do justice to these processes of language production. In a more recent article (2015: 7), Rampton brilliantly brings in the effect of globalised economy on the process of standardisation of language. He cites Bauman (1987) and Urry (2000) in treating governments today as 'gamekeepers' anxious to regulate the mobility of the human flow, rather than concerning themselves with regularity and ordering of 'what is growing and what should be weeded out'. Surveillance is still an important mechanism of governmentality, but instead of Foucault's (1977) 'panoptican' metaphor for controlling population – which is deemed as belonging to the Fordist era and therefore insufficient for Post-Fordist economies (Fraser 2003) – it is the surveillance of the neo-liberal marketisation which has turned the population into consumers in a market economy. Like every cultural production, language becomes commodified, or 'thing-ified', (Rampton 2015: 9). Further, Rampton warns that through this process of commodification and surveillance, language learning becomes a security concern for the state, monitoring the enemy from within. Language standardisation seems less central for the state, as:

> Commercial companies and security services build algorithmic profiles of us all, but it's metadata on the websites we've visited and the transactions we've conducted rather than the specifics of our lexico-grammars. (Rampton 2015: 10)

Canagarajah (2015) argues that since linguistic phenomena are very complex today due to societies becoming more diverse, hybrid and mobile, and also due to the researchers' own evolution in terms of how language should be studied, 'translingualism' can be a term which captures all of these very complex linguistic phenomena, and at the same time allows for more innovative research tools, such as the ones mentioned above. As our understanding of the sociolinguistic reality of communities has not been able to successfully maintain the Herderian mapping of language and nation on the one hand, nor can it successfully maintain the belief that human societies exist with the presence of a mother tongue, and other phenomena such as 'bilingualism', or 'multilingualism' on the other hand, this new understanding allows for conceiving of societies as fluid, intensely mobile and interactive, and not necessarily stable.

Lastly, Abram de Swaan (2001) presents an interesting paradigm on the global status of languages. He brings in the metaphor of a galaxy consisting of peripheral languages whose speakers are multilingual in one or more of the central languages. However, there are also 'supercentral' languages in the world. Among these 'supercentral' languages are Arabic, Chinese, Hindi and others (de Swaan 2001: 5), however, English is a 'hypercentral' language because, for example, if a Chinese person wants to communicate with an Arab, they will both try to communicate in English (de Swaan 2001: 6). As the following chapter will show, Arabic in Israel is far from being the 'supercentral' language it is around the world. In fact, confronted with Hebrew, a central language only in Israel, it is fighting for its presence in the everyday practices of its speakers.

While the book does not attempt to synthesise or challenge any of these terms, it hopes to open up the discussion on Arabic to an application and/or a critique of these concepts, away from the somewhat fossilised discussion of Arabic exceptionalism through the analysis of its diglossia, i.e., the existence of two modes of expression of Arabic for each and every speaker: a formal (*fuṣḥā*) which nobody uses in speaking, and the informal dialectal (*ʿāmmiyyah*). The book is intended for students and experts in Middle East Studies, in Sociolinguistics and in Arabic studies.

Note

1. Available at <http://www.huffpostarabi.com/2015/10/28/story_n_8411604.html?utm_hp_ref=arabi> (last accessed 6 November 2015).

I

Historic Background

This chapter will list the major events of Palestinian history. It will also discuss what each of the following groups of people considers most significant in the history of the conflict. These groups are: Palestinians in Israel, Palestinians in the West Bank and the Gaza Strip, the Jordanians and the Israeli Jews. There is no doubting the fact that the 'Israeli-Arab' conflict has shaped the history and the identity of the people in Israel, Palestine, Jordan, and to a lesser but still significant extent, the history and identity of the people in the Arab world for much of the past century. Often, historians and ordinary people alike chronicle the history in terms of major events, or turning points. For the Palestinian people, these major events often include:

1. the Zionist Basle Conference in 1897 and the declaration of Palestine as the chosen land for the Jewish nation
2. World War I and its aftermath of dividing the Middle East into spheres of influence between the Great Powers of the that time – Britain and France – with Palestine and Jordan falling under British Mandate (1917–47)
3. the related Balfour Declaration which promised the Zionist movement a homeland in Palestine
4. the Arab Revolt against the British and against Jewish migration from Europe on the eve of World War II, between 1936 and 1939

5. the Partition Plan by the UN in November 1947 and the communal strife which followed

6. the establishment of the state of Israel on 78 per cent of historic Palestine in May 1948, and the establishment of borders in 1949

7. the Suez Canal War in 1956

8. the Six Day War in 1967 which resulted in Israeli dominance over the rest of historic Palestine

9. the 1970 civil war in Jordan and its resulting effect on the Palestinian population in Jordan and the expulsion of the PLO from Jordan to Lebanon

10. the 1973 war between Israel, Syria and Egypt, resulting in the opening of a channel of communication with Egypt, culminating in the 1977 Camp David Agreement, in which Egypt signed a peace agreement with Israel and, in effect, departed from Arab consensus regarding the problem of Palestine, for the first time since all of the countries of the Middle East received their independence from colonial powers, after World War II

11. the Lebanese civil war (1975–89) and its effect on the Palestinian refugees in Lebanon

12. 1982 and Israel's invasion of Lebanon and the resulting expulsion of the PLO from Lebanon, and the Sabra and Shatila Palestinian refugee camp massacres in September that same year

13. the first intifada in 1987, which died down once the first Gulf War started in 1990, and the consequent Madrid talks in 1991 in which all Middle East parties gathered, under the auspices of the US and Russia

14. the signing of the Oslo Accords in the White House in 1993, followed by a peace agreement between Israel and Jordan in 1994

15. the eruption of the second intifada in 2000 and its decline by the second Iraq War in 2004

16. Israel's incursion into Lebanon in 2006, and the subsequent incursion into Gaza in 2008–9, 2012 and 2014

17. the Arab Spring in 2011 which resulted in a weakening of the power of the state in the region, to the point of a civil war in Iraq and a genocide in Syria, and the flight of many refugees, including Palestinians as a result of this instability.

This list of events consists of what Paul Ricoeur (1990) calls 'human time', namely the intersection of 'cosmological time' – the forward progression of time, and 'phenomenological time' – time as experienced by humans. Often when talking, Palestinians organise their historic narrative along the 'cosmological time' of the conflict (see C. Suleiman 2011), starting with the Basle Conference in 1997. Palestinian historiographers organise the major events of the conflict in this manner as well (see Khalidi 1997, for example). Jewish historiography lists a similar chronology which appears in the narrative of what shaped the conflict, except for this major departure: the narrative starts with Jewish rights over the land from 3,000 years ago (see Peled-Elhanan 2012, on Israel textbooks). However, when talking to Jewish peace activists the following differences from the Palestinians' narrative appear: (1) Jewish immigration in the late nineteenth century. Participants often mention family members who immigrated to Palestine before the establishment of the state of Israel, (2) 1948 and the establishment of the state of Israel, (3) 1967 and the discomfort among activists regarding the occupation of the West Bank and Gaza, a discomfort which is generally absent in regard to 1948, except with a few of the revisionists such as the historian Ilan Pappé (see C. Suleiman 2011), (4) the 1973 war and the participation of family members in it, (5) the 1977 Camp David agreement with Egypt, (6) the 1982 war, which was considered a mistake by many activists, (7) the first intifada in 1987 and its role in developing an awareness of the ills of the occupation of the West Bank and the Gaza Strip, and the first Iraq War in 1990, (8) the Oslo Accords in 1993, and the Jordan peace agreement in 1994, (9) the second intifada in 2000, and the withdrawal from Gaza in 2002, (10) the Lebanon War in 2006 and the Gaza Wars in 2008–10.

Jordanian historiography, on the other hand, starts with the Hashemite Arab Revolt against the Ottomans during World War I, and the establishment of the state in 1923 under the Hashemite family banner. Historians then highlight 1948 and the creation of the Palestinian refugee problem. They also detail 1967 and the loss of Jerusalem and the West Bank, which then led to the Black September of 1970. They explore the intertwining of political liberalisation in 1989 and the Iraq War in 1990. The Iraq war led to an influx of Palestinian refugees from Kuwait, and later, Iraqis. Historians also study the 1994 accords with Israel (see Lucas 2005), discuss the second

Iraq War and the second wave of refugees from Iraq in the aftermath of 2003, and the current war in Syria and the influx of refugees from Syria.

For Palestinians in Israel, the events of March 1976 in the aftermath of massive land confiscation is considered a turning point in shaping Palestinian consciousness and collective political action (see Jamal 2006). In addition, the killing of six Palestinian citizens in Israel in 2000, right at the start of the second intifada in the West Bank and Gaza, further shaped the collective consciousness of this group. The sentiment among them was that their citizenship was not that meaningful, because of the ease with which these citizens were killed. These two events in 1976 and in 2000 seemed to be of significance to the Palestinians in Israel, furthering their unique situation and at the same time exposing the vulnerable nature of their citizenship (see Jamal 2006, 2011). Jewish historiography, naturally, does not give the same emphasis to these events, nor do the Palestinians in the West Bank and Gaza, as they were experiencing much more brutal oppression at that time, particularly in 2000, and lastly, these two events do not seem to be part of the narrative of the Jordanian part of the conflict. In 1976, Palestinians in Jordan were still licking their wounds from the civil war of 1970, and in 2000 their eyes were focused on what was happening to their brethren in the West Bank and the Gaza Strip, whose own intifada was brutally dealt with while Ariel Sharon was prime minister. Lastly, the 2015 elections in Israel were another turning point for the Palestinians in Israel. All parties including the Communist Party, the Islamic Movement, the Balad Party founded by Azmi Bishara (the National Democratic Assembly) in 1995, the Arab Movement for Change founded by MK Ahmad Tibi in 1996, and others, participated in this election, and for the first time, as one coalition (the Joint List). This resulted in their winning thirteen seats in the Knesset; see Central Elections Committee: Elections for the Twentieth Knesset, 17 March 2015.[1] The reason for their unlikely list was that the Knesset raised the threshold on votes needed to be elected to the Knesset. The change would limit the number of small parties in the Knesset. Arab parties, all of which are small, felt particularly targeted. Indeed, on the eve of the elections, Benyamin Netanyahu, the head of the Likud and the prime minister, urged Jewish voters to go to the polls so that they could prevent the Arabs from winning many seats (Estren 2015). This remark aroused the ire of the Palestinian population in Israel as it was pointing out what they already knew – that their political worth and contribution to the democratic process in Israel is not equal to that of their Jewish co-citizens.

Arab Intellectual Thought during the Arab Nahḍa and its Aftermath

The modern history of nationalism in the Arab world is characterised by the role of the media and journalism in: (1) shaping how people feel about where they belong and who they are, particularly after World War I, and (2) the shaping of standard Arabic common to all Arabic speakers, and facilitated by the spread of the Arab media and the increased access to education. Three strands of modern identity, which are linked to the event where the Arabic language is spoken and what mode of Arabic (dialect or standard), are identified: an Islamic vision of the state, pan-Arab nationalism and state nationalism. Each of these ideas is still negotiating its space in the public sphere (see Suleiman and Lucas 2012).

Suleiman and Lucas (2012) studied eight debates on the status of the Arabic language, aired on *Al-Jazeera* between 1998 and 2010. Three strands of identity emerge out of these debates: Islamist, pan-Arab and state nationalism. These ideas found their expression in Arab intellectual thought in the period prior to World War I, and into the middle of the twentieth century, specifically in what is called the Arab Nahḍa or renaissance. During this renaissance, the Arabic language was revitalised through the spread of the print media, and along with this, notions of the modern citizen emerged. *Al-Jazeera*'s recent debates show that these three competing ideas of nationhood have not been resolved. The debates are summed up as follows:

Islamic: best exemplified in the ideas of Jamal Al-Din Al-Afghani (see ʿAmara 1968) in the late nineteenth century, and his disciple Mohammad ʿAbduh (ʿAbduh 1963), an Azhar scholar and journalist. *Al-Jazeera* aired two interviews with Al-Sheikh Yosef Al-Qardawi, a prominent Azharite Islamic scholar from Egypt, who now resides in Qatar. His position of the dialogic relation between the strength of a nation and the strength of its language is reminiscent of the earlier ideas of Al-Afghani and ʿAbduh.

Pan-Arabist: best exemplified by the writings of Satiʿ Al-Ḥuṣri (see Al-Ḥuṣri 1985), who had a great deal of influence over Baʿthist thought in both Syria and Iraq. To Al-Ḥuṣri, Arabs constitute a nation united by a common history and language (see Y. Suleiman 2003, 2010). The Arabic language is united and unifying, and in *Al-Jazeera* debates this was best exemplified by university professors and authors from Syria. The debates demonstrate that Arab nationalism as a secular state project is not dead, as some scholars such as Fred Halliday have predicted (see Halliday 2009), but rather, has transformed itself into political demands for more meaningful participation, economically and publically (Choueiri 2000). The events of the Arab Spring also testify to this fact. While people emulated each other all over the Arab world, in terms of demands and manner of expression of these demands, there were no calls to erase borders.

State nationalism: exemplified during the Nahḍa by two Egyptian authors, Ṭāha Ḥusayn (1944) and Salama Musa (1928, 1964). Ḥusayn expressed his belief that Egyptian nationalism is unique. Egypt is a nation which has its roots historically and culturally in Egypt and Greece, therefore, it is European. However, it is Muslim too, and its mode of expression is the Arabic fuṣḥā (standard), as Egypt cannot turn its back on its heritage written in Arabic. As for Musa, he called for abandoning the fuṣḥā in writing, in favour of ʿāmmiyyah (dialectical, see Ferguson 1959, and 1991, also C. Suleiman 2016, on the distinction between both modes of Arabic), as ʿāmmiyyah is the expression of the Egyptian people, and he called for writing it in the Latin alphabet. He also finds Egyptians to be closer to Europe culturally than any other place. In other words, the unique nature of Egyptian nationalism is shared by Ḥusayn and Musa, but they come to opposing conclusions as to the language of expression of the Egyptian nation (see Bassiouney 2015 on a fruitful discussion of what makes Egyptian identity). Perhaps the reason for this is Ḥusayn's earlier education as an Azharite, and Musa's Coptic religious affiliation, which does not necessitate tying the Arabic language to Islam. In *Al-Jazeera* interviews the position of Egyptianness and its relation to language was expressed by Faruk Shousha, the president of the Arabic language academy in Egypt. However, his position is similar to Ḥusayn and not Musa, in that he insists on fuṣḥā performing two functions: being a language of expression of Egyptianness, as well as connecting the Egyptians to their Arab neighbourhood and its common heritage.

In addition, in *Al-Jazeera* interviews, the Lebanese author, Rafiq Rouḥana showed a similar view to that of Musa (although substituting Lebanon for Egypt). This is due to the fact that during the Nahḍa Lebanese intellectuals, regardless of their religious affiliation, displayed a similar outlook to those in Egypt. While some gave emphasis to the uniqueness of Lebanon and its connection to Europe and to the ancient history of the Phoenicians, and wished to express that affiliation in the Lebanese dialect (e.g. Ifram Al-Bustani, see Laḥūd 1993, Y. Suleiman 2003), others while not denying the specificity of Lebanese identity, still focused on the shared history of the Arabs in Greater Syria (al-Sham) and Mesopotamia as both constituting the Fertile Crescent, and they generally considered Islam as part of their heritage. They attempted to highlight the Arabness of al-Sham and its cultural continuity and its link to 'being an Arab' even from before Islam (see Ziadeh 1957, Rabbath, 1962).

In other words, because of the particular colonial histories of Egypt and Lebanon, we find that during the Nahḍa, some scholars from both countries gave emphasis to the uniqueness of each identity, but their mode of expression could either espouse fuṣḥā or 'āmmiyyah. At the same time, there were scholars who espoused the idea of pan-Islamic identity, and those who espoused pan-Arab identity. Epistemologically speaking, Arab nationalism derived many of its symbols from Islam. There were many Christians who supported Arab nationalism and considered that Islam is what transformed Arabs into global players. In their writing, they generally emphasised the geographic and ethnic-cultural unity of the Levant, Iraq, Arabia and Egypt (see Kassab 2010).

When the Nahḍa is discussed with its centre in Egypt and Syria, the reference is generally to Greater Syria, or Sham, which includes Lebanon, Palestine and Jordan. Naturally, Palestinian schools played a pivotal role in educating some of the well-known figures of Nahḍa, such as the Nazareth-born 'Mayy Ziadah' (1886–1941), who became a famous essayist and journalist in Cairo, the centre of Arab culture at that time, and Mikhail Nu'ayma (1889–1988), one of the best-known poets of that era from Lebanon, who received his college education in Nazareth. Naturally, Palestinian towns and cities were much wealthier and more cosmopolitan than their Jordanian counterparts. This was facilitated partially by Palestine's geographic location, with Yaffa on the Mediterranean shores becoming the economic hub for the region during the first half of the twentieth century. Journalism also flourished in Palestine throughout the twentieth century and up to the establishment of the state of Israel (see Kabaha 2007). Further, as Rashid Khalidi (1997) argues, Palestinian nationalism was active in the late nineteenth century, not just as a result of the encounter with Zionism, but also for being part of the Naḥḍa intellectual movement. The three strands of nationalism during the Naḥḍa, discussed above, applied to Palestine and to a lesser extent to Jordan: namely, a Pan-Islamic nationalism. This manifested itself in supporting the Muslim State in Istanbul, on the one hand, and by opposing that very rule and accusing it of straying from the tenets of Islam, on the other hand (see for example the 1934 '*The Caliphate or the Great Imamate*', of the Syrian Rashid Riḍa, 1865–1935). The Pan-Arab element was also evident in the press as the research of Kabaha (2007) demonstrates. Lastly, local nationalism, which oscillated between a call for a Greater Syrian unity (see, for example, the 1982 memoirs of Khalil Sakakini) and after World War I, for Palestinian nationalism and its equivalent in Jordan. But while Jordan became its own state in 1923 under the banner of the Hashemites, Palestine continued to be directly ruled by the British until after World War II. Palestinians in the inter-war period had to deal with the British (like every national movement in the Middle East and many other parts of the world at that time, who had to deal with either Britain, France or Italy), but also they had to fight the competing national movement of Zionism. History took its course, and the Zionist movement emerged victorious in this struggle. Its ultimate victory came in 1948, when the state of Israel was established, causing the Palestinians to become dispossessed overnight. So great was their trauma that today they collectively call that year the Nakba (catastrophe) year. After that date, Palestinians were never able to live in one contiguous geographic zone, but rather dispersed, whereas Jews from Europe and, shortly afterwards, from the Middle East migrated to the new state of Israel, a migration which was encouraged by one of the country's first laws (the Law of Return) which stipulated that every Jew in the world has the right to move to Israel and gain Israeli citizenship. Palestinian refugees were denied the right to return to their homes after 1948, in spite of several UN resolutions, starting with Resolution 194 (III), calling for the refugees to go back to their homes (see C. Suleiman 2011).

To make this very complicated narrative briefer, today we find the same strands of nationalism discussed above in both Palestinian and Jordanian politics. For Palestinians in Israel we notice the following: local nationalism manifesting itself in parties which support 'Palestinian nationalism', and parties which support 'Israelisation' (see Smooha 1989, for more detail). The latter also manifests itself in the fact that some Palestinians join Zionist parties such as Likud, Labour or Meretz. The second strand of Arab nationalism is demonstrated no more clearly than in the political thought of Azmi Bishara and his colleagues in the 'Balad' party (Bishara's political path will be discussed in more detail in Chapter 4). Lastly, the Islamic strand is manifested in the political thought of the Islamic Movement founded in the seventies of the past century. All three strands have had representation in the Israeli Knesset.

In the West Bank and the Gaza Strip, we notice the three strands in the political spectrum of the Palestinian National Authority (PA). Palestinian nationalism is expressed clearly in the Palestine Liberation Organisation (PLO), and earlier in 'Fatah' (established by Yasser Arafat and his colleagues in 1959), and began to dominate the PLO in 1969, when Arafat was elected as the head of the PLO (see Cobban 1992). Arab nationalism is expressed in smaller factions of the PLO, such as the Popular Front for Liberation of Palestine 'PFLP', and the Democratic Front for Liberation of Palestine 'DFLP' (see Hasso 2015 for a more comprehensive discussion). Lastly, Hamas (the Islamic movement), founded in the late eighties, is unambiguously expressing the Islamic vision of a state.

In Jordan, the Islamic Brotherhood Movement is expressing the Islamic vision. Since the days of King Hussein, it has had representation in the parliament, but mostly as an opposition party. The Arab nationalism strand is expressed in some political movements such as the Baʿth party in Jordan and others (see Lucas 2005). As for Jordanian nationalism, it is evident in the tension in public discourse about who is Jordanian and who is not, and in the social and political division between Jordanians of east of the Jordan River descent, and Jordanians of Palestinian descent (see, for example, Abu Odeh 1999).

Of the Palestinian Nahḍa intellectuals, I would like to mention Rouḥi Al-Khalidi (1846–1913), who was engaged in the questions of nationalism and the Arabic language and its revivalism. While studying in Istanbul, Paris and Beirut he was much influenced by the thought of Mohammad ʿAbduh whom he met while ʿAbduh was exiled in Lebanon (Ḥadidi 2008), Najib Nassar (1865–1948), who founded 'Al-Karmil' newspaper in Haifa (Kabaha 2007) and who is called the Sheikh of Palestinian journalism. Other Palestinian Nahḍa intellectuals are: Isḥāq Musa Al-Husseini (1904–90), Fadwa Tuqan

(1917–2003) and Khalil Al-Sakakini (1878–1953). Al-Sakakini's life and his political and linguistic positions are a good example of the rapid changes Palestinians had to go through in a short period of time.

Al-Sakakini was born to a Greek Orthodox family in Jerusalem. After graduating from Zion School in his native city, he migrated to New York in 1907, only to return to his home in 1908. In Jerusalem he worked in education and organised the Greek Orthodox community to rebel against the Greek domination of the church. He also called for the Arabisation of all prayers in church. Further, he was a founder of the 'Constitutional School', 'Al-Dustūriyya', which accepted students from all religions and denominations, taking its name from the Ottoman's move towards establishing a constitution for the empire. At that point, Al-Sakakini, like some other Arab Nahḍa intellectuals, was still working from within the framework of an umbrella Ottoman state, but an Ottoman state with a more modern character where all citizens are equal regardless of their religion or ethnicity. However, he joined the Arab revolt against the Ottomans in 1918. He also worked as a journalist and joined the Arabic Academy in Cairo in 1948, where he eventually died in 1953 (Musallam 2003: 358). In his numerous publications and lectures he emphasised the importance of what applied linguists today call 'comprehensible input' (Krashen 2003, 2004). He believed that language (i.e. Modern Standard Arabic) can only be taught by exposing students to the language through reading, using it as a means of communication by teachers, and by activating the language through debates and other activities in the classroom. In other words, he believed in the co-incidental learning of grammar and syntax (Al-Shanti 1967). Further, unlike some other Nahḍa people mentioned above (such as Ṭāha Ḥusayn), he did not call for simplifying the grammar of Arabic, rather, he called for the learnability of grammar through text (written as well as auditory). It is then that some basic rules can be explicitly explained to the students, but not before. He also worked against reforming or changing the Arabic alphabet (unlike Salama Musa in Egypt, for example), arguing instead that it is a highly functioning alphabet, in addition to being aesthetic. However, he did call for simplifying the style of Arabic to fit the new age (Al-Sakakini 1925). Al-Sakakini also recognised the power of the press in language formation and often pointed out grammar mistakes to newspaper editors (Al-Shanti 1967).

Al-Sakakini's understanding of the workings of the Arabic language was historical, comparative and scientific for his time. It was historical in the sense that he tried to compare present usage of Arabic grammar, vocabulary and style with that of earlier ages, in order to show that the use of Arabic has to fit its time, and not keep reproducing the forms of speakers in the past whose lives were very different (Al-Sakakini 1925). His understanding was also comparative in that he called for the comparison of Arabic structure and development to that of Syriac, Aramaic, Hebrew (Al-Sakakini 1925: 20, 22) and even English (Al-Sakakini 1925: 24). He claimed that Arabic grammarians, for example, inherited the Syriac grammatical tradition (Al-Sakakini 1925: 61), just as European grammar derived from Greek and Latin. His claim is significant for two reasons: first, he might have been influenced by the Orientalist thought of comparative linguistics, particularly as it pertains to Arabic and its relation to the Semitic language tradition (see C. Suleiman 2010); second, (speculative on my part), Al-Sakakini was an Eastern Christian who was somewhat familiar with some Aramaic and Syriac through church liturgy. While firm on the relation of Arabic to being an Arab, his Syriac tradition may have created more space for the inclusion of an earlier Christian presence in the region, predating Islam, which was Syriac/Aramaic and Arabic in expression, before it became solely Arabic. As for the scientific, Al-Sakakini (Al-Shanti 1967: 27) relied on the evolutionary theory of the survival of the fittest and interpreted the forms of his contemporary fuṣḥā as the fittest for contemporary life because the language evolved in a way that only the fittest forms have survived for usage.

In regard to diglossia, and long before Ferguson's classic work (1959), the above-mentioned Nahḍa writers seem to have recognised it (but without using the term 'diglossia'), some more explicitly than others. For example, many of them, when they refer to Arabic and the need to strengthen it, refer to the fuṣḥā mode of Arabic (e.g Husayn 1944). Others call explicitly for abandoning fuṣḥā (Musa 1928), while Al-Ḥuṣri (1985) calls for abandoning ʿāmmiyyah as a mode of formal expression, in favour of a fuṣḥā, for one reason – its ability to be used for communication across the Arab world. Al-Ḥuṣri (1985) might be one of the few writers to give a name to it in Arabic: 'izdiwājiyyat al-lugha', 'the duplicity of language', as he finds the phenomenon widespread among languages including French, English and Serbo-Croatian.

As for Al-Sakakini (1925: 95), he recognised that even in journalistic written Arabic, there are Syrian preferred usages, as compared to Egyptian, sometimes in the choice of words, and sometimes even in the verb patterns. He sees these differences as stemming from the evolution of language across a vast region of Arabic speakers. He includes in this evolution both the fuṣḥā and ʿāmmiyyah. For instance, he notes that the expression 'how are you?' is different in Syria, Lebanon, Palestine and Egypt. However, he does believe that the ʿāmmiyyah can corrupt the fuṣḥā, and that students should be sufficiently exposed to fuṣḥā in order to master it, with the ultimate goal of fuṣḥā to possibly replace ʿāmmiyyah in usage as well (Al-Shanti 1967: 26).

It seems that for some Nahḍa intellectuals, the debate of fuṣḥā versus ʿāmmiyyah does not entail a harsh a dichotomy as Ferguson's (1959) model may suggest. One evidence of this is the lack of a name for the phenomenon (except in a few cases, such as Al-Ḥuṣri 1985), and the emphasis on the evolution of language use (Al-Sakakini 1925), or simplifying the grammar (Ḥusayn 1944), or even severing ties altogether with fuṣḥā (Musa 1928), but not the rigid division between what constitutes fuṣḥā and what constitutes ʿāmmiyyah. Research in the English language on Arabic post-Ferguson (1959) is overwhelmingly about the dichotomy of both modes and how structured code-switching is between both modes (see C. Suleiman 2010, and Suleiman and Lucas 2012 for a full discussion). Ferguson himself (1991) laments the state of affairs of Arabic linguistics and how his framework was misunderstood. He argues that what he meant by his model was to offer a theoretical space to discuss language phenomena. What happened in reality was that instead of developing a theory, linguists were caught on the mechanics of code-switching as to how and when it occurs. More than a quarter of a century after Ferguson's lamentation, the field is unfortunately still caught up in this dichotomy. A glance at recent publications can shed light on how Arabic is mostly being studied through the narrow prism of diglossia, without taking into consideration what else is going on in the development of Arabic and its use (see for example Albirini 2016, Hudson 2002 and Wahba et al. 2006).

Zionism as a National Movement

Zionism as a national movement was catalysed in nineteenth-century Europe, and more specifically in Eastern Europe, as a vision of Jewish self-determination. It was a response to the distress of European national-ism as well as anti-Semitism. Within the Zionist movement itself, two major competing strands emerged. However, the ethos of conquering 'the land', 'the market' and the 'labour' became dominant as the twentieth century began to unfold (see Abdo and Yuval-Davis 1995). The first major strand manifested itself in Labour Zionism, which adopted the republican ethos of 'what can you do to the state?' This strand of Zionism also relied on the agricultural settlements and generally socialist values. It also dominated the politics of the state from 1948 to 1977, when the Labour movement lost the elections for the first time to the Likud party (representing the second strand of Zionist thought). Likud, and its predecessor, Hirut, represent revisionist Zionism which focused less on socialism than on expansionism. While Labour defined the frontier of Israeli borders within the 1949 Rhodes Agreement, up until 1967 Six Day War, revisionist Zionism (founded by Ze'ev Jabotinsky, 1880–1940) adhered to a more expansionist ethos. After 1967, prominent members in the Labour movement believed in holding the Occupied Territories (West Bank and Gaza Strip, Egypt's Sinai and Syria's Golan Heights) as a bargaining chip for future peace with the Arab neighbours. However, the Likud won the elections in 1977 and a more rigorous settlement project started, at first through religious messianic movements such as Gush Emunim, which had limited success in mobilising the public. At the same time, the settlements also started to attract people for economic reasons and in effect became suburban enclaves of the major cities, thus opening the frontier again after its closure between 1949–67, in the words of Shafir and Peled (2002). This settlement expansion was combined with neo-liberal principles, at least economically, and the country started moving slowly, but steadily towards less welfare and more privatisation of the economy. The early agricultural settlements gradu-ally declined. Lastly, when Ariel Sharon, the Likud prime minister pulled out of the Gaza Strip in 2002, it was because he also came to the realisation that there is a limit to expansion, and the frontier needs to be redefined. Sharon ended up splitting from the Likud and forming his own party, 'Kadima' or 'forward', and since then Benyamin Netanyahu has become the most domi-nant figure in the Likud party. Today, the Labour movement is significantly weakened and no longer even a major opposition, but at the same time Israeli politics has been fractured for at least the last four decades.

Politically speaking, Labour Zionism tried to include the Arab citizens inside the borders of 1949–67 as a minority in a democratic system. There was no attempt to include the Arabs from the West Bank and the Gaza Strip, as they fell outside of what they perceived as the frontier of Israel. Today, the politics in Israel, to a great extent, reflects these early strands in that we find people calling for: (1) a two-state solution with the Palestinian state in the West Bank and the Gaza Strip, and for respecting the rights of the Palestinians inside the frontier of Israel, (2) ethno-religious groups who call for the expulsion or transfer of the remainder of the Arabs in Israel (Israel is a state for the Jews), (3) a much smaller group calling for opening the frontier completely to that of the 1967 border, and creating a single state for all of its citizens from the Jordan River to the Mediterranean (see Shafir and Peled 2002, C. Suleiman 2011). This last group is best represented in the thoughts of Ilan Pappé (see, for example, Pappé 2006).

Where does Palestinian Identity End and Israeli Identity Begin? Setting the Boundaries for the State Identity

The Zionist movement has been concerned since its inception in nineteenth-century Eastern Europe with the Jewish identity in Europe. While the movement was secular in essence, it relied on the religious connection of the Jews to the Land of Israel. However, how were the boundaries set between what is Palestinian and what is 'Jewish' and later 'Israeli'? Some of the early settlers saw the Palestinian peasants (regardless of their religion) as the true Jews who preserved the Jewish character and the ancient Jewish way of life. They attempted to imitate some of the manifestations of Arab behaviour such as the traditional garb and ways of speaking. But, on the other hand, many settlers were firm about separating and 'Othering' the Palestinian natives. For example, Ze'ev Jabotinsky (see Massad 2006) made clear in his writing his belief that the Arabs are inferior to Jews and that Jews should not necessarily adopt the Arabic guttural sounds when speaking Hebrew. To him, Hebrew and the Jews are of a superior civilisation, that is, Europe.

Setting up the boundaries was not always easy. So dominant was the discourse of separation that Gil Eyal (2006) sees it as prevalent in all spheres of life of the early Yishuv (Jewish settlement) and beyond. For example, Eyal (2006) pays attention to three particularly problematic social categories and how Zionist institutions and later the state of Israel dealt with them: (1) The Arab Jews – Jews who came from Middle Eastern countries, including Jews who were native to Palestine (Sabra), (2) Israeli Arabs – in other words, the native Palestinian Arabs who remained after 1948, (3) the Arabists, among which are the 'Mistaʿravim', that is, those who adopt or even mimic Arab manners, life style and language, and therefore can pass as Arab. The latter group was recruited either in the intelligence services or in the service of the military government from 1948–66. According to Eyal, the difficulties of the state and, by extension, of the Jewish population at large with these groups stem from the fact that they occupy a grey area. In other words, they metaphorically reside in 'shetach ha-hefker' or 'no man's land' between both the Jews and the Arab Palestinians, with 'Kav ha-tefer', 'the seamline' (Eyal 2006: 7) being ill-defined, permeable and changeable across time. Arab Jews are in that 'no man's land' by virtue of speaking Arabic natively and by being from the Middle East; the Israeli Arabs, by being Israeli, but not quite so, as they are not Jewish; and the Arabists, particularly the 'Mistaʿravim', for being able to 'pass' as Arab. Arabists had many manifestations in the history of the conflict, from acting as 'Jewish notables' or 'Mukhtars' (Eyal 2006: 68) who mediate between the Jewish and the Arab communities to actual advisors to Zionists and state leaders. Archival work has exposed the permeability of these boundaries by discussing the extent of Arab 'collaboration' with the state, on the one hand (see Cohen 2004, Saʿdi 2014), by exposing the problems of being an Arab Jew, or 'Sephardi', with the notion that they are the descendants of the Jews expelled from Spain during the Inquisition, by disclosing family histories of working for the pre- and post-state intelligence services (see Shenhav 2006), and lastly, by the ease of which Arabists and even Orientalists were enlisted in the service of the state against the Arab enemy (see Mendel 2014a and 2014b). The 'Mistaʿravim' or 'those who Arabised' in manner and style, first emerged as a 'virtuosi' (Eyal 2006: 90) expression of the newly immigrated Jewish males as a way of connecting to 'Eretz Yisrael' by shedding the European 'diaspora' degenerate heritage and claiming a connection to the land of Israel by adopting the manners of the Palestinian 'fallāḥ' 'peasant', who most Israeli Arabs today hail from, and who was perceived by the early settlers as a hidden Jew, descendant of ancient Jews (Eyal 2006: 11), authentic, uncorrupt and pure. Later, this category included a unit of Jews in the British army during World War II, who could pass as Arab peasants or Bedouin, and who were enlisted for military intelligence. The state of Israel continued this legacy with the 'Mista'ravim' unit. Today, as I write these lines, this unit is still working in, for example, demonstrations in the West Bank, where its members blend in with Palestinian demonstrators, wreaking havoc even at peaceful demonstrations (see Abu Amr 2015).

Lastly, while the Arabists were relied on heavily in administering the Arab population after 1948, they were generally treated with contempt and lack of respect by the establishment. But on the other hand, the 'good old Orientalists' who were trained in Europe, mostly Germany, and who occupied academic positions in the emerging Israeli academia, such as the Hebrew University of Jerusalem, were marginalised by the state and their expertise was not necessarily sought (Eyal 2006: 11, 35, 53, 62) since it was considered to be irrelevant to the demands of nation building, as these Orientalists focused, by and large, on old scriptures of Arabic and other Semitic languages and they were not interested in contemporary Arab affairs and contemporary Arabic language use. At the same time, these Orientalists marginalised themselves by refusing to adapt their field of interest to the demands of the state. Lastly, as a result of setting the boundaries between the above-mentioned three groups, the study of Middle Eastern Jews became the preoccupation of the academic field of Sociology. They were generally discussed as having adjustment problems to the process of 'modernisation', sociologically and economically. They became a subject of study of 'development' towards modernity (see Eyal 2006). This, however, did not prevent the development of critical sociology, best exemplified in the work of Yehouda Shenhav (2006), and many others.

On the other hand, Arab attitudes, society, culture and politics became the preoccupation of the fields of political science as well as security, as the state was surrounded by Arab enemies whose mindset needed to be analysed in order to defend the State of Israel against their aggression. Israeli Arabs were also discussed in relation to the psychological stress caused by the demands of being a modern citizen of Israel and at the same time a traditional Arab. These studies are best exemplified in the works of the well-regarded psychologist at Haifa University in the 1970s and 1980s, Yohanan (John) Hofman (see, for example, his piece with his Arab student on the conflicted social identity of Arabs in Israel, Hofman and Rouhana 1976), and whom this humble author was a student of, in the early eighties. Hofman's research was dedicated to the psychology of the Holocaust, being a Holocaust survivor himself, on the one hand, and interested in the 'well-being' of the Arab citizens of Israel, on the other hand, but without attempting to make connections between both communities, as the dichotomy which separates both the Jewish and the Arab communities was well preserved in Hofman's scholarship.

However, the 1970s and 1980s witnessed a development in the interest in the state of the Arabs in Israel from a politically scientific and sociological point of view. Ian Lustick's scholarship in political science, from the 1970s is well cited, as he used ethnographic field studies and interviews of 'Israeli Arabs' from villages in Galilee, who related directly their experience to him (see Lustick 1980). Sammy Smooha became a leading figure in the study of the process of 'Israelisation' of the Arabs (see, for example, Smooha 1989). He set the tone for the scholarship of the next decade or so, of what is allowable and what is not, as a research discourse. A number of Arab scholars, such as Majid Al-Haj (1995) and As'ad Ghanem (2001), were influenced by him, even though Ghanem is a political scientist. The biggest leap in what is discursively allowable came after the publications of the Neo-historians, with the likes of Benny Morris (1989) and Ilan Pappé (1994). Other disciplines followed suit, though at a slower pace. Today, we do have critical scholarship on how the state has treated its Arab citizens (see Cohen 2004, Eyal 2006, Mendel 2014b, Sa'di 2014 and others). As for the need for the Arabists in the state of Israel, their role has transformed from administering the military regime over the Arab citizens from 1948–66, to participating in the administration of the military regime of the West Bank and the Gaza Strip, at least in the early days of the 1967 occupation. Today, they occupy positions in think tanks and research centres such as the Peres Center for Peace in Tel-Aviv. They are not scholars, but have graduate degrees in Middle Eastern Studies and international relations. They also work in 'Hasbara' that is, explaining the Israeli government's point of view, and in advising the government, as they are often called upon as experts in the region. They also occupy a prominent place in the media, as they are often invited to give their expert opinion on what is going on with the 'Arabs' inside and outside of Israel (see Eyal 2006). This is by no means an exhaustive survey of the fields of sociology or political science or psychology in Israel, but rather a brief summary of existing lines of research in those fields in regard to the question of the 'Arab citizen' in Israel and its problems. It does skip over some important works in the three fields; for example, the work of Baruch Kimmerling in sociology and his struggle with getting his critical research of the Ashkenazi establishment published (see Kimmerling 2008), nor is it an exhaustive account of the critical scholarship in Israel.

In the scholarly critical spirit of the past decade, I would like to highlight three works. First, Gil Eyal's *Disenchantment of the Orient* (2006) defined the contours of citizenship in Israel from a discursive point of view, keeping in mind that discourse in the Foucauldian sense encompasses the inevitable power struggles between the state and its citizens (Foucault 1982). The discursive boundaries of Israeli citizenship is studied by Eyal through the grey area of 'kav ha-tefer' mentioned above. The second work is Ahmad Sa'di's *Thorough Surveillance* (2014), which further illuminates this grey area, more specifically in regard to the Arabs remaining in Israel after 1948. Sa'di excellently and diligently uncovers state archives documenting meetings of the government, the Arabists who counselled the government and in many ways 'ruled' over the Arab population during the military regime of 1948–66, and between the Arabists and the Arab population. The picture one could draw is definitely that of a 'clientele' state in regard to the Arab citizens (see Cohen 2004). The Arabs were treated as mere clients and the democratic process was flawed and only a façade when it came to their political participation. Further, Sa'di demonstrates how the power arrangement, which took roots even before the establishment of the state, set the tone for this clientele relationship to the point where it became inevitable that Arabs collaborated with the state against their own kin. While earlier scholarship exposed the degree of collaboration (Cohen 2004), Sa'di analyses the impossibility of any other dynamics. Further, Sa'di tackles the seeming contradiction in the state's position regarding the 'Arab minority', but at the same time, the elaborate investment of the state in the fragmentation of the Arab community. Thus, Druze and Bedouin divisions were created from the beginning, separating the Druze religiously from the rest of the Arabs, and separating the Bedouin for no reason other than a perceived nomadic way of life, long abandoned by many of those groups categorised as Bedouin by the state. It even dictated how the tribes should be divided. As for the majority of the Arabs who had been

Muslim, further distinctions were made on religious affiliation, distinguishing them from the Christians. Some policymakers despised the Christians and saw the Muslims as the true 'lost' Jews, particularly Muslim village inhabitants (Saʿdi 2014: 20, citing David Ben-Gurion from the archives of the political committees of the ruling party, Mapai, on 24 January 1952). Within the Christian community, the early policymakers favoured the Latin over the Orthodox denomination. Saʿdi does not provide a clear explanation as to why, which leaves one to speculate that the state despised the nationalistic feelings of the Orthodox Christians. Saʿdi, however, rightly points to the fact that many of the Arabs in the Communist Party were Orthodox, and that the party allowed them to marry their nationalistic feelings with socialist ideals, in line with other leftist parties in the Arab world at that time. Saʿdi also exposes the fragmentation, even at the level of the neighbourhood, where the anachronistic 'Ḥamula', or 'family allegiance' structure was revived and encouraged, so much that it became an effective tool in controlling the Arab minority and their political aspirations (see also Eyal 2006 on the mythologising of the Arab village and its social structure).

The third and last work I would like to focus on is Yonatan Mendel's *The Creation of Israeli Arabic* (2014b), as it directly tackles the government practices in regard to studying Arabic. Mendel speaks Arabic fluently as a result of working in the Intelligence unit of the Israeli army (Mendel 2014b: xiii). He, as many others, had been directed into Arabic learning while still in school, in order to later work in the security apparatus of the army. Mendel combines his insider knowledge of how the intelligence in the army works, along with his more recent scholarly work on the matter for his doctorate in Near Eastern Studies at the University of Cambridge (Mendel 2014b: xiii). As a result, he is able to make a compelling argument of how Arabic, as a subject of study in Israeli schools, was emptied of its cultural and civilisational value to be reduced to a 'security' issue. Knowing Arabic meant to be able to translate the press of the Arab 'Other', to penetrate the workings of the Arab mind, and to spy on the Arab. Mendel painstakingly sifts through archival documents from 1935–85 which articulate the state's logic behind teaching Arabic in some select high schools in the country to Jewish students who would later be recruited for the security apparatus (Mendel 2014b: 1). No wonder Mendel finds that Arabic learning in actuality correlates negatively with human values of respect and compassion towards anything Arab. What is ironic is that Mizrachi Jews who were native Arabic speakers were discouraged by the state from nurturing the language and culture and made to replace it with Hebrew instead, but at the same time, Ashkenazi Jews from the best high schools have been recruited for the study of Arabic for military purposes. This irony is resolved through an understanding of setting the boundaries between the two nations. The Arab Jews needed 'de-Arabisation', but the state still needed 'experts' on Arabic and Arab culture, in other words, the Arabists. In this regard, Yehouda Shenhav (2006) recalls the story of Eli Cohen, an Israeli spy in Syria, who after the revelation of his true identity, was hanged by the Syrians in 1965. Cohen's story is told as a story of heroism. However, one fact remains untold: Cohen is an Alexandrian Jew who was a native speaker of Arabic. The omission of this fact from the story is yet another indication of the desire of the state to 'de-Arabise' Arab Jews. However, this did not resolve the need for spies who are fluent in Arabic and can pass as Arab because of this, and perhaps a darker complexion. But, the story of Cohen does not imply that in his time the security apparatus did not recruit from high schools. In fact, Arabists have been predominantly recruited from select high schools and tracked early on for Arabic learning.

One of the most striking examples of the militarisation of Arabic studies is the teaching of Arabic in two Israeli colleges: (1) Givat Haviva which was established by Ha-Shomer ha-Tsaʿir (the Youth Guard), a movement belonging to Socialist Zionism (Mendel 2014b: 181) in 1949, on the one hand, and at (2) Ulpan ʿAkiva, founded and directed by Shulamit Katznelson, an 'ardent' Zionist who was a member of the 'Irgun', a Jewish militia before 1948 (Mendel 2014b: 207). The main purpose of Ulpan ʿAkiva was to teach Hebrew, but it also taught Arabic. Comparing the archives of both institutes, Mendel (2014b) finds remarkable similarities in regard to how Arabic was treated in both institutes: militarised, with a focus on teaching Arabic for the army, and lastly, securitised in terms of contextualising the Arabic learning within the Israeli-Arab conflict, and Israel's need to protect itself from the Arab enemies.

Mendel concludes that the colluding of the Arabists and the state with its security apparatus disallowed the growth of Arabic studies in Israel as a field which positions Arabic in its civilisational context, but rather, and unlike how Arabic is studied in Arab countries, Israeli Arabic:

> instils in its Jewish speakers a fear of Arabic-speaking people, while making the Arab people afraid of those Jewish people who study or who know 'Israeli Arabic'. It is a security-associated language and an Arab-free one, and as such is suspicious until proven innocent. Mendel (2014b: 231)

Lastly, Mendel (2014b: 49) further argues that the academic field of Orientalism itself, as practised at the Hebrew University, colluded with the state in order to create a form of Arabic for the purpose of state security – in other words, Israeli Arabic. He cites the example of Moshe Piamenta, who, while a prolific academic of Arabic, was also a member of the Hagana in 1942, after working briefly as an Arabic teacher. Piamenta also wrote a book in 1968 for learning Arabic, 'Speak Arabic: An Introduction to Eretz Yisraeli-Arabic'. The wording of the title did not escape Mendel's attention (2014b: 136) and he commented that Piamenta, who himself was born in Jerusalem, was also stripping Arabic of its broad context and focusing on an ahistorical Arabic concerned with security. They also focused on Palestinian Arabic, and on listening skills, for the purpose of spying on the Palestinians, and on the Arabic media broadcasts from all over the Arab countries. Mendel states that 'in the 1940s, young orientalists from the institute of Oriental Studies at the Hebrew University "crossed the boundary between academia and official-dom" and took positions in the intelligence services of the Jewish community' (2014b: 49).

The Boundaries of Palestinian Arabic

How does one set the limits of the physical boundaries of Palestine versus Israel, and by extension versus Jordan, which has had the lion's share of displaced Palestinians? And what about the rest of the Arab countries with substantive Palestinian refugees such as Lebanon and Syria? The difficulty is not merely a philosophical question about the state of being a Palestinian, but rather a research question about Palestinians, and more specifically Palestinian Arabic. Most researchers agree that Palestinian Arabic is part of the larger group of dialects of the Levant or 'Al-Sham', which includes Lebanon, Syria, Jordan and northern Iraq as well as historic Palestine. Collecting data and analysing it can be elusive, as Palestinians have not lived in one contiguous area since 1948. Research headlines show different names for the same dialect group: geographic as in Northern Israel (Talmon 2000), who at the time of his premature death was building a dialect atlas of Arabic in Northern Israel, or 'life style' and geographic location categorisation, such as Bedouin Arabic in Northern Israel (Rosenhouse 1984), or the Bedouin of the Negev (Henken 2000, Piamenta 1979), or the rural area of the Triangle in Israel (Amara and Kabaha 1996) who found that the linguistic behaviour of one small village is different from one side to another, as the village was divided between Jordan and Israel between 1948 and 1967, and one half of the residents of the village became Israeli citizens as a result, or the dialects of the Palestinian refugee camps in Lebanon (Hennessey 2011), refugee camps in the West Bank (Hawker 2013), or by religious affiliation such as the Druze or the Christians (Blanc 1953, Bassal 2015 respectively), or by city – Jerusalem (Piamenta 2000, Rosenhouse 2009), and Yaffa (Horesh 2014, 2015), or Gaza (Cotter 2013), whereas the city of Amman is studied not by having a majority of Palestinians residing in it, but rather by the influence of two cities on the dialect of Amman: Salt in East Jordan, and Nablus which parallels Salt on the western slopes towards the Jordan Valley (see Al-Wer 2007). Lastly, Horesh conducts research in Yaffa (2014, 2015), and collaborates with William Cotter (2013, also Cotter and Horesh 2015) who does research in Gaza, a testimony to the physical fragmentation of the Palestinians where it is hard for the same researcher to move between two places to conduct his or her research. Horesh and Cotter have identified similarities and differences between both cities, and they identify these two cities as Palestinian, a political stance, on the part of the authors, rather than a fact these days. Conducting sociolinguistic research in the tradition of William Labov (1966), in a comparative research between Gaza and Yaffa allows both to compare Yaffa features in the speech of the refugees in Gaza who originated in Yaffa (Cotter and Horesh 2015), and in the case of Yaffa, Horesh (2014) investigates the influence of Hebrew on the Arabic of Yaffa.

The confusion of names and boundaries for Palestinian Arabic stems from several facts: (1) Levantine Arabic is identified as influenced by three different lifestyles: urban, rural and Bedouin (see Y. Suleiman 1996), (2) historic Palestine, like the rest of the Levant, in spite of its small size, appears to have diverse dialects, where one village can vary linguistically from the next; this is in addition to class, gender, age and other variations already noted in sociolinguistic research. With the improvement in literacy and its role in standardisation, which the entire Middle East has experienced in the second half of the twentieth century, came the Palestinian dispersion over several countries, each with its own language policies and educational challenges. So, how would a researcher navigate the massive dislocation of Palestinians when studying Palestinian Arabic? And this is just one part of the difficulty of defining the linguistic group under study, and naming it. Not to mention some official and non-official (media and public) naming which has taken place as well: refugees, Israeli Arabs, the Arabs of 1948 (in reference to the 'Israeli Arabs', the Arabs of 'al-Dākhil' or 'the interior' (also in reference to the Israeli Arabs), Palestinian Jordanians, West Bankers, Gazans, present absentees (in reference to Palestinians who were able to come back to the Green Line borders in Israel before the 1949 Rhodes agreement), and perhaps more.

Lastly, the 1948 Nakba remains the main decisive moment for the conflict. So pervasive was the trauma to the Palestinians that they always refer back to it in their collective and personal narrative, wherever they are. Israel, however, celebrates that date as its independence day from the British. But, at the same time, Israelis, regardless of their political inclinations find it hard to recognise the Nakba. In other words, the most formative moment in Palestinian consciousness is far from being recognised by Israeli society (see Jamal 2011, Jamal and Bsoul 2014).

To sum up, this chapter started with a brief overview of historic events and how they are given emphasis by Palestinians in Israel, by Israeli and by Jordanian historiographies, and while the Nakba is the most conspicuous event for both, it is not recognised as such by most Israeli Jews (Jamal and Bsoul 2014). The chapter proceeds to locate Palestinian nationalist thought (and to a lesser extent Jordanian national thought) within the intellectual thought of the Arabic Nahḍa in the Levant and Egypt. The encounter of Zionism interrupted that process, as Zionism in general was an exclusionary movement. Three studies are highlighted in regard to the process of 'Othering' the Palestinian in pre- and post-state Israel alike: Gil Eyal (2006) and his notion of the elasticity of the seamline which divides the Jewish people from the Palestinian Arabs, Ahmad Saʿdi's (2014) emphasis on the methods of surveillance the state of Israel developed in order to control its indigenous Arab minority, and lastly, Yonatan Mendel's (2014a and 2014b) unveiling of the methods the state of Israel has used in order to turn the Arabic language into a security issue, devoid of any civilisational value. The chapter concludes with the difficulties today in establishing the contours of Palestinian Arabic, as the communities who identify themselves as Palestinian do not live in one contiguous geographic entity, and it is often difficult to conduct research on more than one of these scattered Palestinian communities at a time. The next chapter will discuss the minoritisation and securitisation of Arabic in Israel, and how Orientalising Arabic has superseded and facilitated these processes.

Note

1. Available at <http://www.bechirot20.gov.il/error.htm> (last accessed 18 December 2015).

2

Orientalisation, Securitisation and Minoritisation of Arabic

It is not unheard of for state institutions around the world, democracies included, to link language teaching with the national security. For example, it is well known and well documented that US foreign policy and national security have been linked to research centres and departments at various universities. Zachary Lockman (2004) at New York University documents the collaboration between the American government and centres for Middle East Studies, even in elite universities, during and after the Cold War. Further, Lockman (2004) picks up on the relationship between state power and the production of knowledge, where Edward Said's (1978) project on Orientalism leaves off. Said argues that academia aided the state in Europe (and by extension in the US) in reproducing a discourse of 'Othering', and most relevant to us here is the creation of the 'Orient'. Lockman (2004) painstakingly and compellingly shows that after the Cold War, US policy towards the Middle East became wedded to academia, particularly studies in comparative politics. One of his most powerful demonstrations is the collaboration of the Near Eastern Studies centre at Harvard University with the CIA, which caused a scandal in the 1960s because of the illusion of the separation of the centres of learning from 'power'. In other words, Lockman's study (2004) is a testimony to the fact that the discourse of Orientalism at American institutes was fertile soil for the next step of linking the study of the Orient to the American national interests.

However, Lockman's scholarship (2004) does not address the relationship between the teaching of the Arabic language and the American government after 11 September 2001. Soon after 2001, the Department of Defense gave multi-million dollar grants to a number of universities to support the learning of 'Critical Languages', Arabic among them. Initially five major US universities were given this grant to support the teaching of Arabic. The grant did not have any strings attached as far as the students were concerned, but the government wanted these chosen institutions to teach Arabic fluently as part of a five-year programme in the hope that when these students graduated, they would work for the government. These Flagship programmes, as they were called, emphasised the learning of both Standard Arabic 'fuṣḥā', and a dialect, 'āmmiyyah'. The dialects chosen were first the Levantine 'Shami', or Egyptian. As time passed, the plan was refined to enable the students to communicate in both Egyptian and Moroccan Arabic, in addition to the students 'superior' knowledge of 'fuṣḥā' (with the implicit emphasis on speaking and listening skills, for potential work with the government). According to Mahmoud Al-Batal, the director of Arabic Flagship at the University of Texas in Austin, the events of September 11 created a 'Sputnik moment' for the American government for Arabic (Mendel 2014a: 15–16), just as the Cold War resulted in US government support for the teaching of Russian. Further, the support for Arabic at American universities, as well as other critical languages, is seen by many defenders of the academic freedom of Institutions of higher education as a blatant compromise of this freedom (see Stone 2014, see also Mendel and Suleiman 2010, and C. Suleiman 2010). Moreover, the danger of this interference, while not creating a precedent, lies in the fact that many public universities have faced real financial struggles in the years since September 11 and the Iraq invasion. In other words, the desperate financial situation of many institutions has led them to such compromises, where deans and provosts are always chasing potential funding sources, the government included. Having served as the director of an Arabic Flagship programme for four years at a major university, I have witnessed the complicity between university administrators and the government officials in charge of administrating the grant, who have spent millions of dollars of taxpayers' money on this programme at my institution alone.

What is ironic about these millions of dollars is that this spending is happening while Title VI, administered by the Department of Education for the support of area studies and languages is being trimmed, and while the teaching of languages which are not designated by the government as critical to the national security, such as Spanish, the native language of millions of American citizens, is barely supported at all (see Bale 2011, 2014). In fact, when it comes to Spanish, state policies (official and non-official) have tried to trim its presence in the public space in the US. Lastly, at the moment of the inception of these Flagship programmes, it seemed that the government wished to target the heritage speakers of Arabic. Two of the five Arabic Flagship programmes were established in the two major universities of the state of Michigan precisely so that the programmes target the heritage speakers. For example, one of these two major Michigan universities applied for a Chinese Flagship grant. The government rejected their application for Chinese and offered them Arabic instead. Attempts were even made by the administrators of this university (who did not speak Arabic themselves) to recruit students from the Arab community of Dearborn, the town with the largest concentration of Arabic speakers in the US, but these attempts were not successful. However, it seemed that these programmes attracted primarily white American students. As Flagship stands at the time of my writing, most of its students from these five universities are white Americans.

To sum up, as the demand for Arabic knowledge has surged in the past decade and a half, academic institutions in the US (and Europe, see Mendel and Suleiman 2010) have met demands by sometimes seeking money from external sources such as the American government. Students are graduating from Arabic programmes around the US with a decent knowledge of Arabic, and some of them are recruited to work for the government. To a great extent today, the demand for Arabic, and the potential jobs it offers, is interlinked with the US national security interests. In other words, Arabic as a consumer good in US universities has become directly linked to the modern surveillance apparatus, thus, the surveillance of the neo-liberal marketisation seems to be at work here (Rampton 2015). Arabic is commodified to meet American national security interests and its presence is tolerated when it is used for that purpose, but less often in public spaces (see for example the many stories in the American media on Arab passengers being made to get off planes for speaking Arabic, Loller 2011). Young Americans are responding to this commodification by seeking expertise in Arabic in their colleges and they are encouraged by scholarships such as the Flagship to seek jobs related to the government and security after graduation.

A parallel link is found today in Israel between Arabic studies and national security, partly as a result of the joint foreign policy visions of the US and Israel. However, a closer look at the history of Arabic studies in Israel will point to some major differences, in spite of the similarities in the outcome today.

While the connection between the security institutions and the teaching of Arabic to Jews in Israel is known to many experts, Yonatan Mendel (2014a and 2014b) exposes the depth of this connection both structurally for policymakers, as well as historically, since the inception of the state. Mendel's impressive documentation makes a compelling argument for how the state used its power to dictate the terms of how Arabic is taught to Jews. The national obsession for survival amidst of a sea of Arab enemies has made it impossible to teach Arabic in its cultural and civilisational context and it has been reduced to the language of enemies who are after 'us' and want to destroy 'us'. Curricula were not concerned about the massive literary heritage of Arabic, but rather, they were concerned with journalistic Arabic as well as spoken Arabic for security reasons, in a similar manner to the US Flagship programmes mentioned above.

It would be incorrect, however, to think that this view of Arabic teaching only started after the establishment of the state. To the contrary, the roots had already started with the earlier settlers as they were trying to build new communities and revive the 'Hebrew' life and language. Mendel (2014b) calls the ethos of the early settlers: 'conquest of land, labor, market, and language', thus adding the often neglected aspect of the discursive use of language. He also argues that conquering the language was not only a result of the national pressures, but also as a consequence of the Orientalist ethos common among the early settlers in the Yishuv in Palestine. Its driving force is European 'Orientalism' – in other words, Ashkenazi Jews, in varying degrees, were seeking a new identity outside of Europe, but without disavowing Europe and its ideas of racial classifications. This is not uncommon for settler societies and it has been noted by scholars of the Arab-Israeli conflict. Nahla Abdo and Nira Yuval-Davis (1995), for example, note that in settler societies there is often ambivalence towards the 'indigenous' culture of the natives. On the one hand, certain aspects of it are admired and mimicked (food, language forms, cloth-ing, architectural and decorative motifs), but at the same time, the settlers do not wish to sever relations with their original land. Often, in European settlement projects, the settlers were driven out of Europe for various reasons including religious persecution and racism. Israel is no different, according to Abdo and Yuval-Davis (1995). Joseph Massad (2006), influenced by Said (1978) pushed this argument further in claiming that in the case of Israel the specificity of the 'Jewish problem' in Europe contributed to how the settlers viewed the indigenous Arab population and the larger Middle East context: generally as backward, violent, despotic, misogynist and morally corrupt, in line with European Orientalism. This does not exclude some admiration for the Oriental lifestyle, such as the perceived 'simplicity' of peasant life. In fact, some early settlers saw in the Palestinian peasants a form of early indigenous Jewish life, frozen in time (see Massad 2006 and Saʿdi 2014 in reference to the Muslim Palestinian peasant as the descendants of the ancient Jews).

One cannot escape the common roots of Orientalism in both the American and the Israeli contexts – but with a big difference. While Arabs and their language are the Oriental 'Other' in both cases, in Israel they are also the indigenous natives, which adds yet more complexity to the situation of Arabic in Israel. Today, Arabic is linked to the national security of both countries, and the Arabic language for non-natives shares similar positions in the range of languages taught in both places. It also seems that both in the American and the Israeli contexts, heritage speakers of Arabic are viewed with some suspicion. In the American context, at least, right at the inception of Arabic Flagship there seemed to be an interest in the heritage speaker as a tar-get student for such programmes, hence the two Arabic Flagship programmes in Michigan. As the time went by, the interest seemed to move to the recruit-ment of Americans with no Arab heritage. In fact, both programmes were terminated in Michigan and the money moved to other major universities in the country. One can draw a parallel with the difficulty the state of Israel had in recruiting native Arabic speakers for its services from the Mizrachi Jewish population. It seemed that this was done with the first generation of Mizrachi Jews in Israel (see Shenhav 2006), but generally there was an active attempt at dissociating this group from its Arab heritage (Eyal 2006), hence, for example, the effort at recruiting for Arabic in schools with Ashkenazi students such as the 'Reali' in Haifa, one of the best schools in Israel (see Mendel 2014b). Further, looking at the participants in the American Flagship programmes, the majority of the students are white Americans, and not from minorities of any kind.

The minoritisation of Arabic in Israel was obviously facilitated by the mass exodus of the Arab population in 1948. However, the 'management' and 'surveillance' policies which affected all aspects of Arab life in Israel have extenuated the state of this community's powerlessness. What added to this frustration is the 'democratic' gloss which had to be given to every act and decision aimed at furthering the state of powerlessness of this group (Mendel 2014a and 2014b and Sa'di 2014). Further, as Sa'di (2014) notes, successive governments in the first decades of the state believed that the presence of this community inside the borders of Israel was a temporary matter, to be resolved sooner rather than later. Only in the 1960s did the government start thinking of this group as possibly remaining in the state. Thus, the surveillance continued and the management continued, a management which emphasised the compartmentalisation of the Palestinians into 'a mosaic of insular minorities' (Sa'di 2014: 74).

Gil Eyal's (2006) scholarship mentioned in Chapter 1, highlights the state's dilemma in handling the three categories of 'kav ha-tefer', or 'the seamline'. First, the Mista'ravim (those who adopt and mimic the Arab way of life) for the purpose of passing as Arab, to enable better understanding of the Arab. A later reincarnation of this group may include the Arabists, who study Arabic and Arab culture and politics with the aim of becoming the experts who counsel the media and the government on Arab matters, with the security of Israel as the main motivation for this type of expertise. Second, the category of the Arab Jew and the state's difficulty with its Arab identity. Fewer and fewer people who belong to this group today even know Arabic. According to Amnon Levi, a well-known Israeli journalist who is Mizrachi himself, the state does not collect statistics of the third generation of the 'ethnic' origins of the Jewish community and therefore it would be hard to estimate their numbers in society today (personal interview, Levi, 27 August 2014). Lastly, the third group is the 'Israeli Arab' with its attendant problems mentioned earlier.

Eyal (2006) singles out the Orientalist academics for staying outside of the political games of the state and thus marginalising themselves as experts on Arab/Islamic society, delving into ancient texts rather than contemporary affairs and consequentially leaving the field of contemporary interpreters of Arab culture to the semi-scholarly experts who take part in counselling the government and also in administering the Arab community. Mendel (2014a and 2014b), however, shows how some of these Orientalists were actually attuned, if not dedicated, to the power of the state and *did* help in managing the Arab population. Mendel (2014b) gives the example of Moshe Piamenta, who became a well-known Orientalist at the Hebrew University in Jerusalem. Piamenta started his career teaching Arabic to Jews before the creation of the state of Israel, only to join the Hagana in 1946 (along with Yitzhak Navon who became Israel's president in 1978, after similar stunts with teaching Arabic and joining the Hagana afterwards, see Mendel 2014b: 49). But Piamenta was far from being the only one who 'crossed the line between academia and officialdom' (Mendel 2014b: 49), and who in some cases took positions in the intelligence services of the Jewish community and later for the state of Israel.

The difficulty of the state of Israel with the three categories of 'Arab Jew', 'Israeli Arab' and 'Arabist' has involved a constant drawing and redrawing of 'kav ha-tefer' between Arabs and Jews. This act of the 'purification of the hybrid' (Eyal 2006: 8) created ambivalence in all matters pertaining to these groups. These 'manufactured hybrids' (Eyal 2006: 8), or 'monsters' (Eyal 2006: 8, citing Bruno Latour (1993), see also Kymlicka 2001), 'transgressed the carefully outlined boundaries' of the modern state which included the cultural, symbolic classification between groups, and therefore these hybrid groups are generally perceived as a threat to the social order (Eyal 2006: 8). In the case of Israel, 'the twilight zone between Jews and Arabs was dangerous' (Eyal 2006: 129). Academia was inseparable from this common discourse, and rather contributed to the production, reproduction and manufacturing of these hybrids and their precarious boundaries. This is what the next section will discuss.

The (Re)Production of Knowledge of Arabic and the Orient in the Israeli Academia

Arabic studies were established at Israeli universities as early as the founding of the Hebrew University itself in the 1920s. Often the Orientalists were trained in Europe, in the German, French and other European Orientalist traditions, but mostly German (see Eyal 2006: 11, 35, 53, 62). The concern for Arabic was textual in the first place; thus, by definition, not necessarily relevant to the concerns of the Jewish community in the Yishuv and later the security concerns of the state. I do not see a contradiction between Eyal's (2006) argument that the Orientalists generally did not concern themselves with the contemporary affairs of the state, and Mendel's (2014a and 2014b) argument that some of the Orienlists were enlisted in the service of the state and its security apparatus. The reality of their collusion with the state is probably somewhere in the middle between these two arguments. While some, such as Moshe Piamenta, worked explicitly in the Hagana, others might have subconsciously supported the goals of the state in the name of science and scientific scholarship. Further, many of them were interested in the ancient languages of the Orient in antiquity and showed interest in other Near Eastern languages. Naturally, many of them carried with them the European romantic ideas of the Orient and its ancient people, but found a fertile land for their research as they were physically living in this very ancient land. Some also entertained the romantic Zionist idea of the Arab peasant being the 'lost' Jew frozen in time. David Ben-Gurion, the first prime minister of Israel, was a firm believer in this 'imagined' self, but the ideas were spread also among some settlers, academics among them (Sa'di (2014), for example), and therefore they looked for signs of an ancient Jewish life in the dress, mannerisms, and sounds and usages of Arabic of peasants. Some of these Orientalists specialised in Jewish studies, thus focusing on Hebrew at different time periods, and on how it might have been spoken in Palestine in ancient times. Often this expertise was matched with expertise in Aramaic and its sphere of influence on ancient communities, Christian and Jewish included, while others extended their expertise to Samaritan, of the Samaritan community in Mount Gerizim in Nablus, where this community believes the Temple was sited. These Orientalists include: Ze'ev Ben-Hayyim, E. Y. Kutscher, Sh. Morag, Haim Rabin, U. Ornan, M. Bar-Asher and others. Orientalists specialising in Arabic and Islamic civilisation include: D. H. Baneth, Sh. Goitein, Joshua Blau, Haim Blanc, Moshe Piamenta, M. J. Kister, M. M. Plesner and others.[1] Both groups of Orientalists acquired international reputations and each became an authority in their respective fields. Some of the above-mentioned

Orientalists crossed the boundaries between Arabic and Hebrew/Jewish studies, or vice versa, such as in the case of Haim Rabin, or Moshe Piamenta. This was facilitated by the fact that many of these early Orientalists knew Arabic, in addition to other Semitic languages. They also trained generations of future Orientalists.

While this is not an extensive study of Orientalist scholarship and thought in Israel, I will highlight a few works as a representative sample of intellectual trends. But, first, I argue that in Israel we can distinguish three generations today in regard to the study of Arabic, and by extension Hebrew and other Semitic relatives such as Aramaic and Samaritan. The first generation is characterised by the works of the scholars whose names I cite above. The second generation is their students of Arabic. I will mention, for the sake of simplicity Rafi Talmon, Judith Rosenhouse, Aharon Geva-Kleinberger, Sasson Somekh and Roni Henkin. Of this generation I will also mention Haseeb Shehadeh and Ali Watad, two Arabs who specialised in Hebrew, Aramaic and Samaritan. Of the third generation I will simply mention Yonatan Mendel, whose scholarship I have discussed extensively in this chapter and in the previous one, Uri Horesh, and a number of Arab-Israeli scholars, such as Mohammad Amara and Abd Al-Rahman Marʿi, who studied linguistics at Israeli universities. This list also includes Arabs who specifically either studied Arabic or Hebrew, such as Ibrahim Ṭāha and Ibrahim Bassal, respectively. Each generation of scholars shows continuity with earlier thought, yet with significant points of departure. I argue that each generation of these scholars represents the *Zeitgeist* of its time, both academically and politically.

First Generation of Orientalist Scholars

The Hebrew University was founded in 1925 and a year later the Institute of Oriental Studies was created at the same university, with many Orientalist scholars hailing from German universities (Eyal 2006: 62). This generation of scholars generally knew Arabic, Hebrew and Aramaic, as was the German tradition. The emphasis on Arabic was due to the belief of the centrality of the Arabic language in world civilisation. A number of these scholars also came from a scholastic family background in Judaism. Add to this, the affiliation of 'Brit Shalom' or 'Covenant of Peace', which was founded in 1925 and was much influenced by the philosophy of Martin Buber, who emphasised the role of Zionism in bridging the gap between the 'rising East' and the 'declining West' (see Eyal 2006: 65). In that sense, 'academic Orientalism was a form of Zionism', according to Eyal (2006: 65). This was also a defensive response to anti-Semitism. Academics stressed the affinity between Arabs and Jews, the potential of the rising Arab nation, and the role Zionism can play in helping the Arabs and the region in their leap towards modernity, because Zionists are the natural heirs of Western civilisation, but at the same time they are Semite and belong to this cradle of civilisation. Subjects of academic interest varied from Muslim Spain as a high point of Semitic civilisation, with the Jews and Arabs rising to new intellectual and civilisational levels. These scholars also showed interest in the language of the Jews in Arab countries, in other words, their Jewish Arabic, and how it is an expression of their specific identity in the Arab world. Another source of interest was the Yemeni Jews, as an ancient community continuously in interaction with Arab-Muslim communities. These scholars were also interested in the Cairo Geniza and its documentation of the minutiae of Jewish life under Islamic rule, and last, but not least, they were interested in Aramaic and Samaritan, as the closest sisters to Hebrew. Often, many of these scholars did not draw a line between Hebrew and Arabic Studies, but rather, treated both as part of Oriental Studies, as they were knowledgeable about both languages in addition to Aramaic and other Semitic languages. Today, Hebrew and Aramaic are studied in Hebrew departments across the country, while Arabic generally has its own departments. To represent the first generation, I will be discussing the scholarship of Shlomo Dov Goitein (1900–85), David Hartwig Baneth (1893–1973), Moshe Piamenta (1921–), Joshua Blau (1919–), Eduard Yechezkel Kutscher (1909–71) and Haim Blanc (1926–84).

Goitein was born to a family of religious scholars. After completing his studies in Germany, he taught Biblical Studies at the Reali school in Haifa and shortly afterwards joined the Institute for Oriental Studies at the Hebrew University, only to leave the country for the US in 1957.[2] Goitein wrote prolifically about Arabic, Judeo-Arabic, the Yemeni Jews and documents of the Cairo Geniza. As expected, Goitein wrote ambivalently of Arab culture, reflecting the common Orientalist ideas of his time (Eyal 2006: 65), but at the same time, and true to his Zionist beliefs, he saw that the teaching of Arabic

to Jews was part of Zionism, thus contributing to the process of the securitisation of Arabic right from the point of inception of Oriental Studies in Israel
(Mendel 2014b: 34–9). His books generally emphasise the 'Jewish-Arab symbiosis' since antiquity (Goitein 1964: 8) as both belong to the 'Semitic race'
(Goitein 1964: 19) and both have the opportunity to rise with new governments in Arab countries such as Egypt. He cites Ṭāha Ḥusayn's (1944) 'The
Future of Culture in Egypt', as an example of Arab civilisation being historically entrenched in Greek civilisation, thus facilitating the path to modernity
(Goitein 1964: 218), and with Israel having a pivotal role in the symbiosis of
both cultures. He sees no coincidence in the fact that the Hebrew University
in Jerusalem and Cairo University were founded in the same year, in 1925
(Goitein 1964: 217). Lastly, the romantic Orientalist ambivalence towards
Arab culture and civilisation is best exemplified in Goitein's (and others')
'carnivalesque' depiction of the East with its whirling bazaars, and where one
has the ability to disappear in the crowd (Eyal 2006: 48). In the preface to an
edited volume presented to Goitein for his eightieth birthday, Joshua Prawer,
praising Goitein's scholarship on the Cairo Geniza, uncritically reinforces the
carnivalesque image of Goitein's East:

> What were no more than names, geographical or personal, suspended in a
> kind of ethereal void, became under his [Goitein's] vigorous pen a robust
> living world, tangible, busy, bustling, filled with the noises and scents of
> near Eastern bazaars, but also responding with the voices of children in
> schools, of the grown-ups in synagogues and the solemnity of the elders
> laying down the law in court and Academy seven hundred years ago.
> Merchants, craftsmen, bankers, teachers, families which could trace their
> origins over several generations in a great community center or dispersed
> over the vast spaces of Islam, city quarters, streets, houses, and shops were
> resurrected from the dust of bits and pieces of paper and parchment of the
> Genizah. (Prawer 1981: 9–10).

No less impressive of a scholar was Moshe Piamenta, whom I mentioned
earlier. Piamenta, a proud native of Jerusalem, who described himself as
bilingual in Arabic and Hebrew, and who went to Christian Arab schools in
Jerusalem (Piamenta 1966: xv), comments on his affinity with the city and its
sounds (Piamenta 1981: 203):

As a native speaker of Jerusalem Arabic and life-time resident of the city, I have made do with the more or less consistent, and unvocalized Arabic orthography of the text, interpreting it through my own idiolect, for this and earlier studies in the syntax of Jerusalem and Palestinian Arabic, especially the verbal system, in my *The Use of Tenses, Aspects, and Moods* … (Piamenta 1981: 203)

Piamenta, in addition to his post as an Arabic professor at the Hebrew university, served as the General Supervisor of Arabic Studies at the Ministry of Education and, as a result, headed the Piamenta Committee, established in 1976, as a reaction to the 1973 war. This committee recommended the teaching of colloquial Arabic to Jewish students, as well as contemporary Arab affairs, thus merging peace and security together as goals for teaching Arabic to Jewish students and furthering the securitisation of Arabic, according to Mendel (2014b: 134–6). Piamenta (1968) also wrote a textbook entitled '*Speak Arabic: An Introduction to Eretz Yisraeli Arabic*', thus coining the word 'Israeli-Arabic', with all its connotations of securitisation and the historic dispossession of the Arabic language in Israel. Piamenta's later work (2000) focuses on Jewish life in Jerusalem in the first half of the twentieth century, its customs and habits, and its linguistic idiom, through the lens of a community entrenched in its Arab Muslim surroundings. It is a valuable document of the fleeting social mosaic of his beloved city.

A third scholar of this generation is David Hartwig Baneth, who hailed from a family of Jewish religious scholars and who became an immanent scholar of Arabic at the Hebrew University, as well as a librarian of the Jewish National and University Library, and who belongs to the generation which hoped to reconcile Judaism with Islam, albeit Arabs and Jews. Some of his notable students are Yitzhak Navon, who later became a president of Israel, and Joshua Blau, a world expert of Middle Arabic with its Jewish, as well as Christian, texts (Goitein 1979: 1–2). Both Blau and his colleague Piamenta seem also to have been inspired by the work of Michel Feghali (1928) on Lebanese Arabic (Piamenta 1966: xiii). Blau's monumental scholarship (1966) highlights the process between Classical and Modern Standard Arabic through Christian texts from South Palestine since the first millennium. By Christian texts, he means texts written by Christians in order to be read by

Christians. His method was comparative in that he investigated other types of Arabic texts from the same period, most notable of which were Judeo-Arabic texts. The Christian Arabic texts originated from the St Catherine Monastery in Sinai, and other Christian Arabic manuscripts preserved around the world, including the Hebrew University (Blau 1966: Preface).

One of the towering figures of Hebrew Studies at the Hebrew University in Jerusalem is E. Y. Kutscher, with his authoritative book on the history of the Hebrew language, published posthumously in 1982. In this book, he traces the development of Hebrew from biblical times to his day, with an explanation of the social milieu and the linguistic landscape of the languages which co-existed with, and influenced, Hebrew. These languages range from Aramaic to Greek, Persian, Arabic and various modern European languages. As for the Hebrew of his time, he praises the daily *Ha'aretz* for its dedication to two columns comparing phrases in Hebrew as they appeared on its pages 'fifty years ago' and 'thirty years ago', thus providing the readers with a public record of how Hebrew was developing (Kutscher 1982: 243). In his (1976) *Studies in Galilean Aramaic*, he emphasises the importance of examining the generally under-studied Western dialects of Aramaic, which include Galilean, Samaritan and Christian (Kutscher 1976: 5). In a section on place names in Palestine, he claims that the Hellenised names were abandoned as quickly as the Arabs entered the land in the seventh century:

> The Greek Scythopolis – approximately 1000 years old – became once again Beisan; Ptolemais was lost and the ancient name Akko was revived. The reason for this phenomenon is that the peasants – who were close to the Arab conquerors in origin, language, custom, and way of life-assimilated to them over a period of hundreds of years until they became one people – The Arabs of Palestine. (Kutscher 1976: 96)

He continues:

> With the decline of Greek culture and the rise of Arabic culture with its Semitic pronunciation, the Semitic pronunciation of Aramaic was able to recapture its place also among the Jewish class (or in the Jewish places) were it had been forgotten. This took place thanks to the Arabic background. This is in contrast to the Samaritans among whom apparently no one who

had preserved the ancient pronunciation tradition – in any case among the intelligentsia – had survived until the period of the Arabic conquest. Thus their ability to pronounce the gutturals was completely lost, just as their use of Aramaic as their vernacular disappeared, even though geographically they remained in the same area and were not dispersed outside of Palestine. (Ibid. p. 96)

The irony of these statements by Kutscher cannot escape the reader in the light of Israel's rigorous investment in changing Arabic place-names to Hebrew names.

Last but not least is Haim Blanc, a student of Goitein (and also of Roman Jakobson, Somekh 2012a: 91), who became a prominent scholar of Arabic with an international reputation, particularly because of his pathfinding analysis of Baghdadi Arabic (Blanc 1964), long before the study of Variation Analysis took shape with its emphasis on social factors in language variation. This pioneering work attempted to map Baghdadi dialects according to the geographic origin and religious affiliation of the speaker. Collecting his data, naturally, posed serious problems, but he still was able to do it while in the US by interviewing Iraqis there, and by completing his Iraqi interviews in Israel with the Iraqi Jewish community (Somekh 2012a: 93). Blanc was also dedicated to the cause of the state of Israel in that he volunteered in the fighting of 1948, where he lost his vision as a result.

In addition, Blanc published in 1953 a less well-known study, on the Druze community in Israel. Oblivious to the circumstances of the collecting of his data in Palestinian villages in North Israel, shortly after the dispossession of Palestinians, Blanc comments on visiting the village of Rameh where he enjoyed the hospitality of the people, and of Kufur Yasif, where:

> Mr. D. Asboren, formerly with the Military Government of Galilee, kindly offered the use of his office for listening in on the many Christian, Muslim and Druze villagers of the region who had business there. (Blanc 1953: 4)

Needless to say, this was a time of military rule over the Arab community in Israel. The fact that the military government was involved in getting Blanc what he needed for his research is beyond comment. But, at the same time, Blanc treats this involvement as a matter of fact.

To sum up, one can note that for the first generation Orientalists many of the European notions of the 'Orient' continued to survive. Some of these notions were somewhat 'romantic' such as the notion of the historic affinity between Muslim and Jewish civilisations and the hope for reviving this historic legacy, as in the case of the scholarship of Shlomo Dov Goitein. But, at the same time, the positivistic notions of research methods are at work as well, such as in the practice of research that was 'devoid' of the political context of its time. A glaring example is Haim Blanc's research on the Druze of Israel during the military regime to which the Arab community in Israel was subjected. The research does not address any of this, but immediately delves into the features of their language. And even when the military regime is invoked, it is in the context of giving access to the community's repertoire of speakers.

Second Generation of Scholars

Of this generation, I will discuss the work of Judith Rosenhouse, Rafi Talmon, Aharon Geva-Kleinberger, Sasson Somekh, Ali Watad and Haseeb Shehadeh. This generation was mostly trained by the first generation, therefore one notices the similarities of their academic analytical tools and the scope of research, but at the same time this generation also engaged in the new realities of both languages.

The career of Judith Rosenhouse, a professor of Arabic at the Technion, is a good example of this synchronous continuity and change. Her early work, which was based on her dissertation, is an in-depth analysis of the dialects of the Bedouins of North Israel (1984), in which she includes all levels of linguistic analysis: phonological, morphological, syntactic and lexical. It also contains valuable texts of stories of the oral history of these tribes. Similarly, she also studied Jerusalem Arabic (Rosenhouse 2009). Her research can be considered traditional, as she delves into the problem of providing a thorough analysis of these dialects, without the need to provide any context or justification for these data, in a manner typical of the positivistic research of the time, when researchers seldom problematised their subject of study, or for that matter, their relationship to their subject of study. In addition, in consideration of the analytical tools, one can find similarities to those of her mentor, Haim Blanc, but at the same time, her engagement in the linguistic research of the time is quite noticeable. We can see more evidence of this engagement when we examine her remarkable career over the decades. For instance, one of her latest works is an edited volume on the influence of English on various languages, ranging from Russian to Japanese, to French, to Arabic and Hebrew, as well as others (Rosenhouse and Kowner 2008). She finds that while Arabic (in Israel) and Hebrew have borrowed from English since the time of the British Mandate, there are notable differences: Hebrew has more loanwords (Rosenhouse 2008), and these can be found in oral and written language in Hebrew (Rosenhouse and Fisherman 2008), but only in colloquial language in Arabic (Rosenhouse 2008). Regarding language attitudes, Hebrew borrowers associate positive values to English loanwords, values generally associated with the American lifestyle and culture (Rosenhouse and Fisherman 2008), and lastly, that some of the Arabic borrowings come through Hebrew first (Rosenhouse 2008). As a point of departure from her predecessors, the Arabic which Rosenhouse studies is unambiguously from 'Israel'. We do not notice the word Palestinian, as we do sometimes with her predecessors. Lastly, Rosenhouse's breadth and depth of research is such that it covers many aspects of Arabic linguistics. One example is her research on the acquisition of fuṣḥā, as compared to ʿāmmiyyah, in which she argues convincingly that while ʿāmmiyyah is acquired implicitly, fuṣḥā is acquired gradually and explicitly, while foreign languages can be acquired both explicitly and implicitly (Rosenhouse 2011, but see Albirini 2016 for evidence of the opposite).

Another career path is that of Rafi Talmon, who taught at Haifa University. Towards the end of his career, in the early 1990s, he was working on an atlas of the dialects of Northern Israel (Talmon 2000), as a joint German-Israeli project. After his premature death, Aharon Geva-Kleinberger, also from Haifa University, continued with the project.[3] Geva-Kleinberger researches Semitic languages, Judaeo-Arabic (including the first half of the twentieth century Judaeo-Arabic dialect of Galilee), in a manner reminiscent of the research of Piamenta (2000), mentioned above on Jerusalem (see Geva-Kleinberger 2000). He also studies contemporary Arabic from Morocco to India.[4] He started his career studying Arabic at Haifa University, the Hebrew University and in Germany. His connection to the Arabic language, he explains, comes from the early age of thirteen, when he started to work for his father's business during the summer. The workers were Arab and this is how he became fluent and interested in Arabic.[5] Geva-Kleinberger's career is impressive for its access to communities of Arabic not open to his predecessors, or even to his cohorts in other Arab countries who are not able to conduct research outside of their environment for political and financial reasons. At the same time, his career path was inspired by the unequal position of Arabic in Israel: if he had not encountered it through his father's Arab workers, Arabic was likely to have been absent from his life as a youngster. In other words, Geva-Kleinberger's statement as to how he first acquired Arabic speaks volumes for the space Arabic is given in the linguistic landscape of Haifa, the third largest city in Israel and a city which prides itself on being bi-national, having both Arabs and Jews living together.

Sasson Somekh, the well-known scholar of contemporary Arabic can be considered as belonging to this generation, even though his path was somewhat different. Somekh was born in Baghdad in 1930 and arrived in Israel, along with most of the Iraqi community, in the 1950s. He was a native speaker of Arabic, but soon after arriving in the country he immersed himself in Hebrew and Talmudic studies. He studied at the Hebrew University with Yechezkel Kutscher, who encouraged him to continue with his studies and focus on the surviving words in contemporary Galilean Arabic, from Hebrew and Aramaic (Somekh 2012a: 69). He eventually declined, and decided to study Arabic at Oxford with the well-known Egyptian scholar, Muhammad Mustafa Badawi (Somekh 2012a: 76). He described his dilemma in making the decision in his autobiographic account of his life in Israel (Somekh 2012a). However, his love for Hebrew from different time periods was ratified in the invitation he received to join the Hebrew Language Academy. He later joined the Arabic Language Academy when it was founded in 2007, and in that he may have been the only scholar to be a member of both academies. Lastly, Somekh also joined the faculty of Arabic in the newly established Tel-Aviv University in 1968, until his retirement. At the beginning of his career, most of his students were either Arab Jews, or Arab teachers (Somekh 2012a: 103) and his world oscillated between Hebrew and Arabic studies, as he was surrounded by many of the prominent scholars in both fields, such as Haim Blanc, Shlomo Goitein and others. But, he also had the opportunity to meet Arab scholars and writers, first in his native Iraq and later through his studies and interests. For example, he was able to forge a friendship with Najuib

Mahfouz, Egypt's best-known novelist, who received the Nobel Prize in literature in 1988 (Somekh 2012a).

Two notable scholars of Hebrew belong to this generation as well: Haseeb Shehadeh and Ali Watad. Shehadeh is an Arab from Kufur Yasif in the North, who studied Hebrew with Yechezkel Kutscher and Ze'ev Ben-Hayyim. It was Ben-Hayyim who oriented him to the study of Aramaic and Samaritan. Watad, who is from the Triangle, was a student of Shehadeh. Shehadeh today is a retired member of the department of World Cultures at the University of Helsinki, and Watad heads the Arabic Academic Institute for Education at Beit Berl College in Israel. Both specialise in Samaritan, a language which used to be spoken by the Samaritans and whose descendants now live between Nablus in the West Bank and Holon near Tel-Aviv, and who number about 780 people. Shehadeh worked on the Samaritan Torah for his doctorate at the Hebrew University and continued to study the oral and written texts of this community. Shehadeh's work, while focusing on the Samaritan language, also poses questions about the historic influence of the Semitic languages on each other, what facilitated the spread of Arabic in Palestine and how the study of Samaritan can shed light on the transition of the linguistic landscape in the Middle Ages from Aramaic to Arabic (interview on 2 October 2015). Shehadeh continues today to be involved in the Samaritan community and its publications in both Arabic and Hebrew (such as in *Alif Baa, Akhbar Al-Samira*, which is published in Arabic, Hebrew and English, and in four scripts: Arabic, Hebrew, Samaritan and Latin). He also continues to write about the challenges of contemporary Palestinian Arabic (2014a), on Arabic from a historic comparative perspective (2014b) and on the particularity of the morphological structure of his native Kufur Yasif dialect (1995). Shehadeh laments the fact that today there are experts in the field of Semitic languages who do not know these languages themselves, but nevertheless, Israel has a world reputation in these studies. Further, he is of the conviction that a scholar needs to know more than one Semitic language in order to be an expert on Arabic or Hebrew, for example (interview with Shehadeh, 2 October 2015).

Under the mentorship of Shehadeh, Watad also studied the relationship between Arabic, Aramaic and Hebrew, but he focused on Samaritan. When I asked Watad about the general interest in these topics, he told me that he was the only student studying Samaritan with Shehadeh in the 1970s, which enabled him to turn the class into a tutorial session. I also asked Watad whether he found any traces of ancient Hebrew in the Palestinian dialects of today and he said no. Note that I was asking this question because when Watad was a student some scholars at the Hebrew University were trying to find evidence of Hebrew in Palestinian Arabic. In that regard, Somekh (2012a) reminiscences that he was encouraged to do this very study by his mentor Yechezkel Kutscher, as I mentioned earlier. Watad also confirmed to me that the influence on Palestinian Arabic is from Aramaic rather than Hebrew, but that some of the Aramaic words in Palestinian usage are becoming obsolete because of the change in the lifestyle of this community over the past century from agricultural to urban. Many of these words are in the domain of the everyday life of an agricultural community (Watad, interview on 16 May 2015). I chose to discuss the scholarship of Shehadeh and Watad because both of them belong to the indigenous Palestinian community and did not leave the country in 1948, but obtained Israeli citizenship. Both are knowledgeable in Hebrew, Aramaic and Samaritan, and because of this they are a minority among the 'Israeli Arabs'. Both have been the subject of a scientific study which seeks affinity between Hebrew (and Aramaic) and Arabic, as well as between the Arabs and Jews. As discussed earlier, students were encouraged to study the relations between these Semitic languages (as in the case of Sasson Somekh), with the implication that Palestinian Arabic (and Arabs) were related to the land of Israel, and to the ancient Jews in the deep past of the place. This discourse, obviously, does reinforce the legitimacy of the Jews over the country, but at the same time it leaves room for inclusion of the Palestinian Arab population because of a romanticised past historic affinity between both peoples. Just by doing this, both Watad and Shehadeh helped open up discussion for more legitimacy and more inclusion of the Arab population in Israel.

To sum up, the second generation abstains from any explicit political or social context for the research or the researcher. In this, it remains true to the positivism of the earlier generation, which also prevailed through the 1970s and 1980s and which asserts the impartiality of science. However, this generation is characterised by a background of nation-building in Israel which is less critical of the hegemonic mainstream Zionism (if at all critical). It was at a time when Labour Zionism had not yet been critiqued publicly. Chapter 4 will deal with this point more extensively, as it relates to the generational shift in the public discourse regarding Zionism. Suffice it to say, in brief, that Labour Zionism and its hegemony was challenged in the late seventies by Mizrachi Jews as well as by the feminist movement (Shafir and Peled 2002). In the 1990s the political environment opened up in Israel in a way that was unprecedented for several reasons, the most important being economic liberalism and the direct talks with the PLO. But, according to Pappé (2014), this window of opportunity closed again after the 2000 Al-Aqsa intifada. Today, the political situation is more fragmented, but with a clear right-wing Zionist hegemony. The third generation scholarship reflects clearly the opening of the 1990s in public discourse and, at the same time, the fragmented political agenda which followed. Note that the state of scholarship in the West was also going through the 'discursive turn' around the same time, when every aspect of research was problematised, challenged and critiqued, and when the objectivity of science was no longer a given.

Third Generation of Scholars

In this generation, we find people educated in linguistics in addition to those educated in the fields of Arabic and/or Hebrew. We also find a number of indigenous Arabs who work in academia in Israeli institutions. I will discuss the scholarship of Mohammad Amara and Abd Al-Rahman Marʿi, who both teach at the Arab Academic Institute for Education at Beit Berl College. I will also discuss the scholarship of Ibrahim Bassal, who teaches Hebrew at the Arab Academic College in Haifa, and Uri Horesh who teaches in the US. Amara studied at Bar-Ilan University with Bernard Spolsky, one of the world's best-known contemporary linguists (in both Sociolinguistics and Applied Linguistics). Lastly, while some come with an academic background in Hebrew/Aramaic, as is the case of Bassal, others have a background in Arabic studies such as Mendel and Horesh. All of these scholars know both Arabic and Hebrew, and some know Aramaic as well. This group of scholars is also familiar with the critical work of Elana Shohamy at Tel-Aviv University, in regard to language policy, globalisation, language acquisition and multilingualism. In other words, they are all familiar with a wide range of academic fields.

Amara and Marʿi discuss the effect of Hebrew on the Arabic of the Palestinians in Israel. Generally, their data is drawn from the Triangle population, where they both reside. In an early work by Amara (co-authored with Sufian Kabaha 1996), he discusses the effect of the partition of the small village of Bartaʿa in the Triangle on the linguistic behaviour of its population. Bartaʿa was divided between Israel and Jordan shortly after the Rhodes Agreement in 1949, with half the village becoming Israeli citizens and learning Hebrew in school, and half the village becoming Jordanian citizens. In 1967 the village united, but the population continued to carry two different citizenships. Amara and Kabaha observed that the linguistic behaviour of the village was different between both parts of the village: the Palestinian and the Israeli. In the Israeli part people borrowed from Hebrew and demonstrated their knowledge of Hebrew in their daily lives, whereas in the part of the village which belonged to the West Bank people did not borrow from Hebrew, but rather looked to fuṣḥā for borrowing into their local dialect, and then to English. In other words, there were clear differences in language choice between both parts of the village in the 1990s.

Amara's career produced a number of studies on the linguistic behaviour of the Arabs in Israel, their patterns of borrowing, language attitudes and the pervasive influence of Hebrew on their behaviour. His later work surveys the language education policy for the Arabs in Israel (Amara and and Marʿi 2002). It takes a historic view of the language curricula in Palestine during the British Mandate, and of the establishment of the state of Israel. Amara and Marʿi conclude with the statement that the language policies in Israel:

> Have failed to consider the needs and attitudes of the minority students towards the various languages taught and their motivations for learning them. While the symbolic aspects are emphasized by the subjects in relation to Arabic learning, the emphasis on the curriculum is on the pragmatic aspects. The opposite is true in Hebrew: while the subjects emphasize the pragmatic aspects for learning the language, the curriculum emphasizes its cultural and national aspects. (Amara and Marʿi 2002: 137)

Marʿi (2013), on the other hand, discusses extensively and intensively the pervasiveness of Hebrew words into everyday Arabic of the Palestinians in Israel. In other words, his discussion focuses on the lexical influence of

Hebrew on Arabic. Marʿi (2013: 15) states that Hebrew is one of the cultural and behavioural cornerstones of Arab life in Israel today.

Ibrahim Bassal, much influenced by the work of Ali Watad and Yechezkel Kutscher, explores the influences of Aramaic on the Palestinian dialects. He classifies the domains in which Aramaic and Hebrew lent words to Arabic, and this includes the agricultural domain. However, he also admits that some of the borrowed words from Aramaic are shared in Levantine Arabic, and sometimes they also entered the fuṣḥā; therefore, they are not specifically Palestinian. Bassal classifies the lexical borrowings in Palestinian Arabic in these domains: land, agriculture and seasons, weather, agricultural tools, house tools, crops and fruits, food and clothing items, animals and their habitats, residences and buildings, and lastly Christian religious terms (Bassal 2012, 2015). Just like Shehadeh before him, who comes from the same village in Galilee, Kufur Yasif, he gives a morphophonemic description of the dialect of Kufur Yasif (2008).

While researchers are so far focused on lexical changes, Uri Horesh focuses on the phonological changes currently occurring to the Arabic of the Israeli Arabs as a result of contact with Hebrew. The community he focuses on is the Arab community of Yaffa, a mixed city. Horesh found that the contact with Hebrew has affected the length of some vowels for the Arabic speakers who speak Hebrew. In addition, he claims that an entire constellation of sounds is adjusting to Hebrew phonology, most striking of which is the deletion of the pharyngeal voiced fricative. This deletion is compensated for by lengthening the vowel, for example, baʿdeːn changing to baːdeːn 'later' (Horesh 2014). Horesh also observed that the Arabic emphatic sounds are becoming non-emphatic, as a result of language contact with Hebrew (Horesh 2014, 2015). To test his observations further, Horesh compares the Yaffa speech in Yaffa with William Cotter's study of the speech of the Yaffa refugees from 1948 in Gaza (Cotter and Horesh 2015) and confirms his observations of the changes in Arabic phonology for bilingual speakers of Arabic and Hebrew. The Yaffa speakers in Gaza did not demonstrate any of the above-mentioned changes.

To sum up, this generation of scholars is equipped with the scientific tools of their time, in addition to the knowledge of at least Arabic and Hebrew. However, they did not participate fully in the discursive turn of linguistics and social sciences. In the case of Amara, Marʿi and Horesh, they are still confined to the empirical sociolinguistic research methods of the previous generation. But while Amara and Marʿi confine their research questions and conclusions to a permissible level of discourse (Arabic influenced by Hebrew, or the Arabic of a divided village influenced by Hebrew on one side, and by Standard Arabic and English on the other), Horesh pushes the boundaries of his research to make a comparison of two interrelated communities such as Yaffa and Gaza (Cotter and Horesh 2015). In other words, Amara and Marʿi in their subordinate political position in Israel reproduce scholarship which appeals to Jewish readers, such as the subordination of Arabic in the state to Hebrew. At the same time, both of their research projects seem to seek more proximity and more understanding between both peoples. As for Bassal, while his scholarship can be characterised in the same vein as that of Amara and Marʿi, it has the potential for being used politically to further fragment the Arabic community in Israel into religious identities, by separating a possible Christian 'Aramaic' identity from that of the Muslim.

Arabic Departments in Israeli Universities

The language of instruction in the Arabic departments of Israel's major universities is Hebrew, with the exception of Haifa university where 80 per cent of its classes are offered in Arabic and even master's theses and doctoral dissertations are written in Arabic (Ibrahim Ṭāha, Professor of Arabic at Haifa University, interview, 15 May 2015).[6] Ṭāha also stated in the same interview that only two professors in this department do not teach in the Arabic language. Further, 95 per cent of the students in this department are Arab. A quick look at the official websites of Arabic departments in the major universities show the following: the website of Haifa University is the most comprehensive in Arabic, but it also offers the same information in English and in Hebrew.[7] The website of the Hebrew University does not offer information in Arabic, but rather in Hebrew and in English.[8] Tel-Aviv University *does* offer information in Arabic, but it is incomplete compared to the information offered in Hebrew and in English.[9] Bar-Ilan University *does* offer information in the three languages, in a manner similar to that of Tel-Aviv University's presentations.[10] And lastly, the department of Middle East Studies at Ben-Gurion University of the Negev offers information on its website in both

Hebrew and English, but not in Arabic.[11] Thus, while Arabic is visually present in most of these major universities, it is subordinate to Hebrew and sometimes even English.

Arabic in the Knesset: The Case of (MK) Ahmad Tibi

Ahmad Tibi, born in Taybeh in the Triangle, is a medical doctor who studied at the Hebrew University and who became a politician and advisor to Yasser Arafat in the 1990s. He also founded the 'Arab Movement for Change', 'Ta'al', and became a Knesset member representing this movement in 1999. During the last elections in 2015 his movement joined the 'Joint List' when Arab parties decided to unite for the elections in order to maximise their presence, as the threshold needed for a party to be considered an eligible to run for the Knesset was raised for that election period (mentioned in Chapter 1). Tibi believes that the state of Israel should be a state for all of its citizens if it still wants to consider itself a democratic state (official website of the 'Ta'al' movement).[12]

Tibi is known in the Knesset for his quick wit and humour. His Hebrew is impeccable, and he often corrects Jewish Knesset members when they are speaking Hebrew.[13] He has a following for his speeches in the Knesset: one of the excerpts I checked had 184,000 views.[14]

Tibi does not speak Arabic in the Knesset, but rather he peppers his Hebrew with Palestinian Arabic for emphasis. This generally irritates his Jewish peers in the Knesset who start shouting that he should speak in Hebrew, an effect he might have intended all along.[15] In this particular example, Tibi uses one sentence in Arabic at that point when the chairman of the Knesset session asks him not to speak in Arabic. Tibi explains to him that maybe because he is a new MK, he does not know that Arabic is permitted in the Knesset and that it is an official language. The chairman of the Knesset session asks him to leave the platform. Tibi says that he will finish what he had to say first, in Arabic, and then leave the platform. At this point he speaks in Arabic, addressing the Knesset with 'Arabic is an official language. I am proud of it, in spite of you (the chairman of the Knesset session), and I will continue to speak and repeat the sentences which irritated you, do you like that? I don't care if you don't like it.'

In another excerpt, Tibi pays tribute to MK Israel Eichler from the religious party 'Agudat Yisrael', in Yiddish. Eichler had spoken in Arabic saying that he supports the Arabs in their struggle for democracy. Tibi pays him back by stating in Yiddish that he supports the religious party in its struggle for equal rights.[16] At that point, all Knesset members burst into laughter.

The use of Arabic by Tibi is generally not in order to communicate in Arabic, but rather, it is part of a performance to create an effect on the listener, beyond the words uttered in Arabic. He uses mostly Palestinian idiom. In his defence of the Bedouin of the Negev who have been forced to dislocate from what Israel calls 'illegal towns', he recites Mahmoud Darwish's poem 'ābirūn fī kalām 'ābir', 'passersby in passing words'. At that point, the chairman of the session asks him to leave the platform.[17] Leaving the platform as punishment seems to be a ritual he and his other opponent MKs seem to expect and relish.

In another example, Tibi comments on a proposal for a bill which distinguished the citizenship of the Arabs according to their religious affiliation. He peppers his argument with a quote of Naji Al-Ali (1938–87), the Palestinian cartoonist, who uses the image of what seems to be a Palestinian boy wrapping his arms behind his back and commenting on the absurdity of the Palestinian presence. The image of this boy, 'Ḥanthala', is well recognised by Arabs and certainly by Palestinians. For the Knesset, however, Tibi had to give some context in Hebrew before he cites Ḥanthala in Arabic as saying 'Ana 'Arabi, Ya Jaḥsh', 'I am an Arab, you mule', in reference to those who insist that there is no Arab unity, but rather fragmented religious identities, such as was happening in Lebanon at the time of Naji Al-Ali, who had to live there as a refugee.[18]

Lastly, in a speech in the Knesset, in reaction to MK Yaron Mazoz, the Deputy Minister of Interior in the last elections who proposed a bill to take away the identity cards of Arabs in Israel (in effect stripping them of their citizenship), Tibi gives the Knesset a lesson in what the word 'izrach', citizen, means in Hebrew and in Arabic. In Hebrew, it refers to the contract between the state and the individual. In Arabic, the word 'muwāṭin' is derived from 'waṭan', 'homeland'. At that point, another MK asks him to explain the difference between 'waṭaniyya' (local nationalism) and 'qawmiyya' (ethnic nationalism) in Arabic. Tibi playfully responds that he will give him or anyone else a private lesson in Arabic after his speech. He declares in Arabic that 'the identity card is important, but the identity is more important, and we are the people of this place', 'al-hawiyya aham min biṭāqit al-hawiyya, wa iḥna aṣḥāb al-balad'. He continues in Arabic, 'my name is Ahmad Tibi, Arab, Palestinian, and my identity number is 56775', 'Ana ismī Ahmad Tibi, 'Arabi wa-falasṭīnī, wa-raqm hawiyatī 56775', in an allusion to one of Mahmoud Darwish's best-known early poems 'Identity Card'. Tibi then switches back to Hebrew and declares: 'I am proud to be from this place', 'ani ga'eh shi-ani ben ha-makom', perhaps as a tribute to his complex identity.[19] To sum up, Tibi abstains from giving full speeches in Arabic from the platform of the Knesset, but uses Arabic in subordination to Hebrew, often to create a dramatic rhetorical effect. The success of these linguistic strategies is apparent in the manner of the reception of his speeches by both Arab and Jews alike, yet, in spite of these strategies, Tibi's usage remains within the confines of the discursive reality of Arabic as subordinate to Hebrew.

Interviews during Fieldwork

I interviewed a number of students, writers, and journalists mostly from Nazareth in 2013 and 2014, in regard to their thought on the Arabic language and bilingualism with Hebrew. The interviews were informal and the questions were open and not scripted. I generally opened with a question of what they think of the situation for the Arabic language in Israel, whether they have any concerns and what it means to them to be bilingual with Hebrew. I let the interviewees reflect on the situation without much interruption on my part, unless I felt that I wanted clarification or elaboration on a certain point. Most interviewees spoke of the concern for the loss of the Arabic language, as Hebrew was taking over domains reserved in the past for Arabic. They also expressed fear of the pervasion of Hebrew words into Arabic speech, and of the amount of code-switching which Arabs do, a fear that this is creating a new language, incomprehensible to people outside of the Israeli Arab communities. But there was one point they all emphasised: the relationship of the language situation to the Palestinian conflict and to the fact that they live as a minority in a state that defines itself as Jewish, and considers the Arab identity as 'antithetical' to Jewish identity. All the interviewees can be considered middle class people who have succeeded in their education in Israeli institutions and who have successful careers.

In other words, all can be considered as successfully integrated in Israeli institutions.

For example, the poet and writer of children's books, Jawdat Eid (interviewed 8 July 2013), who is educated in social work, expressed his dismay at the reaction he gets when he takes his children to Jewish cities, such as Tel-Aviv, and speaks to his children in Arabic. He is generally confronted with stares in Jewish public spaces. He says, 'I open my mouth and I am immediately transformed into a suspect, an unwanted person, and possibly a terrorist.' He even wrote a short story of how he was sitting in a restaurant with his father in Tel-Aviv when he was a child, and while speaking to his father in Arabic everyone in the restaurant became very quiet, and as a child he could not understand why. The same thing is happening to his children today when he takes them to Jewish places. Eid expresses his agony in a poem he calls 'Disharmony' (Eid 2003: 12) as: 'I am a crusader-descendent, Phoenician, Arab, Palestinian, Canaanite, Terrorist' (my translation of Ṣalīby, Phīnīqy, ʿArabiy, Falasṭīny, Canʿāny, Irhāby). Eid explains this poem to me as 'I am the clothes hanger which they (the Jews) throw all of these identities at. I did and do not choose these identities for myself.' This particular poem was translated into Hebrew and he was invited to a poetry reading in Tel-Aviv. He said that among the audience there were people who genuinely appreciated it as they wanted to know the 'Arab other', but there were also people who expressed anger at his 'alleged' ingratitude to the state that gave him citizenship. He also mentioned that some of these particular identities, such as the 'crusader-descendent' and 'Phoenician' are thrown at him because he confessed the Maronite faith (interviewed 8 July 2013).

Ruba Warwar, the broadcaster in Arabic on Israel's Channel 1 (interviewed 8 July 2013), expressed her conviction that language is the expression of a political reality. 'Whether we want it or not, there is a significant influence of the Jewish culture and the Hebrew language on us as Arab citizens of the state.' She also stated that the Arab minority in Israel is and should be resilient, bringing in the Nazareth proverb of 'we should summer in the summer and winter in the winter' which means that people need to make adjustments to the times and circumstances that they live in. Ruba Warwar believes that 'we are culturally Arab in our collective memory, language, history, habits and customs, but we are at the same time Israeli in our citizenship and that must express itself as a component of our identity'. When I asked her where the Palestinian component was in all of this, she emphasised the inseparability of the Palestinian component from the Arab component of her identity. I then probed for identities which preceded the Arab identity in Palestine. Her reaction was that they *do* exist, but one should not dig that deep in history for these identities, and instead one should deal with the reality of Arabness in a Jewish state. I received this same reaction from Jawdat Eid. They are both aware of the discourse of a minority of Arabs who wish to go back to a pre-Arab identity such as the Aramaic, but this is not a successful project in their opinion, and it is clearly motivated by politics meant to divide the Arab public in Israel. Warwar laments the institutional encouragement of fragmented identities such as 'Muslim, Christian, Druze, and Bedouin'. In her opinion, 'in spite of our differences, we must all remain under the Arab umbrella, but at the same time, adjust it to the fact that we are Israeli citizens'. Warwar, as a broadcaster, likes to choose a combination of fuṣḥā and ʿāmmiyyah. In her opinion, the problem is the lack of an effective academy or authority which would guide her and other broadcasters in the appropriate usages of Arabic.

This same concern was expressed to me by Zuhair Bahloul from Akka, who became a Knesset member from the Labour party in the twentieth Knesset elections, after my interview with him. Bahloul used to be a very popular sports broadcaster in Hebrew, but at the time of my interview he was working as an Arabic broadcaster in 'Al-Shams', a private radio station located in Nazareth, and popular with all Arabs in Israel. I interviewed him on 12 August 2013. In his opinion, while the Hebrew Language Academy is strong and has an influence on the media, 'we don't have that with Arabic, in spite of the fact that there is an Arabic Language Academy in Israel'. He brings as an example the word for identity in Arabic. He doesn't know, and there is no authority to turn to, whether he should pronounce it as 'hawiyya' or huwiyya'. So he has to make that decision on his own. Lastly, Bahloul also commented that the average Arab in Israel turns to the Hebrew media for news as it is perceived to be more accurate, in spite of the prevalence of media outlets in Arabic.

All three (Eid, Warwar, Bahloul) expressed that the ʿāmmiyyah has a huge presence among Israeli Arabs, at the expense sometimes of the fuṣḥā. For example, Arab politicians try to speak in fuṣḥā, only to switch to

ʿāmmiyyah because their fuṣḥā is not good enough. Eid commented that Ahmad Tibi (mentioned above) is hesitant to speak in fuṣḥa and he generally confines himself to ʿāmmiyyah when he has to speak in Arabic. The three also lament that the Arabs in Israel read very little in Arabic, if they read at all. In this regard, Amir Abu Jabal, another broadcaster at Al-Shams radio, who is originally from the Golan Heights (interviewed 12 August 2013), brings the example of the Lebanese poet, Said ʿAql (1911–2014), who promoted a Lebanese Phoenician identity and who wrote in Lebanese ʿāmmiyyah as he considered it an expression of the uniqueness of the Lebanese nation. But ʿAql also wrote in fuṣḥā, and according to Abu Jabal, some of his poems are considered to be among the most beautiful contemporary Arabic poems in fuṣḥā. ʿAql described fuṣḥā as a very beautiful language, and he knew it well, but that did not stop him from believing that the Lebanese ʿāmmiyyah is the language of the Lebanese people. In other words, Abu Jabal does not see why fuṣḥā should be competing with the Palestinian ʿāmmiyyah.

A slightly different but no less rich perspective on language and 'living together' comes from the veteran broadcaster on Channel 1 of Israeli television, Roger Tabor. Tabor came to the country in the fifties, when he was five years old, with his Lebanese Jewish mother and his French father. The family settled in Akka, where he went to school with Arab children. Ironically, Tabor comments that in the early days of the state, there was much less racism than there is today. His classmates were Muslim and Christian Arabs, and he grew up to be bilingual in both Arabic and Hebrew. He describes his Arabic as belonging to Akka, 'Akkiyya'. He studied Medicine after school for a few years, until he realised that his inclinations were linguistic and not scientific, and so he went to study Arabic, Middle East Studies and Communications. In the 1970s he had a programme entitled 'Alā Fikra', 'By the Way', which he presented in both Arabic and Hebrew, with subtitles. This programme was broadcast on Israel's Channel 1 during the time allocated for Arabic broadcast. Any of his guests could speak in either language on the programme. At one point he even had guests speaking in Arabic, Hebrew, English and French, with translations to and from each of these languages. Tabor translated to Hebrew some of Mahmoud Darwish's poems, Adonis and others. He also co-edited a bilingual literary journal with Anton Shammas, which was published in Ann Arbor, Michigan. The journal was called 'Delos' after the birthplace of the Greek god, Apollo. He continued to use Arabic and Hebrew in his daily life without any conflict. However, he does make a comment about his cohort Sammy Mikhail, the Iraqi Jewish writer who used to write in Arabic to 'Al-Ittiḥād', the communist newspaper in Israel (edited by Emile Habibi at that time). Mikhail at some point stopped writing in Arabic as it interfered with his sense of identity in Israel. His children felt embarrassed by it and so he abandoned it (interview with Tabor on 16 May 2015).

Raja Marjiyeh, a student at the Technion, laments that while one of his professors at the Technion in Haifa is an Arab, neither of them can communicate in Arabic about academic topics even when they try. The reason is a lack of knowledge of scientific terminology in Arabic. He added that he was able to find science books written in Arabic, but they were old and unhelpful. As for Rayeq Bawardi, who also studies at the Technion, he is happy that Arabic grammar has not fundamentally changed much throughout the centuries, because it has enabled Arabic speakers to read old texts in Arabic. He compares this to Italian and English (he learned both). In English it is hard for him to understand Chaucer, but he can easily understand Dante in Italian. Another comparison he makes between Arabic and Italian is that both languages have many dialects, yet the standard is so prevalent that at least it is enabling greater numbers of people to communicate in the same language, particularly in writing. To both Bawardi and Marjiyeh, Aramaic is a component of the Arab Palestinian identity, but at the same time to dwell on this ancient identity is a form of escapism from the reality of 'us' as Arabs 'here' in a country which is built on Zionist myth and nationalism, and which denies the Arab 'Other'. Bawardi also expressed dismay at his unsuccessful effort in trying to distinguish the boundary between Arabic and Hebrew, as many words exist in both languages but with slightly different connotations and sometimes denotations. His inability to distinguish where Arabic ends and Hebrew starts, and the possibility of a language loss, causes him discomfort.

Lastly, Siba Khatib, a law student at Haifa University, expressed the necessity of mastering the Hebrew language in order to succeed in her studies and to have a future career in law, as the language of the law and of the courtroom is Hebrew. The same sentiment was expressed by Maroun Maalouf, in respect to his studies in Economics at the University of Haifa and his future career success.

To sum up, this chapter discussed the affinity between the teaching and the scholarship of Arabic and the nation-building in Israel. The three generations of scholars identified in this chapter have contributed to the discourse of subordination of Arabic. Academia has also played a role in strengthening the ties between the Arabic language and the national security of Israel. For example, research questions have been tied to the dominant discourse of each of these time periods. It seems that the opening up of discourse on the history of Israel and its relationship to the indigenous Palestinian community which marks the 1990s (Pappé 2014) did not touch Arabic studies. They seem to have been immune to the critical turn of the 1990s as it was perhaps safer to stick to a discourse of mutual respect of both peoples at the time of the Oslo Accords. As for Ahmad Tibi's style in his Knesset speeches, Arabic is used for making or reinforcing a point he is generally expressing in the Hebrew language, thus Tibi, while getting attention for his message, is still confining Arabic to a subordinate position to that of Hebrew. Ironically, Arab Knesset members in the early days of the state spoke in the Knesset in Arabic, on the rare occasions that they were asked to speak. Those members were hand picked by the Israeli political elite and were considered as mere tools in the hands of the government (see Sa'di 2014). Moreover, for the journalists and the students I interviewed, the mood in regard to the Arabic language seems gloomy, as they sense its subordination to Hebrew, as well as their subordination as a group to the Jewish hegemony of the majority. At the same time, however, these interviewees demonstrate a linguistic repertoire that is highly sophisticated and diverse.

Notes

1. I thank Haseeb Shehadeh for his helpful suggestions; however, I remain responsible for the text analysis.
2. Available at <https://en.wikipedia.org/wiki/Shelomo_Dov_Goitein> (last accessed 12 November 2015).
3. Available at <http://arabic.haifa.ac.il/staff/ageva-Kleinberger.html> (last accessed 25 October 2015).
4. Available at <https://www.youtube.com/watch?v=UIZoS8Y93TY> (last accessed 25 October 2015).
5. Available at <https://www.youtube.com/watch?v=UIZoS8Y93TY> (last accessed 25 October 2015).

6. In contrast to the Arabic presence in 80 per cent of the Arabic classes, Arabic is non-existent in signs around the university where Arab students constitute 30 per cent of the student population, a percentage which is even higher than that of the population in general (Shohamy and Abu Ghazaleh-Mahajneh 2012). Both authors add that when asking the Arab students how they felt regarding the absence of Arabic on campus signs, they expressed alienation and unhappiness. In other words, they took the absence of Arabic as a political attempt to marginalise the presence of Arabs on campus and in the country. Lastly, the lack of Arabic signage at Haifa University is also in contrast to the city of Haifa, which was the first to include Arabic in signage across the city.

7. Available at <http://arabic.haifa.ac.il/index.php/en/> (last accessed 25 October 2015).

8. Available at <http://www.hum.huji.ac.il/english/units.php?cat=823> (last accessed 25 October 2015).

9. Available at <http://humanities.tau.ac.il/arabic_eng/> (last accessed 25 October 2105).

10. Available at <http://arabic.biu.ac.il/en> (last accessed 25 October 2105).

11. Available at <http://arabic.biu.ac.il/en> (last accessed 25 October 2015).

12. Available at <http://www.a-m-c.org/> (last accessed 27 October 2015).

13. See for example <https://www.youtube.com/watch?v=6WujhH6KQFs> (last accessed 27 October 2015).

14. Available at <https://www.youtube.com/watch?v=tIWPUd0hsbY> (last accessed 27 October 2015).

15. Available at <https://www.youtube.com/watch?v=9gqrMgj8ois> (last accessed 27 October 2015).

16. Available at <https://www.youtube.com/watch?v=YkZo84HMcrU> (last accessed 27 October 2015).

17. Available at <https://www.youtube.com/watch?v=tIWPUd0hsbY> (last accessed 27 October 2015).

18. See <https://www.youtube.com/watch?v=g6Z9GLtG5CY> (last accessed 27 October 2015).

19. See <https://www.youtube.com/watch?v=HWOye_umCCo> (last accessed 27 October 2015).

3

The (in)Visibility of Arabic:
The Linguistic Landscape

A Linguistic Landscape (LL) analysis of the symbolic presence of Arabic in public spaces presents a picture of a marginalised language struggling for legitimacy, in spite of its official status. A broad understanding of the context which includes historic, political and social dimensions enables LL to be a formidable tool of analysis regarding the place of a language in a community. As mentioned earlier, the status of Arabic as an official language along with Hebrew has been continuous since the times of the British Mandate in Palestine, which considered English, Arabic and Hebrew as the official languages (see, for example, stamps issued during that period, Figure 3.1). As for the legal aspect of signage in Israel, I will discuss that in more detail in Chapter 4.

This chapter studies the Linguistic Landscape, or the arrangement of the public symbolic space of a community, in Israel through examining the general signage on major highways, as well as in Haifa (a mixed city), Nazareth (the only remaining Arab town after 1948) and Jerusalem. Much has been written on language policy in Israel (see Spolsky and Shohamy 1999, Spolsky 2004 for example). Spolsky and Cooper (1991) have already discussed signage in their book on the languages of Jerusalem, thus initiating a conversation on the importance of signage, which later evolved into the study of signage through the lens of LL. Elana Shohamy, a pioneer and advocate for LL prefers a wide definition of LL (Shohamy et al. 2010), which can even include

Figure 3.1 Old stamps from around the Arab world, Oman, May 2014.
(Photo: Russell Lucas)

body tattoos, while Spolsky prefers to tighten up the definition (Wiley 2014). Regardless of this seeming difference, both scholars account for the conditions of inequality among languages and their speakers through the visual presence of these languages (Trumper-Hecht 2010). Some researchers make a distinction between the top-down (official and placed by government or institutional bodies) and bottom-up (unofficial and placed by private businesses or persons) of LL (Gorter 2006: 4).

Further, Eliezer and Miriam Ben-Rafael emphasise the social aspect of LL, with the related issues of cultural hybridisation and human movement among, for example, French Jews in Israel (Ben-Rafael and Ben-Rafael 2010). Their research revives Fishman's notion of 'linguistic domain' in regard to the organisation of LL (Ben-Rafael and Ben-Rafael 2010: 336). Other researchers may focus on the political aspect of LL and on the conditions of inequalities among groups (Coupland 2003). Nonetheless, all agree on the symbolic aspect of LL (Ben-Rafael et al. 2006). Ben-Rafael et al. (2006) argue that LL is driven by three forces: self-presentation (Goffman 1981), power relations of dominance and subordination among groups (Bourdieu 1993), and lastly, by forces of reason, such as, but not exclusive to, the linguistic signs targeted at consumers. Generally, this type of signs appeals to the rationality of the consumer (Boudon 1990). In my analysis of Arabic LL in Israel, I use both top-down and bottom-up signs, as both are necessary for the analysis. I also find the three forces which Ben-Rafael et al. (2006) mention as generally illuminating the LL analysis.

I argue in this chapter that an overview of LL in Israel through signage sheds a light on what it means for Arabic to be an official language in Israel. The study of signage points to a process of marginalisation of the Arabic language and its speakers inside the borders of the Green Line in Israel. I will first give a brief summary of the legal-political status of Arabic in Israel (discussed in Chapter 4 in more detail), then I will discuss the validity of LL as a concept, the practices of place naming in Israel, an analysis of some signage from different parts of the country and finally, I dedicate a section to the signage in Jerusalem. The chapter concludes with the necessity of sufficient contextualisation of the visual aspect of a language in public spaces, as the context of LL reproduces the power relations among groups and their respective languages, but at the same time, the very particular arrangement of LL can influence the public perception of a language (see Marten et al. 2012). Thus, LL gives us access to 'what is going on?' in regard to how a language might be minoritised.

Arabs and Nationality in Israel: Minoritised People, Minoritised Language

Arabic has been referred to as a minority language since the establishment of the state in 1948. The irony of calling Arabic a minority language compared to Hebrew does not escape Shohamy and Abu Ghazaleh-Mahajneh (2012). Further, as mentioned in earlier chapters, the Palestinians in Israel have generally viewed themselves as a 'minority' and have demanded equal rights from within the institutional system of the state of Israel (Ghanem 2001), as they participate in elections and are represented in the Knesset. Also, since the Oslo Accords, many organisations have been formed to speak for and protect the rights of the Palestinian 'minority' in Israel, such as the HRA[1] or Adalah.[2] The rationale for these organisations, as Mohammad Zaidan, the founder of the HRA organisation explained to me, is that when the Oslo Accords were signed, he, among others, felt that the Palestinians in Israel were left behind, hence the need for such organisations to deal specifically with Arab affairs in Israel (C. Suleiman 2011). These organisations have become even more important today, as the Knesset, since the beginning of the second intifada in 2000, has been proposing various bills in an attempt to change this group's citizenship status. These bills range from removing Arabic as an official language, to Israel becoming a Jewish state, to a proposal for a loyalty oath for the state of Israel. Further, the events in the summer of 2014 in Gaza Strip have intensified the anxieties of the Jewish politicians, as well as the media and the public. Racist remarks about Arabs and Arabic have become more vocal and public. About 40 per cent of Jewish people in a 2014 poll said that they have never spoken to an Arab (Jibreal 2014) and many Arabs have expressed discomfort at speaking Arabic in public spaces, and even at continuing to live in mixed cities among Jews, out of fear for their safety and the safety of their children (see for example, Kashua 2014).

The Linguistic Landscape of Arabic

Linguistic Landscape is defined as 'the scene where the public space is symbolically constructed' (Shohamy et al. 2010: xi). It covers a wide array of linguistic-symbolic phenomena in public spaces, such as the demographic concentration of ethnic groups and languages, signage and the organisation of public space and the language representation in it. As a term, it is fluid in that it can capture the demographic changes across time and space in a certain community. Different methods aid the researchers in operationalising the LL concept: historic demographic data, google maps and signage, among other things. The investigation of LL involves ethnographic work with the community. For instance, some of the questions asked are: what is the focal point of the community – a store, a cultural centre or a religious centre? What types of printed materials do people in the community get and read? What is advertised and in what languages? How does the community organise the signage in roads, shopping areas, stores etc.? In other words, the visual organisation of a space gives an important clue as to what is going on in terms of the demographic/linguistic structure of a community (see Wiley 2014). This leads to larger questions about linguistic rights, minority rights and practices of marginalisation and exclusion or inclusion. This type of analysis is multilayered as it examines a community in its space, over time, but it also pays attention to the discourse from within the community in the 'here and now' regarding its interaction with other communities in its proximity. The urge for such broad analysis is the result of general dissatisfaction with the linguistic analysis of a community based solely on its language practices, or on the context of its linguistic practices, but, generally, in a narrower sense than the LL would allow, and where the physical spatial dimension is not taken into consideration.

However, by utilising LL, we must never forget the auditory presence of a language. For instance, as I write this chapter, a bill has been proposed in Israel to ban the Muslim call for prayer in mosques in Israel, on the pretext that the sound annoys non-Muslims. This bill is a significant indication of the diminishing public space of Arabic in Israel, yet research cannot capture it visually (see *Al-Jazeera* 2014a).

Moreover, if Arabic is unwelcome in public spaces in Israel, one cannot capture this other than by its conspicuous absence in public spaces, or by ethnographically interviewing people to find out whether they use Arabic in public and how comfortable they feel, or not, about using it. In other words, the concept of LL, while enriching our understanding of a community's linguistic rights, or lack of rights, still cannot provide a full explanation unless we combine various methods of analysis to account for the visual as well as the auditory space of a language, in both the literal and the metaphorical sense. I take LL to be metaphorical as well as literal.

The Practices of Naming of Public Spaces in Israel

With the establishment of the state, a process of renaming places began. This went side by side with the practice of making Hebrew the first language of the state. The revivification of Hebrew in everyday life had started decades earlier with the advent of settling the land. Every once in a while, Zionist ideologues debated what the language of the new nation in a new homeland should be, and what innovations are needed to make that chosen language modern and up-to-date. Once the argument for Hebrew was won, disfavouring the two major competitors, German and Yiddish, a process of lexical and grammatical innovations started. Ze'ev Jabotinsky, a revisionist Zionist (mentioned in Chapter 1), for instance, argued for distancing Hebrew from Arabic, even in the pronunciation of certain sounds, such as the pharyngeal sounds which both languages share (see Massad 2006), as he perceived Hebrew to be an Ashkenazi/European language, thus ignoring the fact that Judaism existed outside Europe as well.

The process of naming has taken the following forms: (1) translation from the Arabic name, (2) finding a phonetically similar Hebrew name to that of the Arabic, (3) removing the Arabic definite article from the name, (4) reviving biblical names sometimes already in usage by the Arab population in an Arabised form, and finally, (5) inventing new names for modern items, rather than borrowing from Arabic (Mar'i 2013). As for English, the Hebrew names appear in transliteration, but not consistently, in spite of the fact that many of the place names in the country have an English equivalent. For example, Akka in Arabic (Akko in Hebrew) is Acre in English, and Yaffa in Arabic (Yaffo in Hebrew) is Jaffa in English.

Over the years, and particularly in the 1990s and beyond, several bills were proposed in the Knesset regarding the nature of the state, the status of the Arab citizens in a Jewish state, and the status of Arabic in relation to other languages, such as Russian. A debate was also initiated regarding Arabic in public spaces, such as road signs, signs at Israel's international airport and place names. Also discussed was what type of Arabic names should appear on road signs. The argument for Arabic appearing on road signs, including the country's international airport, prevailed (Marʿi 2013). The presence of Arabic is also attributed to Arab human rights organisations in Israel, such as 'Adalah'. Arabic, however, always appears below Hebrew and generally in smaller letters (see Figures 3.2, 3.3 and 3.4).

English appears on most road signs too (Figures 3.2, 3.3, 3.4), below Hebrew and Arabic. Arabic names often appear in transliteration of the Hebrew name; in other words, the Hebrew name appears in Arabic letters, below the Hebrew (Figures 3.2, 3.3, 3.4). Sometimes the Arabic name appears in parentheses next to the Arabic transliteration of the Hebrew name, but not in a consistent manner (Figures 3.3, 3.4), and sometimes the Arabic name does not appear in parentheses. For example, in Figure 3.5, the painted-over Arabic name is the name of one of the gates to the Old City of Jerusalem ('Bab Al-Khalil', Hebron Gate), and not a transliteration of the Hebrew name, which is 'Yaffo' (Jaffa) Gate.

Bernard Spolsky and Robert Cooper (1991) noted that in old Jerusalem the order of Arabic, Hebrew and English are an indication of the age of the sign; in other words, whether the sign goes back to the time of the British Mandate, or the Jordanian rule of the Old City between 1948 and 1967 (when Hebrew was not present on the sign), or whether it is an example of more recent signage (see also Y. Suleiman 2003).

As for Haifa, a city which prides itself on being mixed and peaceful at the same time, Figure 3.6 shows a common municipal road sign in the city. Note that the Arabic script is smaller than the Hebrew. However, Figure 3.7 has the three languages appearing in the expected order, but the instructions as

Figure 3.2 Multilingual road signs in Israel.[3]

Figure 3.3 Multilingual road signs in Israel.[4]

Figure 3.4 Multilingual road signs in Israel.[5]

Figure 3.5 West Jerusalem, July 2009. (Photo: author)

to how to get to a car park in the area are solely in Hebrew, another powerful indication of the primacy of Hebrew.

However, on the western slopes of Mount Carmel in the city, in an upmarket area which is mostly Jewish, an Arab-owned restaurant gives primacy to its sign in Arabic, and second to English, an indication of perhaps who the main customers are in that restaurant, as Figure 3.8 shows.

In comparison, in Tel-Aviv, the most important truly Hebrew city, municipal signs generally do not show Arabic, as Figure 3.9 indicates.

It is interesting to note that in Tel-Aviv not even the sign at the site of Yitzhak Rabin's murder in 1995 has any Arabic (see Figure 3.10). The Hebrew simply says that it is the site of the murder of Yitzhak Rabin, who was prime minister and minister of defence, and to whom peace was a mission. It also indicates the date of the murder according to the Jewish, as well as the Western calendars. The words on the wreath say 'remember and remind'. Needless to say, at the murder site of the man who is perceived as a peacemaker with the Palestinians, the conspicuous absence of Arabic is beyond comment.

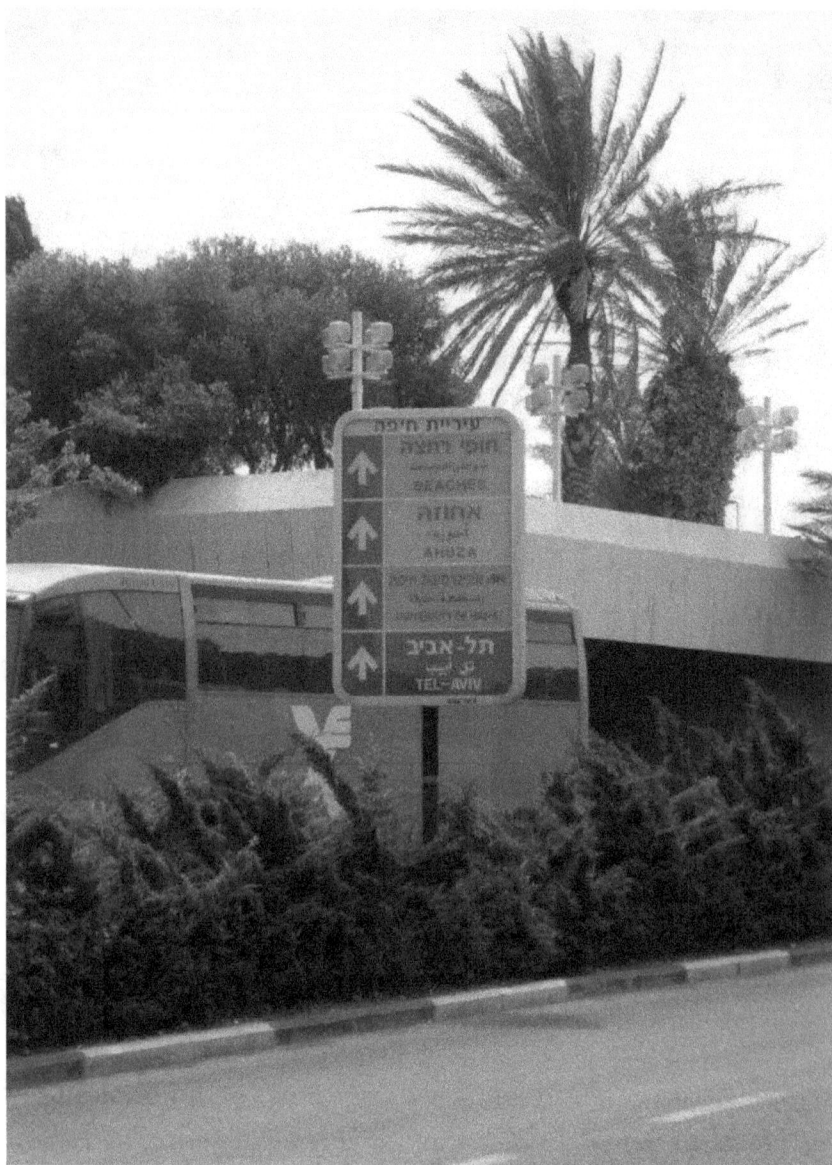

Figure 3.6 A municipal road sign in Haifa, May 2015. (Photo: author)

Figure 3.7 A municipal road sign in Haifa with instructions on how to get to a car park in Hebrew only, May 2015. (Photo: Aman Onallah)

Figure 3.8 Sign of an Arab-owned restaurant in Haifa, July 2008. (Photo: author)

THE (IN)VISIBILITY OF ARABIC | 83

Figure 3.9 Road sign in Tel-Aviv, July 2008. (Photo: Russell Lucas)

In groundbreaking research of signs in three Israeli cities, Nira Trumper-Hecht (2010) utilised the concept of LL in her analysis. She distinguished between LL as an empirical visual sign that can be observed, and the LL as perceived by the community. In the mixed city of Upper Nazareth, Jewish residents, for example, thought that Arabic is over-represented, while the Arab population thought the opposite. Further, the Jewish population viewed the presence of Arabic as a threat to the character of the state as Jewish, while the Arab population viewed the presence of Arabic in a positive sense. Arabs thought that both Arabic and Hebrew should appear on road signs, while Jews

Figure 3.10 The site of Yitzhak Rabin's murder. (Photo: author)

thought only Hebrew should appear. One could well speculate that this is an indication that (1) the Arabs indeed view themselves as a minority in Israel, in a similar manner to other minorities in other parts of the world, and in addition, they view their linguistic rights as human rights, also akin to other minority language contexts (Skutnabb-Kangas and Phillipson 1994), and, (2) that the Jews have internalised the 'securitisation' and 'nationalism' associated with Arabic in Israel and encouraged by the state institutions, at all levels of public life; thus, the Jews of the city view the presence of Arabic negatively.

In support of Trumper-Hecht's (2010) finding on the undesirability of Arabic in public signage for the Jewish community, the city of Jerusalem has many road signs appearing in the three languages: Hebrew on top, below it is Arabic, and last is English. However, the Arabic on many signs is painted over in black as an act of vandalism (see Figure 3.5). This act of vandalism creates a powerful image as one drives across Jerusalem and sees one sign after another with black paint over the Arabic words, and undoubtedly, it gives a powerful message that Arabic and its people need not be part of the landscape of the land of Israel. However, Trumper-Hecht (2010) also finds that the Jewish community in the city of Yaffa does not view negatively the presence of Arabic on signs. She attributes this to the history of Yaffa, a thriving Arab city until 1948 and the establishment of the new Jewish city of Tel-Aviv. Today, Yaffa is a mixed city after the exodus of its most Arab residents in 1948 and that particular history seems to make its Jewish residents more tolerant of the presence of Arabs and Arabic, unlike Upper Nazareth, which was built after 1948 as a Jewish city. Lastly, one would expect the national tensions to show themselves in Jerusalem, perhaps, more than in any other place.

Further, in historic Nazareth, a city of about 70,000 Arab citizens of Israel, signs appear in Arabic, Hebrew and English. However, when the sign has only Arabic, it is, for example, advertising a supermarket in Hebrew 'kimʿat chinam', which means 'almost free of charge'. This sign is seen in Arabic transliteration of the Hebrew with the added borrowed adjective 'perfect' from English. So, in effect the expression means in Hebrew 'perfect, almost free of charge', with Hebrew borrowing the English adjective, but lending it to Hebrew syntax and word order, and Arabic, in its turn, transliterating the Hebrew phrase into Arabic letters (Figure 3.11). In other words, the forces of rationality of consumerism seem to prevail in this example, as the Hebrew connotes a participation in the Israeli consumerism culture (see Ben-Rafael et al. 2006).

Figure 3.11 Sign advertising a supermarket in Nazareth, July 2014. (Photo: Russell Lucas)

Even though Upper Nazareth was built as a Jewish city in the 1950s, on mountainous land (Mount Sikh, in Arabic) that used to be olive groves mostly belonging to Nazareth families and some families from the surrounding villages, up until 1948 historic Nazareth remained demographically Arab. Over the years, meanwhile, due to a lack of land to expand Old Nazareth, many Arabs moved to live in Upper Nazareth, thus in effect transforming it into a mixed city. I was visiting in July 2014, during the Hebrew book month and advertising for this was in Hebrew in Upper Nazareth (Figure 3.12).

However, some of the shoppers, as well as the salespeople, were Arab and therefore there were also Arabic books advertised, but in Hebrew (Figure 3.13).

Lastly, Figure 3.14 shows some of the book titles in Arabic in one of the bookshops at a mall in Upper Nazareth, during the Hebrew book exhibition in July 2014.

The titles of the books exhibited varied from dictionaries to novels and books of poetry from different Arab countries, to books in translations such as Harry Potter, or the works of Paulo Coelho (as the picture shows). But the numbers were limited, as was the variety. Most likely, these books were purchased in Jordan, where there is a larger market for books in Arabic.

I personally find that the signs in Jerusalem are the most interesting. For example, on a sign showing the name of the major commercial road in

Figure 3.12 Hebrew book exhibition, Upper Nazareth, July 2014. (Photo: author)

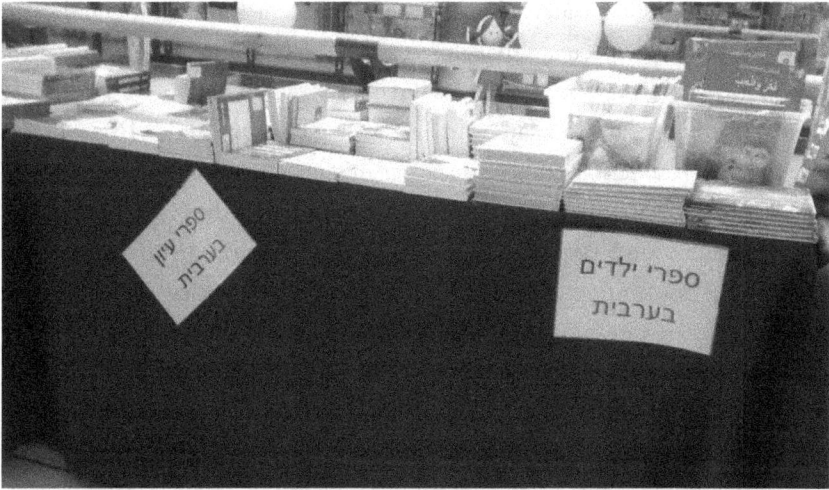

Figure 3.13 Advertisements for Arabic books at the Hebrew book exhibition in Upper Nazareth, July 2014. (Photo: author)

East Jerusalem, 'Saladin Street', the three languages appear in the expected order, however, with a twist. First, the English name appears in transliteration of Arabic, rather than the Anglicised name of this historic figure. Second, underneath the Arabic name, in smaller Arabic script and only in Arabic, the

Figure 3.14 Books in Arabic at the Hebrew book exhibition in Upper Nazareth, July 2014. (Photo: author)

sign says, 'a Muslim leader who liberated Jerusalem from the Crusaders in 1187'. One could speculate that this is a very powerful message of defiance, considering that everyone in Jerusalem knows who Saladin was. In other words, it is not meant to relate who he was (Figures 3.15 and 3.16).

Further, Arabic sometimes appears as misspelled or with incorrect grammar or choice of words, as Figures 3.17, 3.18 and 3.19 show.

The Arabic for Artists Workshops in Figure 3.17 appears with the incorrect nominative case ending appearing for the genitive. Note that spoken Arabic uses the genitive case for all grammatical positions, and does not use the other case endings used for the nominative and the subjunctive, which fuṣḥā uses. In other words, this sign is an example of 'hypercorrection' where the sign writer knows the rules of Standard Arabic, but is not competent in producing them. The next example shows a sign with no meaning in the Arabic translation.

This sign carries the diacritical marks for short vowels in Arabic. These marks are optional in Arabic writing, and they are used to assist the reader with the correct pronunciation. The marks appear incorrect in the word for trees (Khashab is written as Khushub). Further, 'Khashab' means wood and

Figure 3.15 Saladin Street in East Jerusalem, July 2013. (Photo: author)

Figure 3.16 Saladin Street, May 2016. (Photo: Aman Onallah)

not trees. Finally, the adjective for 'petrified' appears in the feminine plural, when it should be in the masculine singular. In other words, the writer of the signs is somewhat familiar with Arabic rules for grammatical agreement, but does not seem competent enough to use these rules correctly. This is in addition to misusing the word for wood. This is a phenomenon that is prevalent in Israel: many typographical, grammatical or lexical errors in Arabic. Another example of a typographical error in Arabic can be seen on a road sign at an junction between Haifa and Nazareth (Figure 3.19), which has misplaced dots above the word 'Haifa' in Arabic.

These common mistakes are perhaps a result of non-native speakers writing these signs. But, more importantly, it shows a carelessness regarding how Arabic should be represented, a carelessness akin to the Arabic spoken by Israeli soldiers at the various military checkpoints which dot the West Bank. The equivalent of such mistakes in Hebrew or in English is not as visible. The misspelling or misuse of language can get a whimsical turn as on a Yaffa Port sign which says in both English and Hebrew 'you are here', but 'you were

Figure 3.17 Sign with incorrect Arabic grammar.[6]

here' in Arabic (Tamari 2015). Tamari, whose family was forced out of the city in 1948, and who now lives in Ramallah, even notes that the word for 'map' in that port is spelled in Arabic as 'kharbata', instead of 'khareeta'. It could be an honest mistake as the 'b' and the 'i' (ee) sounds in Arabic look the same except that the 'b' has one dot, and the 'i' has two. However, 'kharbata' means 'scrambled mess' in Palestinian Arabic.

Another sign with perhaps less of a whimsical twist is at the border with Lebanon in Ras Al-Naqoura/Rosh Ha-Niqra on the Mediterranean. The sign first appears in Hebrew, then English and Arabic last, unlike the more customary order of Hebrew, Arabic and then English. This is perhaps because many UN envoys pass through this border point. The Hebrew and English say that water entry is forbidden, but the Arabic says that recreation is forbidden, thus, in effect, the sign is more restrictive of the movement of the Arabic speaker than it is of the Hebrew or English speaker. Again, this is likely to be an innocent mistake as the word for swimming in Arabic is 'istiḥmām' and for recreation it is 'istijmām'. The pharyngeal 'ḥ' and the 'j' sound are similar

Figure 3.18 Sign with Arabic translation that makes no sense.[7]

in Arabic writing. Adding a dot underneath the pharyngeal 'ḥ' makes it a 'j'. See Figures 3.20 and 3.21.

Jerusalem: 'Within the Ancient Walls'

> In Jerusalem, and I mean within the ancient walls,
> I walk from one epoch to another without a memory
> To guide me. The prophets over there are sharing
> The history of the holy ascending to heaven
> And returning less discouraged and melancholy, because love
> And peace are holy and are coming to town.
>
> (Mahmoud Darwish)[8]

The wall of Jerusalem was last built during the reign of the Ottomans (Spolsky and Cooper 1991), specifically during the rule of Sultan Suleiman the Magnificent, on the ruins of more ancient city walls (Figure 3.22 shows a view of the Old City with its wall). The size of the city 'within the ancient

Figure 3.19 Road sign at a junction between Haifa and Nazareth with misplaced dots on one of the Arabic letters. (Photo: author)

walls' is no more than 0.9 square kilometres, or 0.35 square miles <https://en.wikipedia.org/wiki/Old_City_%28Jerusalem%29>. The only pathways to it are the gates, particularly the two major ones: Damascus Gate (Bab Al-ʿAmoud in Arabic, or Shaʿar Shekhem in Hebrew) in the north and Jaffa Gate (Bab Al-Khalil, 'Hebron' in Arabic and Shaʿar Yaffo in Hebrew) in the south-west. Putting the issue of naming aside, the streets are nearly all narrow and inaccessible to vehicles and donkeys and carts still carry merchandise in the narrow streets of its souk (market). British historians commented that when the British army entered the city in 1917, they thought it the best-preserved Middle Eastern city from earlier centuries (Keay 2003). Most of the vendors and shopkeepers are Arab, but many tourists from all over the world walk through the gates on any given day. Arabs and Jews seem to have minimal interaction, in spite of the shared narrow space.

In a groundbreaking study, Spolsky and Cooper (1991), in the 1980s asked their students to walk through the city streets inside the walls and listen

Figure 3.20 Sign at the Israeli-Lebanon border, July 2013. (Photo: Aman Onallah)

אזהרה

זהו שטח צבאי סגור

חל איסור מוחלט על כניסה למים.

איסור זה נכון לכל שעות היממה.

עוברי החוק צפויים להיענש בדין הקבוע בחו

WARNING

This is a restricted military area

water entry is forbidden at all times

trespassers will be prosecuted

according to the law

منطقة عسكرية مغلقة

ممنوع الاستجمام بتاتا

في كل ساعات النهار والليل

من يخالف القانون يعاقب

كما القرار في القانون

Figure 3.21 Close up of sign at the Israeli-Lebanon border, July 2013: notice the word 'istijmām'. (Photo: Aman Onallah)

Figure 3.22 The Old City of Jerusalem, from Mount Scopus, summer 2008. (Photo: author)

to the languages spoken. The students reported that Arabic was the most used language (549 occurrences), followed by Hebrew (430 occurrences) and then by English (375 occurrences). The remaining languages consisted of German and French, followed by Scandinavian languages, Greek, Yiddish and Spanish (Spolsky and Cooper 1991: 98). At the time of the research, 90 per cent of the residents of the Old City were Arab, but only 40 per cent of the observed participants were Arab. In spite of the importance of the research, I do not know of a follow-up study in the Old City. Judging from impressionistic observations, Russian probably has a presence today as well. The research also does not seem to mention Armenian, which is also spoken in the Old City. Armenians generally speak Arabic with the local community, but Armenian among themselves. They also own some of the small businesses in the souk. Further, it is not uncommon to be sitting in a restaurant in East Jerusalem and to hear Armenian at the next table. In addition, many stores sell everyday goods to the local community, but the souk is also dotted with religious souvenir shops, mostly for Christian tourists. Outside of Al-Aqsa Mosque, many stores sell Muslim religious artifacts, while outside of the Western Wall many Jewish religious artifacts are sold. A typical interaction between Arabs and Jews in the city the 1980s, is captured beautifully by Spolsky and Cooper's students (1991: 101–2), at Damascus Gate, as an indication of the bilingual transactions which take place in the Old City:

> *Buyer* (female, 40, pointing, in Hebrew): *Kamah zeh?* (How much?)
> *Seller* (female villager, 40, showing three fingers, in Arabic): *Tlat miyat, kilo.* (300 a kilo)
> *Buyer* (in Hebrew): *Kamah?* (How much?)
> *Seller* (raising hand, adding emphasis and a pause, in Arabic): *Tlat miyat, kilo.* (300 a kilo)
> *Buyer* (leaving): Ah.

I do not know if today these moments of human interaction still exist between both groups in the Old City, due to the changing demographic landscape and the decline of political forces for co-existence.

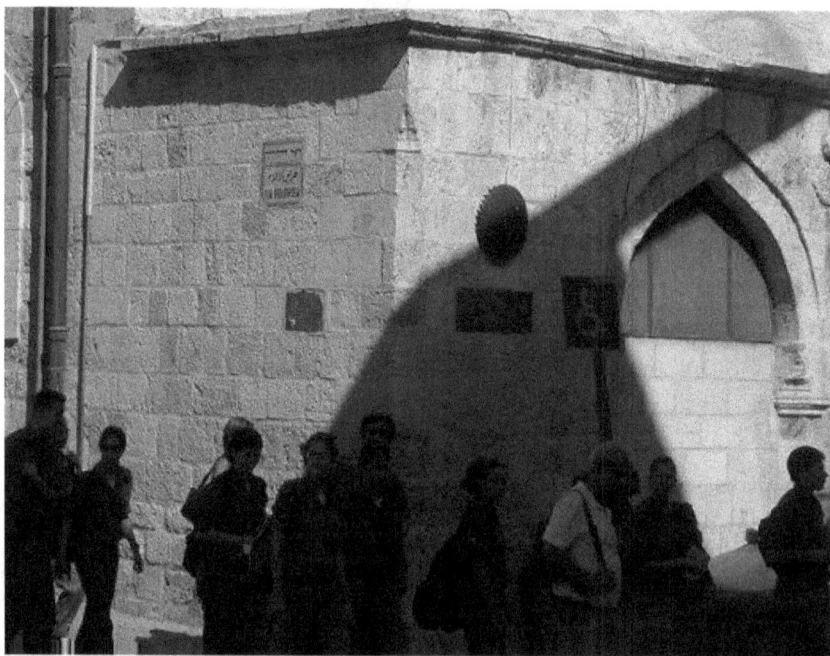

Figure 3.23 Via Dolorosa, Jerusalem, summer 2008. (Photo: author)

A walk which probably takes about twenty minutes between Damascus Gate and Jaffa Gate shows the following linguistic landscape: soon after walking through Damascus Gate a sign to the left shows Via Dolorosa in the three languages; while the Hebrew and English are a transliteration from Latin, the Arabic is a calque translation of Latin, 'Ṭarīq Al-Ālām'. The reason could be that the Arabic phrase has been in use for more than a millennium, due to the early translations of the Bible into Arabic (Griffith 1992). The Arabic script is also in block print rather than artistic calligraphy, as is sometimes the case with signs in Jerusalem (Figure 3.23). The heavy presence of the military could also be noticed in this narrow street during the summer of 2008. The same sign appears on the other side of the alley (Figure 3.24). The sign right below it is a municipal instruction forbidding pedestrians from leaving rubbish in the alley. It is only in Hebrew and Arabic. At a distance, an Armenian-owned souvenir shop advertises itself only in English, as tourists are its target customers.

Walking in the alley, the pedestrian will be faced with many shops, some selling vegetables or groceries, others selling souvenirs. Figure 3.25 shows the

Figure 3.24 Via Dolorosa, Jerusalem, summer 2008. (Photo: author)

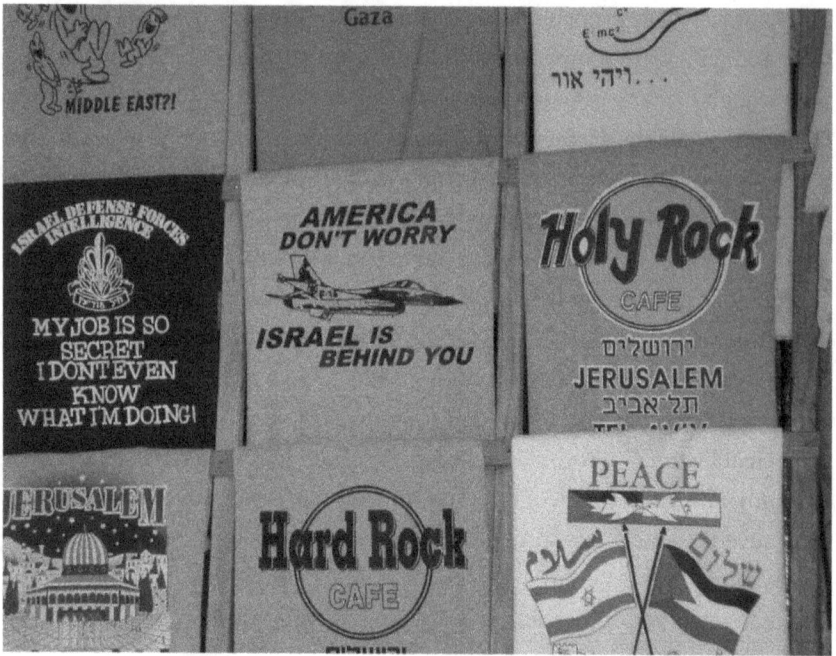

Figure 3.25 Shop display near Damascus Gate, Jerusalem, summer 2008. (Photo: author)

display of one of the souvenir shops, selling T-shirts primarily in English, secondarily in Hebrew and then in Arabic; aiming at tourists with different religious and political affiliations. Note that the owner of the shop, like most in that alley, is an Arab.

A few metres down the alley, a pharmacy advertises to the Arab residents, only in Arabic, that it accepts prescriptions from the Israeli health-care fund, 'Kupat Holim' (Figure 3.26). This is only intended for the Arab residents of Jerusalem. Arabs in Jerusalem are not Israeli citizens and therefore do not carry Israeli passports, but they hold Israeli identity cards, which allow them to participate in the municipal elections and to benefit from the health-care system. Thus, a simple sign, comprehensible to the locals, can help us to understand an entire system of politics and demography.

In the background, behind the sign, Ariel Sharon's house can be seen, with the big Israeli flag and the Minoura on top of it, all of this behind a minaret of a mosque. Another flag appears on one of the balconies of a house with the lion sign, the symbol of Jerusalem, in the middle of the flag.

Figure 3.26 Arabic sign of a pharmacy in the Old City, summer 2008. (Photo: author)

Further along the alley towards Al-Aqsa Mosque is a water fountain, probably owned by the Muslim Waqf. Water fountains are common in Islamic cities because the building of such fountains by individuals is considered a meritorious deed in Islam. The fountain is decorated by calligraphy of an unknown period (to me) and it is hard to read, especially for someone (like myself) who is unaccustomed to Muslim artistic calligraphy. I could only decipher a few words, which may indicate who the donor was (Figure 3.27).

About a hundred metres further, the Dome of the Rock peeks from behind the walls of Al-Aqsa Mosque. The dome, while dominating the skyline of the Old City, is itself dominated by Quranic verses in blue tile (Figure 3.28). The dome underwent major renovations in the 1980s, and again more recently.

The alley finally leads to the Western Wall. Figure 3.29 shows the trail of pieces of prayer paper in many languages, including Hebrew, worshippers leave behind as they pray at the Wall.

But, if someone decides not to exit the Old City, and turns right instead, towards the Church of the Holy Sepulchre (itself dominated primarily by

Figure 3.27 Water fountain in Old Jerusalem, summer 2008. (Photo: author)

Figure 3.28 The Dome of the Rock, summer 2008. (Photo: author)

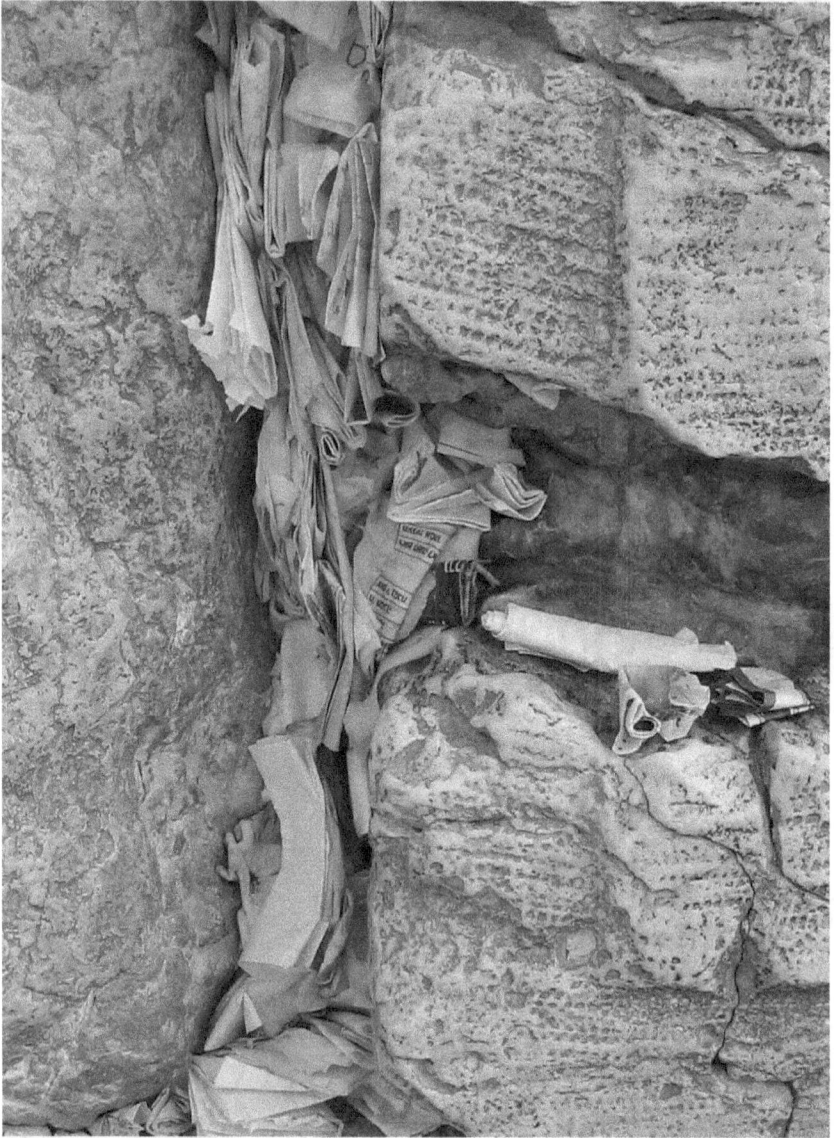

Figure 3.29 Prayer papers at the Western Wall in Jerusalem. (Photo: Yarin Kirchen)[9]

imagery, and secondarily by Latin and Greek calligraphy) and the many souvenir shops which sell Christian religious artifacts, they will end up at the
other major gate of the Old City, Jaffa Gate, towards Mamilla. Figures 3.30
and 3.31 show Jaffa Gate in the three languages, first English, then Arabic in

Figure 3.30 Jaffa Gate. (Photo: Marina Shemesh)[10]

artistic calligraphy and in the Arabic name 'Bab Al-Khalil' or Hebron Gate, while the Hebrew shows 'Sha'ar Yaffo'. Spolsky and Cooper (1991: 7) analysing this sign, argue that:

> the sign on the Jaffa gate appears to date from the British Mandate period, which lasted from 1919 until 1948, which is why it is written in the three official languages of the Mandate government; English first; Arabic second; and Hebrew third. The use of calligraphic script for the Arabic suggests that the sign-writer did not assume that Arabs would actually need to read the sign.

Underneath the Jaffa Gate sign (Figure 3.31) another sign can be seen indicating Omar Bin Al-Khattab Square, named after the second Rightly-Guided Caliph who visited the city during his reign in 637.[11] As Spolsky and Cooper (1991) observe about other signs in the city, this sign seems to have been made when the city was under Jordanian rule, with Arabic in block print

Figure 3.31 Jaffa Gate, summer 2008. (Photo: author)

above the English, and with Hebrew added on later. Turning towards the gate, the visitor will notice advertisements for the Light Rail in Jerusalem in three languages: English, Arabic and Hebrew. The Light Rail was in the state of early planning in summer 2008 (Figure 3.32).

Today the Light Rail links different parts of the city, with a stop in Mamilla outside Jaffa Gate, allowing easy access for both the Arab and Jewish population to Mamilla. on a recent visit to Mamilla (May 2015), where an upscale

Figure 3.32 Jaffa Gate, summer 2008. (Photo: author)

shopping mall has been built, I noticed both Arab and Jewish shoppers barely interacting, while momentarily sharing space (see for example Figure 3.33), and where stores advertise only in Hebrew and English (Figure 3.34).

However, the entrance to Mamilla does have Arabic signs, in addition to English and Hebrew. The Arabic name of 'Ma'man Allah' appears in aesthetic calligraphy (Figure 3.35).

Leaving Mamilla for Jaffa Street, a major Jewish commercial street, the visitor is faced with the sign below (Figure 3.36). This sign seems to be new, with the three languages in the expected order and with Arabic written in block print. As mentioned earlier, Spolsky and Cooper (1991: 7) argue that the block print for Arabic has appeared on signs since the Jordanian rule of East Jerusalem. The choice of block print is attributed to the improved literacy rate, as the signwriters are expecting people to actually read the sign. This is in contrast to the Mandate period, when the literacy was lower than it is today, and when more calligraphic print was used for Arabic (Spolsky and Cooper, 1991: 7). However, about fifteen years after this observation, new

Figure 3.33 Palestinians at Mamilla shopping mall. (Photo: Zeev Tamir)[12]

Figure 3.34 Mamilla shopping mall. (Photo: Brian J. McMorrow)[13]

Figure 3.35 Mamilla in three languages. (Photo: Manuel Schneider)[14]

Figure 3.36 Jaffa Street sign, Jerusalem, May 2016. (Photo: Aman Onallah)

signs could still be found in East Jerusalem, written in calligraphic print for the Arabic. Thus, in spite of the increasing literacy, the choice of calligraphy may also indicate that the aesthetic value of Arabic script is still highly valued by the Arabs of Jerusalem (Figure 3.37).

Across from the mall in Mamilla, is a very old Islamic cemetery (Ma'man Allah Cemetery). A walk through this cemetery reveals headstones with Arabic script for the name and year of death of the deceased. Even though the graves are old, the headstones seem new (Figure 3.38). The city of Jerusalem has been trying to take the cemetery from the Muslim Waqf in order to use it for some building projects. One could speculate that the new tombstones in Arabic are yet another act of defiance against any erasure of Arab presence in the city, akin to the defiance of the sign of Saladin Street mentioned above.

The tombstone shown in Figure 3.38 is that of Ahmad Agha Duzdar, the Ottoman governor of Jerusalem (1838–63). The tombstone is new and the inscription appears in Arabic with English below it. According to Wikipedia, the tombstone was made in 2005 in collaboration with the Muslim Waqf in Jerusalem and the Turkish government.

Figure 3.37 Nablus Road sign, Jerusalem, May 2016. (Photo: Aman Onallah)

Figure 3.38 Mamilla Muslim cemetery in Jerusalem. (Photo: Sfrantzman)[15]

Lastly, leaving the city, one is faced with another wall, the separation wall. This wall is much more recent and it surrounds the city and most parts of the Green Line (the Rhodes Agreement border line). Graffiti in Arabic and in English on the Palestinian part of the wall is immediately noticeable, as there is none on the Israeli side. Figure 3.39 shows the south side of the wall separating Jerusalem from Abu Dis village, at the time of its building, with the graffiti seen from afar.

Figure 3.40 is a closer view of the same graffiti. It shows the face of Che Guevara next to declarations in English and in Arabic. The Arabic says 'let the Apartheid Wall fall'.

Figure 3.41 shows the northern part of the separation wall at the entrance to Shuʿfāt, another Palestinian village, at the time of building, and the construction sign of a sewage line built on the road to Ramallah. This sign is in Hebrew and in Arabic and displays the phone numbers of the construction companies involved in the project, along with the expected completion date. Note how the separation wall divides Shuʿfāt into two halves.

Figure 3.39 The separation wall at Abu Dis, November 2005. (Photo: Sally Ragep)

Figure 3.40 The separation wall from Abu Dis, November 2005. (Photo: Sally Ragep)

To sum up, a LL analysis of signage indicates a language in distress. While Arabic appears second to Hebrew on most road signs, and this is generally followed by English, one can note the following: (1) the Arabic script is mostly a transliteration of the Hebrew name of a place, and not the Arabic name, (2) Arabic is generally written carelessly, with mistakes in spelling, grammar and/or lexical choice, (3) many signs in Jerusalem appear with the Arabic crossed out with dark paint. I have observed these signs since at least 2004. The ubiquity of these painted-over signs, has a powerful visual effect on the viewer, (4) in spite of the municipal regulation of signage in a city like Jerusalem, subtle acts of resistance which escape the regulator, can still be noticed, such as in the Saladin's sign in East Jerusalem's main commercial street, (5) in Nazareth there are signs in Arabic letters, but with Hebrew and English structures given Hebrew syntax (and Arabic, as the noun-adjective agreement works in a similar manner in both languages). This syntax was noticed on commercial signs, perhaps to reflect the desire of the consumer to integrate with the larger Israeli economy. This last point needs further investigation.

Figure 3.41 The separation wall at the northern end of Jerusalem in Shuʿfāt, summer 2006. (Photo: Aman Onallah)

Lastly, this chapter followed the narrow streets of the Old City of Jerusalem from Damascus Gate to Jaffa Gate. While the distance is short between these two major gates, the different signs and their organisation, along with the choice and order of languages, tell the story of a city where Arabic and Hebrew are present (along with English). The representation of Arabic and Hebrew reveals a divided city where speakers of these languages live separate lives as they share this very sacred sliver of space, which is home to all three Abrahamic religions. In other words, the signs are further testimony to what Butler (2012: 4) calls: 'the conditions of unwilling proximity, the modes of being bound together in antagonism and without contract,...'

Notes

1. HRA, The Arab Association for Human Rights: association in service of the Palestinian Arab minority in Israel, <http://www.arabhra.org/hra/Pages/Index.aspx?Language=2> (last accessed 7 November 2014).
2. Adalah 'Justice': the legal centre for Arab minority rights in Israel, <http://adalah.org/> (last accessed 7 November 2014).
3. Available at <https://commons.wikimedia.org/wiki/Category:Road_signs_in_Israel#/media/File:Directions._Boy_walking_israel_highway_desert_autoroute_beersheva_(2454582241).jpg> (last accessed 31 July 2016).
4. Available at <https://commons.wikimedia.org/wiki/Category:Multilingual_road_signs_in_Israel#/media/File:Beit_Hashita.jpg> (last accessed 31 July 2016).
5. Available at <https://commons.wikimedia.org/wiki/Category:Multilingual_road_signs_in_Israel#/media/File:PikiWiki_Israel_37219_Vacation_Experience.JPG> (last accessed 31 July 2016).
6. Available at <https://commons.wikimedia.org/wiki/Category:Multilingual_road_signs_in_Israel#/media/File:Omanim_and_Bazalton_Sign_090529.JPG> (last accessed 31 July 2016).
7. Available at <https://commons.wikimedia.org/wiki/Category:Multilingual_road_signs_in_Israel#/media/File:1000_words_to_the_big_crater_(12).JPG> (last accessed 31 July 2016).
8. Trans. Fady Joudah, <http://www.poetryfoundation.org/poems-and-poets/poems/detail/52551> (last accessed 21 May 2016).
9. Available at <https://en.wikipedia.org/wiki/Western_Wall> (last accessed 22 May 2016).

10. Available at <http://publicdomainpictures.net/pictures/20000/nahled/jaffa-gate
-sign-jerusalem.jpg> (last accessed 24 May 2016).

11. See https://en.wikipedia.org/wiki/Umar (last accessed 2 September 2016).

12. Available at <https://commons.wikimedia.org/wiki/File:PikiWiki_Israel_883_
Mamila_shoping_center_%D7%9E%D7%A8%D7%9B%D7%96_%D7%A
7%D7%A0%D7%99%D7%95%D7%AA-%D7%9E%D7%9E%D7%99%
D7%9C%D7%90.JPG> (last accessed 31 July 2016).

13. Available at <http://m8.i.pbase.com/o2/93/329493/1/124274368.5hLIFj6w.
JerusalemMay100402.jpg> (last accessed 22 May 2016).

14. Available at <https://commons.wikimedia.org/wiki/Category:Mamilla_Mall#/
media/File:031_2010-09-04_15-10-00_Jerusalem_Mamilla.JPG> (last accessed
31 July 2016).

15. Available at <https://en.wikipedia.org/wiki/Mamilla_Cemetery#/media/File:
AhmadAghaDuzdar.jpg> (last accessed 11 August 2016).

4

Modernisation, Globalisation and Citizenship in Israel

The land loss for Palestinians in Israel is entangled with the process of twentieth-century modernisation (Hobsbawm 2008). Israel's nation-building for the Jews appropriated Arab land, and turned villagers in Galilee and the Triangle into day-labourers dependent on the Israeli market. In other words, the process of modernisation, along with Jewish nationalism, meant that the Arabs lost their livelihood, in addition to not having the opportunity to build an autonomous economy after 1948. Today, the Arab sector is poorer. However, an educated middle class has emerged, with higher education received from Israeli institutes or abroad. Such people usually moved from the villages to towns like Nazareth or to mixed cities like Jerusalem, Akka, Haifa and Yaffa, where the job opportunities have generally been better.

As the world moved towards a free market and globalisation in the late twentieth century, the state of Israel started adopting the neo-capitalist model by privatising some of its former domains which were built on social-welfare principles. Israel entered the world market with heavy contribution in terms of companies, and high technology. This period coincided with a window of liberal and critical thought regarding Zionist nationalism. As mentioned earlier, Pappé (2014) describes this period of the 1990s as offering a genuine opportunity for Israelis to revisit the exclusiveness of Zionism. The movement was led by academics, particularly from History departments, but the media and the public were open to this debate as well. What it meant for

Palestinians in Israel is further integration into the economy for young people. Some Palestinians started working in high-tech companies and became part of a new class of businesspeople with offices in India, Europe, South Africa and the United States. Many Jewish CEOs saw in this an opportunity to integrate the Arabs with what they believed to be Labour Zionism. Most of these CEOs were from urban centres around Tel-Aviv and Haifa, and from the Ashkenazi elite. The economic opportunities were a natural continuation of a general discourse of openness and hope for the future, a future of Israel as a solid democracy which is making peace with the PLO (these changes coincided with the signing of the Oslo Accords) and is 'tolerant' towards its own Arab minority. That was the image of the 1990s. Young Palestinians from Israel also dreamed of a future with more integration and equality. A number of organisations emerged which enhanced and protected the legal status of Arabs in Israel. Young Palestinians from Israel also started to call themselves Palestinians without fear of institutional retribution. This is also the backdrop for important Arab organisations such as Adalah,[1] Musawa,[2] The Arab Association for Human Rights (HRA),[3] I'lam media centre,[4] Mada Al-Carmel[5] and others. These organisations took advantage of the relative openness of Israeli political culture. Nonetheless, and in spite of this opening, the absorption of Israeli Arabs into Israeli academia does not exceed 1 per cent today (*Al-Jazeera* 2014b).

However, Pappé (2014) masterfully shows how this project came to an end due to the internal contradictions of this cultural project. Today the pendulum has swung in the other direction. Since 2009, for example, a number of bills have been proposed with the intention of stifling the public and political lives of Palestinians in Israel (see *Al-Jazeera* 2014a and 2014b, also see Strickland 2014). For example, it is a state offence to commemorate the Nakba and organizations doing so will be deprived of any governmental funding. Also, anyone engaged in activities which harm the state (however this is defined) can have their citizenship revoked.

Literature abounds with the failure of Israeli institutions to integrate the Arabs fully into the state, and in the 1980s, Israeli academia was examining the successes and failures of the Israeli state in this regard. Sammy Smooha (1989), a sociologist at Haifa University dedicated his career to the study of the 'Israelisation' of the Arab citizens, a process which his research aimed to further. Some Arab sociologists, also from Haifa University, and mostly in conjunction with its 'Jewish-Arab Centre', followed suit in their research. However, in the aftermath of the Oslo Accords, many Israeli Arabs felt that they were overlooked in negotiations for a resolution with the Palestinians, on the part of both the Israeli and the Palestinian authorities. Thus, NGOs emerged (such as the ones mentioned above) with the aim of speaking for the Palestinians in Israel and for protecting their rights. This was facilitated, to some extent, by the money donated from the EU after the signing of the Oslo Accords, and poured into Israeli and Palestinian organisations which help push for human development, human rights and peaceful discussion between both groups (C. Suleiman 2011). More importantly, however, this was facilitated by the unprecedented openness in Israeli society in dealing with the 'Palestinian' other. Admittedly, this openness was mainly confined to the urban middle and upper classes, which are mostly Ashkenazi, and from the salons of their comfortable homes. Palestinians in Israel picked up the change and started self-identifying as 'Palestinian' rather than 'Israeli Arab' which the state had previously designated for them. They also started to revisit the 1948 Nakba, meaning 'Catastrophe', calling it openly as such, and commemorating the Nakba day at the sites of their ruined villages. The Arabic media, enjoying more freedom than in the rest of the Arab world, was also discussing the Nakba and using such terms as 'trauma' to describe it. Young Palestinian graduates from Israeli universities were speaking out about discrimination, marginalisation and the psychological trauma caused by the Nakba since their parents' time. There were even attempts at dialogues between Nakba generations from Israel and the West Bank, Israeli Jewish descendants of Holocaust survivors, and descendants of Nazis. This major project was carried out by a psychologist at Ben-Gurion University, Dan Bar-On, and it stopped after his premature death (see Bar-On 2006).

However, as Pappé (2014) states, after the second intifada in 2000, the Israeli public became less open to these debates and the mood in Israel changed completely. Pappé (2014) discusses the sociological and historic reasons as to why this openness did not continue, and draws a very complex picture. However, with the risk of simplification, the Israeli society closed in on itself again, as the changes in the 1990s were not genuine and deep. In other words, the Israeli public consciousness became critical of the occupation of the West Bank and the Gaza Strip and its attendant evil, but never to the point of disavowing Zionism as a national project, and never fully admitting the responsibility of the dispossession of the Palestinian people in 1948.

Azmi Bishara: An Alternative View of Citizenship

Against the backdrop of the 'openness' of the 1990s, Azmi Bishara emerged as a spokesman for the ills of the Israeli state, with regard to its Palestinian citizens. Bishara grew up in Nazareth and studied at the Hebrew University and upon graduating from Humboldt University in Berlin in 1986 with a doctorate in philosophy, he worked at Birzeit University in the West Bank and at Van Leer institute in Jerusalem. He formed the Democratic Party, an Arab party (Balad), in 1995 and served as a Knesset member from 1996 to 2007, when he abruptly left the country, eventually settling in Qatar. Through his political activism, as well as his writing and numerous television appearances, Bishara pointed out the inherent contradictions of Israel being democratic and Jewish at the same time, a point that many others have commented on. However, the difference is that he turned this observation into a political project by establishing his party. Bishara's ascendance and fall are yet another indication of the 'special aura' which prevailed in the 1990s, and the impossibility of its continuation to the present day.

Further, Bishara is a prolific writer with a following not only in Israel, but also throughout the entire Arab world. In the 1990s he presented a vision for Israel and for its Arab citizens. In his opinion the Communist Party, as well as many Arab political activists in Israel, focus on the political rights of Arabs as a minority in the state of Israel. He argues that this is a flawed vision for Arabs, as the state never hid its Zionist character. Instead, he calls for the Arabs in Israel to strengthen their ties to other Palestinians, particularly in the West Bank and the Gaza Strip, and also to other Arab countries, as one should not deny the fact that the Arabs in Israel are part of larger collectives. He attacks Jewish and Arab Israeli scholars alike who argue for the 'Israelisation' of the Arabs in Israel, meaning that the state, while being Jewish in character, has democratic values which have helped the Arabs in Israel to be integrated into the state and its institutions (see, for example, Smooha 2001). Bishara argues that the state, which defines its nationality as 'Jewish' and not 'Israeli', is unable to integrate the Palestinian Arabs in the state-building project (see Jamal 2011). Moreover, a state which only recognises the individual, and not the collective, rights of ethnic Palestinian Arabs cannot exist as democratic either (Jamal calls this 'hollow citizenship' as far as the Palestinians in Israel are concerned (see Jamal 2007)). Bishara calls for the state of Israel to recognise the collective rights of the Palestinian Arabs, its indigenous ethnic minority. Only then, can it become a true democracy, a state for all of its citizens.

In addition, Bishara argues that the Palestinian society was undergoing a process of modernisation during the first half of the twentieth century, and that the Nakba of 1948 is what interrupted this process (Ghanim 2009, Jamal 2011, Bishara 1993, 2003, 2004). In other words, not only did Israel not encourage modernisation for the Palestinian society in Israel, but it also prevented it from succeeding. A necessary condition for modernisation is a viable urban middle class, and this class ceased to exist as a result of the mass exodus of the Palestinians from their homeland in 1948. The remainder of the Palestinians who became Israeli citizens consisted primarily of a rural society, deprived of its land. By not recognising the collective rights of Palestinians in Israel, Bishara argues that the state encourages a process of reversion to more primordial fragmented identities: religious, familial, tribal and so on, all fighting among themselves over the resources that the state is willing to give them.

However, it took more than a generation for a new urban middle class to put down roots, a class which is educated in Israeli universities, fluent in Hebrew and often in English too. Bishara calls for this class to be mobilised for political action. They can and should put pressure on the state to change its character and become a state for all of its citizens. This can happen only through recognising the differences and the unique character of the Palestinians in Israel. He calls for those Palestinians to also support the rights and the struggle for self-determination of their fellows in the West Bank and Gaza Strip. But at the same time, whether justly or not, they should also recognise the right of the Jewish self-determination within the borders of the armistice of 1949.

Bishara was vilified in Israel and had to face accusations of treason, as a result of his breaking the taboo of visiting Arab 'enemy' countries, such as Lebanon and Syria. He chose exile first in Jordan and later in Qatar, where he now resides. In Qatar he became a fixture on *Al-Jazeera* network as a political analyst and advisor to the young Emir of Qatar. He is also the General Director of the Arab Centre for Research and Policy Studies in Qatar,[6] where he heads research teams publishing books and periodicals in both Arabic and English. In addition, he established an Arab graduate university, where the language of instruction is Arabic, unlike the new private universities in Qatar, which teach in English. It is clear from this that Bishara sees Arabic as integral to 'Arab identity'. While many institutes of higher education in the Arab world do not teach in Arabic, but rather in English or French, Bishara makes a point of using Arabic as a vehicle for higher education, and for publishing, through his Arab Studies Centre for Research and Policy Studies in Qatar. Moreover, in spite of his self-exile, he still has a following inside and outside of Israel. As for the party he established, it still has representation in the Knesset.

The Centre for Research and Policy Studies in Qatar (which also has offices in Beirut) offers a wide range of studies in sociology, political science, media, economics, education, Israel Studies, Turkey and Iran, the environment and others. It also conducts its own polling, and publishes its research in books and several journals. The staff consists of some of the best scholars from various countries in the Arab world, and effort is dedicated to translations between Arabic and English.

In May 2013, Bishara also initiated the Arabic historic dictionary and brought Ramzi Ba'albaki, a well-known Arabic scholar, from the American University in Beirut to head the project. At the opening conference, both Bishara and Ba'albaki confessed to the absence of a modern historic dictionary for Arabic, ironically, a language with a long history of dictionary production that goes back to at least the eighth century,[7] a project which complements Bishara's interest in an Arab intellectual revivalism, expressed in the Arabic language, yet at the same time without denying the role of English as a global language. Bishara is also one of the visionaries behind the Doha Institute for Graduate Studies.[8] The Institute's goal is to support the production of Arab/Arabic knowledge, and Bishara emphasises this in his message on the Institute's website. He adds that the main teaching is conducted in Arabic, but a knowledge of English is also necessary at the institute.[9]

Lastly, and in regard to the collective consciousness of the Palestinians and who they are, Bishara emphasises that it is not, and ought not to be, that of Canaan. In other words, Palestinians can identify with Saladin, Jamal Abd Al-Nasser, the Algerian revolution, with Egypt and Iraq and with Jerusalem, with its Al-Aqsa Mosque and the Church of the Holy Sepulchre, but not with the Canaanites. A past which cannot be imagined cannot be remembered either (Bishara 1997, Ghanim 2009: 141). This is an answer perhaps to the attempts at either seeing the Palestinians as the ancient people of the land and the descendants of the Jews, or at fragmenting them into different sects and religious groups, perhaps with different collective histories (discussed in Chapter 2).

To sum up, Bishara's rise and decline in the Israeli political scene is perhaps a testimony to what types of indigenous citizenship projects the Hobsbawmian (2008) state institutions can and cannot handle. However, Bishara's thought continues to inspire Palestinians in Israel, as the next section will demonstrate.

In the Aftermath of Bishara's Exile

As mentioned earlier, the 1990s brought NGOs into the social and political scene in Israel. Further, since 2002 some Arab academics and politicians (particularly from al-Balad, the party Bishara founded and from Hadash, a descendant of the Communist Party in Israel which Bishara used to be a member of before forming his own party, as well as activists for NGOs such as 'Mada Al-Carmel', 'Musawa', 'Adalah' and others) issued four documents (three of them in a matter of a few months in 2007) regarding a future vision for living in the state of Israel. The culmination of all of these documents is in the fourth, which is called 'The Haifa Document'. All of these documents articulate a vision for a state of Israel which is democratic and not Jewish, but rather, bi-national, and based on equality among all of its citizens. It asks the state of Israel to recognise the crimes of the Nakba, and its responsibility for the dispossession of the Palestinian people. However, it also recognises the right for self-determination of the Jewish people, as well as the horrors of the Holocaust. In addition, it asks Israel to withdraw from the territories it occupied in 1967 and to allow the Palestinians in the West Bank and the Gaza Strip to have their own state. But, at the same time, the documents emphasise the bonds between the Palestinian people in Israel and in the West Bank and the Gaza Strip. It also articulates the Nakba as the one single event which dispersed and dispossessed the Palestinian people. Lastly, it defines the Palestinians in Israel as a 'minority that suffered a historical injustice in the Nakba of 1948 and seeks to voice its interests and aspirations' (Jamal 2011: 175), thus rearticulating Bishara's political project.

Not surprisingly, the documents were attacked by both the Palestinian and Arab press, as well as the Israeli Jewish press (see Jamal 2011: 185). On the Palestinian side, for example, the Islamic movement in Israel rejected it, as it saw in it a secular vision which contradicts the teaching of Islam (see Jamal 2011: 171). On the other hand, the Arab press called it an attempt at 'normalising' Israel as a state and abandoning the understanding that all of 'Palestine' is occupied land, and not just the 1967 borders (see 'Alosh 2007). Nonetheless, the importance of all of these documents, in the view of one of their drafters, Amal Jamal, is symbolic and moral, even if the writers of the documents are not representatives of the Arab public in the formal sense of the word (Jamal 2011: 167).

It is significant that this type of activism drew some support on the Israeli side. Public figures such as Yehouda Shenhav (mentioned in Chapter 1) and others have been vocal in their support for a more just society in Israel and for more meaningful civil rights. Shenhav, for example, has been campaigning for adding more Arab professors to the faculty at Tel-Aviv University where he teaches. In a letter to the Director General of the University, Mordachai Kohn, he states that it is shameful that only 0.5 per cent of the university faculty is Palestinian (email, 23 June 2015). He also asks him to create a more inviting environment for the Arab students at Tel-Aviv University and to take such steps as having the university's website accessible in Arabic, and not only in Hebrew and English. Lastly, he urged Kohn to help implement Arabic on some signs at the university. The request was, of course, rejected, but that does not stop Professor Shenhav and some of his colleagues from continuing to fight for more justice and more rights, including the linguistic, for the Palestinians in Israel. Lastly, Shenhav does indeed find a connection between himself being a dispossessed Iraqi Jew and the Palestinians, a stance that is perhaps not too common among Mizrachi Jews.

As expected, the documents are part of the larger picture of demands for equality for the Palestinians in Israel. One could argue that Israeli politics has hardened its stance towards its Arab minority, as well as towards the Palestinian right for self-determination in the West Bank and the Gaza Strip. Needless to say, the Palestinians in Israel constitute a marginalised community, which gets ignored in the bigger picture of Israeli politics. In fact, according to Jamal (2011), this sense of marginalisation played a pivotal role in pushing for these documents.

Lastly, these documents pay special attention to the Arabic language and its place in Israel, and they emphasise the indigeneity of the Palestinian collective identity for the Arab citizens of Israel, and its unique cultural, linguistic and religious character (Amara 2013: 115). The documents add that the Arabic language is an important part of the Palestinian identity, and therefore maintaining its official status is not only in the spirit of Israeli law which already recognises Arabic as an official language, but it is also necessary for the practical purpose of expressing the Arab culture in the public sphere in Israel, as the language of Israel's indigenous minority. The bilingual situation of English and French in Canada may be used as an inspiration for the future of Arabic in Israel (Amara 2013: 115). The Palestinians in Israel as an indigenous minority should be full partners in decisions regarding their autonomy in education, which also includes the bilingual schools. Lastly, the documents call for Israel to change its definition from 'Jewish and democratic' to 'democratic' and to apply the equality of the Arabic and the Hebrew languages at all levels, guaranteeing at the same time the multicultural nature of the state (Amara 2013: 116). As for organisations, such as the ones mentioned above, which advocate Palestinian rights in Israel, the current minister of justice, Ayelet Shaked, who represents the far-right 'Jewish Home' party in the Knesset, is targeting their activities by attempting to pass a bill which bans any foreign funding for NGOs in Israel (*The Jerusalem Post* 2015), perhaps as an indication of the changes in Israeli politics to further disfavour the Palestinian citizens of the country.

Changes in the Israeli Political Scene

Yehouda Shenhav, a sociologist with Iraqi-Jewish roots at Tel-Aviv University, and an ardent supporter of Palestinian rights inside and outside of Israel proper, belongs to a cadre of Jewish intellectuals who are critical of the Israeli 'incomplete democracy' and the ethno-religious nature of it. Jews of Arab origin belong generally to the poorer strata of society and live in the geographic periphery of Israel, away from Tel-Aviv and its surrounding urban and sub-urban centres. They are generally discriminated against in education, employment, social mobility and places of residence, even though they constitute the majority of Jewish society. However, they were not part of the nation-building ethos early in the twentieth century and were not brought into Israel until the 1950s. The melting pot of the state aimed at 'de-Arabising' them from their Arab identity. Many Orientalist stereotypes were applied to them and they were considered backward and primitive societies in need of modernisation (see Shenhav 2006, Chetrit 2013). Many of them have turned to the right-wing Likud party since the 1970s, which has expressed a more militant stance towards the Palestinians. The Likud party also opened the country for neo-liberalism, economically speaking. So the question is: how is it that the strata who are discriminated against still follow right-wing parties such as the Likud and some of its allies, for example, Shas, the religious party representing Mizrachi Jews? The answer to this seeming contradiction is to be found in Uri Ram's analysis of Israel's neo-liberal age (Ram 2008). On the one hand, economic liberalisation brought about a process of globalisation, mainly in Tel-Aviv. The affluent class who benefited from the neo-liberal policies became more open to a resolution with the Palestinians, as well as to integrating them fully in the Israeli economic order. The outlook of this class is towards the global economic order and the place of Israel in it. Naturally, globalisation in Israel (as in many other places) meant Americanisation. Israelis look to the US as a cultural and economic model, and appreciate US support (First and Avraham 2009). On the other hand, the neo-liberalism entailed an inclusionary/exclusionary rhetoric which redrew the boundaries of the nation in Israel excluding the Mizrachi Jews from the economy, but at the same time including them as part of the nation, in such a way that the Labour party, with its contempt and disdain for the Arab Jews, was not able to get their support at any moment of its domination of Israeli politics. In other words, the nationalistic stance of the Likud was able to include the Mizrachi Jews as part of the nation. Shas has become an important partner in Likud governments and uses a combination of religious and nationalistic rhetoric which appeals to the Mizrachi masses. Add to this mixture Israel's move towards populism, and the charismatic personality of Benyamin Netanyahu, the Likud leader who has won three elections in a row since 2009. Netanyahu and his government play to the racist fears of the Jewish masses (see Filc 2010). The Arabs are seen as a threat to the national unity of the Jews in Israel, and to the nature of the state, as a state of the Jews. Netanyahu uses the Arabs inside Israel as a scapegoat, whenever his politics require, such as in the last elections of 2015 (which he won). As mentioned earlier, in this round of elections, all Arab parties united in order to maximise Arab representation in the Knesset. Netanyahu unapologetically urged Jewish voters to go to the polls in order to overcome the large Arab turnout in the elections. His rhetoric succeeded in convincing Jewish voters to participate in their masses (Kershner 2015). What does all of this political narrowing of the scope of civil participation mean in relation to the official languages of the state? This is what the next section will try to address.

What does an Official Language Mean?

What does it mean for a state which defines itself as Jewish to have Arabic as an official language, in addition to Hebrew? In order to understand this 'riddle' (Saban and Amara 2002: 6), Ilan Saban, a law professor and Mohammad Amara, a linguist, analyse the official status of Arabic in Israel through the following three lenses: history, socio-reality and legality. Historically speaking, Article 82 of the Palestine Order-in-Council in 1922 was a British Mandatory legislation which gave English, Arabic and Hebrew official status. Article 82 states the following:

> All ordinances, official notices and official forms of the government and all the official notices of local authorities and municipalities in areas to be prescribed by order of the High Commissioner shall be published in English, Arabic and Hebrew. The three languages may be used in debates and discussions in the Legislative Council and subject to any regulations to be made from time to time, in the Government offices and the Law Courts. (Saban and Amara 2002: 10–11)

This Article was adopted into Israeli law in 1948 with one important change: the 'dilution' of English as an official language. According to Saban and Amara (2002: 11): 'It is obvious then, that retaining the status of Arabic as an official language was a conscious decision on the part of the Israeli legislator.' Israel does not have a constitution, and as a result, Arabic does not have a constitutional basis as an official language, but rather, its 'officiality' is '(merely) a statute' (Saban and Amara 2002: 21). In other words, the legal standing of Arabic, while symbolically forceful, is still more susceptible to changes because a statute is weaker than a constitutional law, legally speaking. Second, politically and socially speaking, the status of Arabic has been undermined in Israel in many ways. To mention one, a person can testify in Arabic in court and it will be translated into Hebrew. However, the court procedure will be conducted in Hebrew. Another way of undermining Arabic is that road signs until relatively recently were in Hebrew and English, and not in Arabic. Third, the 'practical significance of the status of Arabic has for many years diminished to basically the level of protecting of the internal life of the minority, especially the right of education in Arabic' (Saban and Amara 2002: 25). However, with no Arab university, higher education remains in Hebrew in reality. What can be understood from this is that the Arabs in Israel (just like many other minorities in the world) have to be bilingual in both Arabic and Hebrew, while the Jewish population does not, and in fact does not know Arabic.

Adalah (an organisation for the legal rights of Arabs in Israel), went to the supreme court against the municipality of Tel-Aviv Yaffa and petitioned for major road signs to include Arabic. Up to that point, road signs were in Hebrew, and sometimes in English as well. The court, headed by the Chief Justice, Aharon Barak, ruled in favour of Arabic on major road signs. Barak's reasoning was that the basic values of Israel as Jewish and democratic include the right for 'human dignity' (Saban and Amara 2002: 31). In other words, the ruling in favour of Arabic fell short of recognising the rights of Arabs as a collective inside Israel. However, in answer to the question of whether any language could be added to road signs – for example, Russian – in areas where many Russian Jews reside, the Chief Justice's reply was negative. His reasoning for this was that Arabic is the language of the indigenous inhabitants of Israel, from before the establishment of the state, and therefore it has a special status, unlike other languages such as Russian, which are immigrant languages. In other words, Arabic is a 'homeland (native) minority' language (Saban and Amara 2002: 32). However, in spite of this ruling, Saban and Amara express their concerns for the future of Arabic. They conclude that it is a vulnerable language both internally and externally: internally because most Arab students do not specialise in the Arabic language for their state matriculation (Bagrut) exams (about 80 per cent), as they do not see it as valuable for their higher education. They also know that they need to focus on their Hebrew skills for the job market. A linguistic analysis of the landscape conducted by Amara in the Arab town of Umm Al-Faḥm (in the Triangle), also showed that half the notices and commercial advertisements were in Hebrew, and on about a third of the signs, Hebrew was above Arabic (Saban and Amara 2002: 34). Externally, Jewish society is 'as far away from bilingualism as ever' (Saban and Amara 2002: 34). They conclude that, legally speaking, the very deriving of the status of Arabic from the basic law of 'Human Dignity and Liberty' – which is in itself a derivative of Israel being 'Jewish and Democratic' – is in itself problematic to the future of Arabic (Saban and Amara 2002: 37–8).

Hebrew as the National Language

It is well established that the Hebrew language is associated in modern history with the Zionist state building in Israel. Ironically, Theodor Herzel, the father of Zionism, did not see language as a component of national identity, but others in the Zionist movement did (Liebes and Kampf 2010). The early Yishuv had a choice between keeping its multilingualism: German, Russian, Polish, Yiddish and so on, or focusing on the idea of 'one nation-one language', which was prevalent in nationalistic ideologies in Europe at that time. Yiddish was rejected as a national language as it symbolised European Jewry with its 'submissive' and subordinate position in regard to various racist ideologies in Eastern Europe (Spolsky 2014). Reviving Hebrew for every day usage had a following, as it linked the ancient history of the Jews with the land. This movement culminated in the efforts of Eliezer Ben-Yehuda (1858–1922) who took it upon himself to speak the language with his family and to teach it as well. In 1916, 40 per cent of the Jewish population in Palestine spoke Hebrew (Kampf 2013: 2), but the population still relied on other languages for various functions. However, the community of the Yishuv, for ideological reasons, had a strong desire to expand the functions of Hebrew, and to write in Hebrew, even when it was not the the writer's strongest language. Take, for example, the poet Leah Goldberg (1911–70). She insisted on writing her poetry in Hebrew, even though her languages of expression were

Lithuanian and Russian, as well as German, which she used for her doctoral dissertation when she was a student of Semitic languages in Berlin (see Weiss 2014). The decision to make Hebrew central to the life of the Yishuv did not go uncontended. A language 'war' ensued between those who espoused Hebrew as the language of the Yishuv, and those who wanted the national language to be German. Hebrew won the language war and became the language of education in 1914. At the core of this conflict was the Technion, Israel's Institute of Technology. When the board of governors of the institute decided on German as the language of instruction, the faculty and students walked away from classes in protest (Neuman and Gueta 2014). After this, when the Hebrew University was established in 1925, there was no question regarding the language of instruction at the *Hebrew* University. However, the success of Hebrew was not going to be the same without the media: first the printing press, and later, in 1936, the radio, then the television in 1966. In 1939, there were nine dailies, six bi-weeklies and thirty-four monthlies published in Hebrew. In contrast, there were eleven dailies, fourteen weeklies and nine monthlies published in Arabic in Palestine at that time (Kampf 2013: 4). It should be noted that the population of Palestine was roughly 70 per cent Arab and 30 per cent Jewish in those days (see Smith 1996).

Following the British Mandate's making of English, Arabic and Hebrew the official languages of Mandate Palestine, 'Jerusalem Calling' established Kol Yerushalayim (the Voice of Jerusalem) the Hebrew station of the Palestine Broadcast Services (PBS). It was inaugurated on 30 March 1936, and it broadcast a daily *Hebrew Hour* (Ha-Sha'a Ha-'ivrit). According to Liebes and Kampf, this daily hour provided the much needed public space for Hebrew: a public space for an 'imagined community' (Liebes and Kampf 2010: 138). Jewish people from inside and outside the Yishuv were able to listen to programmes in Hebrew. Special attention was paid to teaching 'correct' Hebrew, and to explaining grammatical as well as stylistic matters of Hebrew. New words were also coined to fill the gap in the Hebrew lexicon, and they were discussed on the radio. The Sephardic pronunciation was also adopted on the radio, with its stress generally on the ultimate syllable, as compared to the penultimate for Ashkenazi Hebrew. The Hebrew radio worked closely with the Hebrew Language Committee (which was founded in 1890 and functioned as a language academy). When the Hebrew language academy was founded in 1953, it cooperated with what was to become 'Kol Yisrael, (Voice of Israel) and continued to have a fruitful cooperation furthering the development of Hebrew as a language for modern life. Moreover, the printed press also established a dialogue with the radio, as there were often commentaries on how Hebrew was used on the radio. These commentaries were shared by experts in language and lay people as well. In other words, the media (press and radio) played a pivotal role in the development and spread of Hebrew as a functional language for everyday life. According to Liebes and Kampf (2010: 140), Hebrew was founded by the Yishuv, but at the same time the Hebrew language founded the Yishuv. This dialectic was, to a great extent, mediated through the press and the radio.

The Arabic equivalent of 'Kol Yerushalayim' was 'Ithā'at Al-Quds', Radio Jerusalem, broadcasting an Arabic hour as well. The last broadcast of 'Ithā'at Al-Quds' was in 1967 when Israel took the West Bank and East Jerusalem. According to Zohar Kampf (personal communication, 22 May 2015), it is not clear what happened to the Arabic radio archives, particularly of the period 1936–48, but it might have been considered a sensitive security issue in Israel to make these archives available to the public. Just as Kol Yerushalayim was an important public platform for Jewish nation-building, one would assume that the same could be said about 'Ithā'at Al-Quds', particularly because Ibrahim Ṭuqan (1905–41), a much-loved poet in Palestine and the Arab world in general, worked in this radio station for the Arabic programme from 1936 until he was released from his job by the British authorities in 1940 (Ṭuqan 1991). Ibrahim Ṭuqan was known for his nationalistic poetry and arguments and his poem 'Mawṭinī' (My Homeland) is still recited by Palestinians everywhere. It was also adopted by Iraq as a national anthem.

From 2004 to 2011, an average of 6,410 books were published each year in all languages in Israel. Of these, 86 per cent were in Hebrew, 6 per cent in English, 3 per cent in Arabic (188 books), 3 per cent in Russian and 1 per cent was in French, Yiddish, Spanish, German, Romanian, Dutch and others. From 2007 to 2011, between 83 and 89 per cent of the books written in Hebrew were original and not translated (Kampf 2013: 7). Note that while the major Hebrew publishing houses *do* publish in English and Russian as well (see Modan or Keter publishing house web page), they do not publish in Arabic. Arabic books are published either at small presses in Israel, or they are sent to places such as Jordan to be published. As for literacy in Israel, among the Jewish population in 2007, 63 per cent of Israelis bought at least one book. In 2009, Israel had twenty-one dailies; thirteen of them were in Hebrew and only two were in Arabic (Kampf 2013: 9). As for weeklies, of the 274 published in 2003, only two of them were in Arabic. In regard to the radio, of the twenty-six channels existing in 2013, twenty-three of them broadcasted in Hebrew. As for television, as of 2013, there were three main nationwide Hebrew channels for television, (channel 1 'public' and channels 2 and 10 (commercial)), in addition to the educational channel, the parliament channel and the Arabic channel (33), broadcasting for half of each day (Kampf 2013: 11). Concerning television, the commercial channels are obliged to have Arabic (broadcast, or subtitles), for only 5 per cent of their allotted broadcasting time (Kampf 2013: 18). Lastly, regarding internet use, 66 per cent of Jews prefer to read online in Hebrew, as compared to 56 per cent of Palestinian Arabs who prefer to do so in Arabic (Kampf 2013: 14). In 2013, there were 150,000 websites in Hebrew, the equivalent of about 0.1 per cent of the million most viewed websites (Kampf 2013: 15).

The figures above give a rosier picture of Hebrew literacy for Jews than Arabic literacy for Arabs. This is indeed the case, as the data corresponds with other sources on literacy in Israel. For example, Shoshana Brosh-Vaitz (2005), in a report submitted to the United Nations Education, Scientific and Cultural Organisation (UNESCO) on the state of literacy in Israel, finds the following: (1) 'Israel was placed 23rd out of 35 countries' at a 2001 Progress in International Reading Literacy (PIRLS) test (Brosh-Vaitz 2005: 38), (2) a similar picture emerged from the Indices of School Efficiency and Growth (ISEG) examinations conducted in Israel (Brosh-Vaitz 2005: 38), (3) Arab students are underachievers compared to Jewish students, with the Bedouin students being the worst. Brosh-Vaitz (2005: 39) summarises this last finding as follows:

The PISA (Program for International Student Assessment) 2002 test also reveals very great disparity between the Jewish and the non-Jewish sectors for all subjects. The reading achievements in the Jewish sector were 50 points lower than the OECD (countries which signed the convention on the organization for economic co-operation and development) average,

while those of the non-Jewish sector were 125 points lower … About 62%
of the Arab students could read at level 1 (the lowest of five levels) or worse,
compared to some 30% within the Jewish sector. Similarly, no Arab students were found who could cope at level 5 for any of the reading skills.

According to Brosh-Vaitz (2005), many factors contribute to these results for
Arabic literacy among Arab students. These factors range from the effects of
diglossia on literacy, to the influence of Hebrew, to the allocation of resources
for Arab schools compared to Jewish schools, and to the quality of curricula
for Arab schools. The curricula are generally translated from Hebrew with the
least adaptation to an Arabic learner. Thus, in spite of the universal literacy in
Israeli schools, other factors have been at work to undermine the obligatory
schooling for all citizens in Israel.

It seems that in a little more than a century after the revivification of
Hebrew, the language is solidly established as a first language for most Jews
in Israel, as well as a second language for the Palestinian Arabs in Israel. But,
as in the past, when the language played a pivotal role in the Zionist 'nation-
building', it is still doing so. In other words, the language is used to rally people against a common enemy. Considering the ongoing conflict, the enemy
is the Palestinian people, the neighbouring Arab countries and Muslims in
general. For example, when the young Likud minister of education, Gideon
Saʿar, took office in 2009, he declared the year 2010 as the year for Hebrew.
He stated that 'language is culture' and that mastery of the mother tongue
not only contributes to the cognitive development of students, but it also
constitutes the necessary framework for identity and sense of belonging. He
added that the goal of announcing 2010 as the year for Hebrew in schools is
to improve speaking and writing skills of students, encourage correct use of
language, raise an awareness of the importance of Hebrew, improve commu-
nicative skills and educate students on the linguistic and historic tradition of
Hebrew. In effect, the minister is doing two things: spelling out the connection between Hebrew and nationalism, and, more importantly, the conspicuous absence of any mention of Arabic and the need to strengthen it, which
is furthering the marginalisation of Arabic in Israel, despite its legal status.
This minister is also known for encouraging Christian Palestinian Israelis to
identify themselves as Aramaic, as I will be discussing later in this chapter.

As mentioned earlier, since the 1990s, neo-liberal policies have been progressing in Israel at the expense of social and economic equality. Uri Ram (2008) distinguishes between two processes resulting from neo-liberalism: nationalism and a stronger stance against Palestinians, and, at the same time, globalisation and opening up to the world, including the Palestinian and the Arab world. Ram calls the first process 'Jihad' and the second 'McWorld', in reference to the Americanisation factor in globalisation in Israel. Demographically speaking, Ram argues that Tel-Aviv has become a global city, whereas Jerusalem attracts ethno-nationalists. As expected, Hebrew *does* play a role in both processes. For example, since 2004, Israeli higher education institutes have been offering some courses in English, as a sign of Israel's opening up to the outside world. The Israeli press calls this debate about teaching in English 'language war II' in reference to the language war between German and Hebrew which ensued at the Technion in 1913, and which I discussed earlier in this section (see Yadid 2013, 'Etser 2009). The Technion itself was considering offering an MBA degree in English, in order to attract foreign students (Liphshiz 2008). Further, for a discussion on whether Israeli universities should offer law courses in English, the Council for Higher Education appointed a panel of law professors to discuss the issue and, as a result, Hebrew won the day (Skop 2014b). It is interesting to note, however, that Aharon Barak, the (former) chief justice who ruled for road signs to include Arabic, voted for enabling the universities to offer law courses in English (Skop 2014a). Proponents for English cite the importance of connecting with top-notch institutes in the world, as well as of attracting foreign students to Israel, particularly in fields that Israel excels in, such as archaeology, crisis and trauma studies, Holocaust studies and biblical studies (Maltz 2012). Gad Barzilai, the dean of the University of Haifa law school (who also headed the panel appointed by the Council for Higher Education in 2014 to discuss allowing English in higher education), is cited as saying 'they (world institutes) should treat us like Albania?' in reference to Israeli academics becoming isolated, if Hebrew is considered more important than English (Hovel 2012). Opponents to teaching in English cite the fear of emigration from Israel and of weakening the link to the land. The also cite 'self-respect', in reference to Hebrew's connection to the sense of belonging to a nation (Hovel 2012). It is interesting to note that the Iraqi Jewish writer, Sammy Mikhail, who is a native speaker of Arabic, protested against speaking in English when he was asked to do so at a conference of the International Association for Israel Studies. He wanted to deliver his speech in Hebrew (Hovel 2012). Note that this is the same writer who had to abandon his native language, Arabic, in favour of Hebrew because he could no longer reconcile the presence of both languages in his life (see Chapter 2).

In the English-only debate in the United States, where the indigenous languages of native America were the first casualty, it seems that, as is often the case, the same may be true in Israel. While Arabic is the victim of the insistence of the Hebrew-only movement, at the same time globalisation and the opening up of the market is giving more space to English at the expense of Arabic. The presence of English is significant in, for example, malls around the country. Shop signs are sometimes in English and sometimes in English and Hebrew (Ram 2008). This includes, for example, the mall in the Arab town of Nazareth (which took the spot of a former school) and which is called 'Big' in English, so that it is often referred to as 'al-Big', that is, 'The Big'. It caters to the population of Nazareth, but some of the shoppers and salespeople are from Upper Nazareth (which is now a mixed town). Songs played at the mall are in English and cafes at that mall *do not*, or *are not* allowed (by the company owning the mall) to play Arabic music (field observations in summers 2013–15, and talking to Arab shoppers at the mall). Nonetheless, the language of the shoppers is Arabic, with a mixture of Hebrew. Jewish salespeople at the mall speak Arabic to the Arab customers (field observations in summers 2013–15). In other words, the language situation is more fluid than the dichotomous situation observed at first glance. Lastly, Neftali Bennett, the right-wing leader of 'Ha-Bayet Ha-Yehudi', 'the Jewish Home', upon becoming Israel's minister of education in the 2015 elections announced that he wants to pay special attention to Arab schools in terms of resources. He considers the economic inequality to be a national threat in Israel. Improving the education system in the Arab sector can help tackle the issue of inequality (Arlozorof 2015).

The effect of Jewish-Israeli nationalism, as opposed to globalisation, is also felt in the different styles of Hebrew usage. For example, in a seminal work in 1986, Tamar Katriel, a professor of communication at Haifa University, discussed the ethos of the 'Sabra' (Arabic for prickly pear, but refers to Jews born in Israel, in Hebrew) speaking style of Hebrew. It was identified by her and by her informants as 'dugri' speech. The word 'dugri', originating in Turkish, is borrowed via Arabic. While it simply means 'straight' in Palestinian Arabic usage, it signifies that the speaker is about to suspend 'face-work' for the sake of telling the truth, in Hebrew. Katriel analyses the socio-political catalysts for this style, which was viewed positively, by her informants in the 1980s. More recently, she observes that this style is giving way to two new styles: more politeness in speech, and a somewhat negative attitude towards 'dugri' speech. In fact, speakers now seem to prefer the English word 'fair' when they want to suspend 'face-work', but without the negative connotation of being 'brute' when the word 'dugri' is used. In addition to the influence of English on Hebrew, the speaker signifies the desire to be perceived as more cosmopolitan in attitude. Moreover, a more militaristic style of speaking has emerged, particularly on television and in public debate: the 'Kasaḥ' (pronounced kasach in Hebrew) style. The word 'kasiḥ' is an Arabic adverb, used in Hebrew as an adjective. It is from the root 'k,s,ḥ', which has the meaning of incapacitating, and it is used when brute linguistic force is used to silence the other speaker. Katriel attributes the emergence of this style to the culture of militarism and force that prevails in Israel, as well as the lingering unresolved conflict with the Palestinians. She also states that Hebrew speakers are not necessarily insecure about Hebrew and that Hebrew is alive and healthy in the twenty-first century. Rather, speakers of Hebrew feel insecure about their style of language and whether Hebrew, a new 'speaking' language, has developed all the nuances for social interactions (Katriel 2004). In other words, Hebrew speakers *do* borrow today, mainly from English (as compared to German, Yiddish and Arabic in the past century), as there is a recognition that it is in need of innovation, but they feel less confident about the style of usage. Note also that Israeli Jews in general do not view 'globalisation', or rather 'Americanisation' negatively. In fact, Israelis tend to admire the American way of life and appreciate the American political support of Israel (First and Avraham 2009).

Lastly, Katriel notes that 'dugri' speech, and one could also assume 'kasaḥ' speech, conflict with the Arab society 'musayara' style. Musayara, according to Katriel and her informants, means a style where the speaker suspends the truth in order to save the face of the conversational partner. In other words,

Palestinian Arabic speakers pay attention to saving face, in situations where it is completely suspended in Hebrew. This, according to Katriel, can add to the misunderstanding of both people when interacting face to face, just to add to the already existing national conflict (Katriel 1986).

To sum up, it seems that the competing forces between Hebrew as a national language and English as a language of globalism are not in conflict, as the general mood, to a great extent, welcomes the 'intense globalisation' (Ben-Rafael et al. 2006), and its symbols, side by side with the national symbol of the state, the Hebrew language. However, national tension, predictably, is noticed in regard to the space allocated, or even allowed, for Arabic in Israel. In other words, Arabic is seen as a threat to the national symbolism of Hebrew and not English, which ironically has penetrated the public life and the Hebrew language in a much more noticeable manner than Arabic has. In that sense, do the respective language academies of the two languages play a similar role in their goals of strengthening each language? The next section argues that while the Hebrew language academy has had a noticeable role in providing a standard for language use, the Arabic language academy in Israel does not play a similar role. Further, the Arabic language academy in its stated goals expresses subordination to Hebrew, and at the same time a negligence of the natural geographic and historic space of the Arabic language.

The Role of the Language Academy

The Academy of the Hebrew Language was established in 1953,[10] as the continuation of the Hebrew Language Committee established in 1890. Both organisations played a significant role in modernising and standardising Hebrew. Sasson Somekh, an Iraqi Jewish academic who joined the academy as a member in 1963, expresses his excitement at admission to the academy in his second memoir 'Life after Baghdad' (Somekh 2012a), which was originally written in Hebrew a few years earlier. What is interesting about his joining the academy is that he thought that the Ashkenazi Jews, who have had the language more naturally while growing up in Mandate Palestine, were much better at Hebrew than he was. He considered his Hebrew to be unnatural and learned. Somekh much later also joined the Arabic Language Academy, when it was established in Haifa in 2007.[11] The Academy of the Hebrew Language, which is hosted at the Hebrew University in Jerusalem, also has a guiding role in relation to broadcasting to the public, in matters of grammar and style, as well as innovation in the Hebrew lexicon to enable it to deal with modern vocabulary. One ongoing project of the academy has been building a historic dictionary of Hebrew. In contrast, the Arabic Language Academy in Israel does not have a university hosting it, nor does it guide the media on the correct use of Arabic. In fact, one popular radio broadcaster, Zuhair Bahloul, mentioned to me in an interview on 21 August 2013 that the lack of guidance from any linguistic authority often confuses the broadcasters as to how they should use the language. Note that Bahloul, who grew up in the mixed city of Akka, made his career as a sports commentator in Hebrew. In spite of Arabic being his native language, he does not express the same confusion when it comes to language choices in Hebrew (see Chapter 2 for more on Bahloul). The same sentiment was expressed by Ruba Warwar, who grew up in Nazareth and who works in Arabic broadcasting on Israel's Channel 1 (interview 8 July 2013; see also Chapter 2 for more on Warwar).

The Arabic Language Academy in Israel was founded by a Knesset law approved on 21 March 2007,[12] with the purpose of strengthening the presence of Arabic in the 'general linguistic scene, and at the scientific, cultural and educations circles' (the official website of the Arabic Academy in Israel, p. 2).[13] The statement of goals mentions the historic context of Arabic, the need to innovate terms in science and other modern fields, the different Arabic genres such as poetry and fiction, and the need to cooperate with the Hebrew Academy in Israel, as well as the ministry of education. Conspicuously absent is the reference to the geographic natural extension of Arabic beyond the border of Israel. One could well speculate that Arabs in Israel do indeed view themselves as a minority. The most important goals of the academy are specified as:

> Studying the Arabic language in different epochs and branches; working in the field of terminology; grammar, vocabulary, pronunciation, transliteration, spelling; dealing with neologisms and linguistic innovations and their suitability to technology, computerization; compilation of general purpose and specialized dictionaries; studying the language in the Arab culture, especially in poetry and fiction; *establishing relations and exchanging information with the Academy of the Hebrew Language and research institutes*

of Arabic and Hebrew in Israel and the world; cooperation with the Ministry of Education and institutes of higher education and providing counselling to them in the different linguistic fields; publishing books and monographs and holding conferences on themes pertaining to the Academy's interests and activities. (Emphasis added)[14]

At the same time, Al-Qasimi Academic College for Education[15] also has an Arabic language academy. The stated purpose of this language academy is to strengthen the Arabic language and its use, and to offer guidance regarding all contexts of the language: grammatical, literary, scientific, social and political.[16] Al-Qasimi College is a private college which was established in 1989 in Baqa Al-Gharbiyya, an Arab town in the Triangle, and its purpose is to contribute to an education in Arabic for the Palestinian Israelis. One of the goals in its covenant of 2010 is to establish academic connections between the Palestinian Israeli local community and its surroundings: local, state-wide, Arab, Muslim and international. It also aims at nurturing dialogue among different groups in the Israeli society: a dialogue built on mutual respect.[17] The college received recognition from Al-Azhar University in Egypt in 1995 (thus investing in the Arabic language in its natural civilisational and geographic surroundings), and accreditation for its BEd (Bachelor of Education) from the Israeli Council for Higher Education in 2002.

In comparison, the Arabic Language Academy, focuses on coordinating and establishing connections with the Hebrew Language Academy as discussed above, and in a clear articulation of the subordinate status of Arabic to Hebrew.

So far, I have discussed the receding space for Arabic in the country, in spite of its official status. The next section will discuss bilingual schools and their attempt at giving space to both languages.

Bilingual Schools

Arabs in Israel attend Arabic-speaking schools, and Jews attend Hebrew-speaking schools. It is well documented that the state of Israel practised heavy surveillance of the Arab schools and up until the 1990s state intelligence had a say in the employment of Arab teachers for the ministry of education. Further, the Arab sector in education has also been divided into Arab, Druze and

Bedouin (see Al-Haj 1995 for a full account of Arab education in Israel). The curriculum in Arab schools was created in order to educate the Arab 'Israeli' on Jewish history and culture, the Holocaust, and on the idea of 'Israel', in an attempt to 'de-Palestinise'; in other words, to 'Israelise' young people (Smooha 1989). There is an ongoing debate as to how much Israel has succeeded in the process of 'Israelisation'. The combination of 'Jewish' and 'democratic' is often cited as a major obstacle in the process of 'Israelisation', which for an Arab living in Israel can mean full equality, as well as a recognition of the collective rights of Palestinians in Israel, but more often it means a process of marginalisation of the Palestinian and the Arab context of the Arabs in Israel. Nadim Rouhana (1997) notes that the process of 'Israelisation' resulted in some changes in social values, such as the status of women, which used to be more traditional. On the other hand, the 'Palestinian' collective identity and its national rights does not seem to have been affected by the encounter with the process of 'Israelisation'. Rouhana attributes the changes in social values to the fact of accelerated modernisation, resulting from living in Israel. This academic stance is in stark contrast to Azmi Bishara's claim that Israel interrupted and hindered Palestinian society's process of modernisation (see Jamal 2011).

Note that Arabs can study in Jewish schools, but at the expense of the Arabic language. Moreover, in order to be accepted at Israel's universities, students must demonstrate a high level of proficiency not only in Hebrew, but also in English. Jewish students take English as a second language, whereas Arab students take both Hebrew and English, resulting in less emphasis on Arabic, even in the Arab schools. As mentioned earlier, for the high school matriculation tests (Bagrut), most Arab students do not major in Arabic, but rather take the minimal units required for graduating. Note that Christian Arab schools continued to operate after 1948, but gradually accepted the ministry of education curriculum. Today, as during the British Mandate, these schools serve about a quarter of the Arab population from all religious sects (Pores 2015). Some of these schools excel academically, such as St Joseph's, or the Baptist schools in Nazareth. Azmi Bishara for example, graduated from one of these schools in Nazareth. A good number of the Arab academics at the Israeli universities graduated from some of these schools, however, few Arab parents opt to send their children to Jewish schools. The author Sayed Kashua (Chapter 5) graduated from a Jewish school in Jerusalem.

Jewish schools in Israel educate students on the history of the Jews, their rights to the land, the Holocaust and the Jewish literature and culture. In an exhaustive account of textbooks in Israeli Jewish schools, Nurit Peled-Elhanan (2012) painstakingly deconstructs the Zionist nationalist narrative in history, geography and civic studies. The results of her analysis come as no surprise at all. These textbooks 'Other' the Palestinian, whether a citizen or not, and put him or her in contradiction to anything Jewish and Western. The Palestinians are terrorists and primitive, whereas the Jews are enlightened and civilised. The racist depictions of the Palestinian 'Other' are represented both verbally and graphically in schoolbooks.

The Hebrew language and its teaching was at the core of the Zionist nationalist agenda, as stated earlier. This language ideology finds its way even in bilingual schools: schools that attempt to build a better Israeli society, a society which is inclusive of Arabs and yearns for full equality. The first bilingual school was built in 1984 in the village of Neve Shalom/ Waḥat Al-Salam/ Peace Oasis, near Jerusalem. It was followed by one other school in Galilee in the north (1997), one in Jerusalem (1998), one in the Triangle (1998) and lastly, one in Beersheba in the Negev (2009). The first four schools mentioned above are run by an NGO called 'Hand in Hand Centre for Jewish-Arab Education in Israel', while the last one is run by a sister NGO called 'Hagar' (see Romano-Hvid 2015). The aim of these schools is to give the students an education in Arabic and Hebrew concurrently. At first, equal numbers of Arab and Jewish students, as well as teachers, were sought. In reality this did not happen, but the schools, while marginal to both Arab and Jewish societies, attract more Arab students than Jewish. For example, the school in Jerusalem, which has classes up to the 6th grade, has attracted an average number of 30 Jewish students and 120 Arab students since 2009 (personal correspondence with Zvi Bekerman, a scholar at the Hebrew University who has been researching these schools since their inception, 11 May 2015). Arab parents of students at these schools are generally educated at Israeli universities, belong to the new Arab middle class and are mostly Muslim, like the writer Sayed Kashua who sends his children to such a school. According to Bekerman (personal correspondence, 11 May 2015), these parents 'all seem committed to having their children not suffer as they did when going to university, that they are happy with the emphasis on Hebrew so much so that a few even were happy mentioning how their children when speaking Hebrew sound Jewish'. None of the Arab parents expressed fear or worry about language loss in Arabic. Most speak to their children in Arabic at home, but few do so in Hebrew. Further, the power relation between both societies is reproduced and maintained to a great extent inside these schools. In reality, Hebrew is used more than Arabic and Arab children become fluent in Hebrew, but not the converse. Jewish children are far from becoming fluent in Arabic in these schools (Romano-Hvid 2015, Rajuan and Bekerman 2010; see also Bekerman 2016). Lastly, these parents consider English to be a very important part of their children's education, as they recognise its global significance.

The ratio of Arab to Jewish children in these schools, in addition to being an indication of the majority-minority relation between both groups, can be explained further in light of Dafna Yitzhaki's research on language policy in Israel (2008). The attitudes of the Arab respondents and the Jewish respondents diverged greatly. For instance, the indigenousness was important for the Arabs in regard to decisions on language policy, but not for the Jewish respondents (Yitzhaki 2008: 183). Arabs emphasised the importance of learning both Hebrew and Arabic, but Jews favoured multilingualism, which may or may not include Arabic learning. Further, a linguistic hierarchy which guarantees the supremacy of Hebrew was important to the Jewish group, but predictably, not to the Arab (Yitzhaki 2008: 189). Lastly, the ethnic situation between Arabs and Jews overshadowed the discourse of 'minority language rights' for both groups (Yitzhaki 2008: 190).

To sum up, bilingual schools depict an unequal language status, even when the goal is coexistence and mutual respect for both cultures. The reality of the situation outside the schools does in the end dictate their outcome, and it is not improving, when one examines the Zionist teaching which goes side by side with the teaching of the Hebrew language, as well as other subjects, such as history, for Jewish children. As for the teaching of Arabic, it is limited in Jewish schools and diminishing for Arabs. In spite of the fact that schools for Arabs teach in Arabic, the students do not attach much importance to the language itself. The next section will discuss one of the attempts at fragmenting the Palestinians in Israel through the introduction of a new nationality: 'Aramean'.

The Case for Aramaic

Amal Jamal (2006) argues that the political leadership for Arabs in Israel, while part of a democratic process, can be identified by the following three characteristics: it adheres to the clientele relationship with the state, as Hillel Cohen describes in his (2004) *Army of Shadows: Palestinians in the Service of Zionism*. Second, the Arab leadership is personalised, which by itself, however, does not necessarily undermine democracy and the democratic process. Further, Israeli politics, since at least the time of Menahim Begin, can be characterised by populism (Filc 2010). Third, the Arab leadership is patriarchal and does not allow much space for Arab women in politics. Jamal (2006) concludes that in spite of the common cause of the Arab leadership and the public – the struggle towards full citizenship and recognition of their collective rights as Palestinians – the leadership is nonetheless fragmented and does not unite, as a result of the above-mentioned three features. The early elections in 2015 proved to be the exception to Jamal's argument. All Arab parties united, suspended all differences and followed what Spivak (1999) calls 'strategic essentialism'.

However, the picture of unification is not as rosy as the 2015 election results suggest. In the autumn of 2014, the Likud minister of the interior, Gideon Sa'ar (the same minister who declared 2010 as the year for strengthening Hebrew when he was minister of education) added a new official nationality for Israelis. This concerns the Christian Arab minority of the Eastern Churches,[18] who can register as 'Aramean' on their identity cards and the birth certificates of the newly born, if parents choose to do so. The Arabic press, generally, did not pay much attention to this, as it was seen as yet another cheap plot by Netanyahu's government to divide the Palestinian Arab community. The Muslim Nazareth mayor, Ali Sallam, was very dismissive of it, on the grounds that Netanyahu should be more concerned about Israel's citizens in general.[19] This was the last act of Gideon Sa'ar, just before he stepped down from his position as minister of the interior. Israel's channel 24 announced the news as the birth of a new nationality (same source). In October 2014, almost a month after the minister's decision, Yaakov Hallol from the Arab Christian village in the north, Jish (or Gush Halav in Hebrew) became the first child to be registered as 'Aramean'. His father, Shadi Hallol (Risho), a Maronite Christian is one of the advocates for this new nationality.

He also serves as the head of the Christian IDF (Israeli Defence Forces) Forum, an organisation which recruits Christian Arabs into the Israeli army (note that this attempt failed in 1957, see Saʿdi 2014: 89). The advocacy for Aramaean and for joining the IDF are both linked together with Hallol and his following.[20] His argument revolves around an imagined community of Christians in the Holy Land, who spoke Aramaic, until the Islamic conquests of the seventh century. Islam forced the Arabic language and Arabism on this community and Hallol yearns for a return to that pristine era before Islam. He also links his community to the Aramaic community in Iraq and Syria (some of these communities indeed preserved the Aramaic language). His 'we' in the interview cited above is inclusive of the Christians in Syria and Iraq and the Islamic threat they are facing from 'ISIS'. In his opinion, Israel's democracy is a guarantee for protecting minorities, like his, from the Muslim threat. In other words, Christians should join the IDF because the state of Israel is their protector, and they should participate in all of the state's institutions. Note that Christians, as Arabs, have been joining the IDF for decades, in small numbers but optionally and not by law, as the case is with the Druze. Note also that there are more Muslims in the IDF than there are Christians.[21] Hallol estimates that about 250 Christian families are interested in registering as 'Aramaean' and would like to join the IDF as well. Hallol also uses Hebrew rather than Arabic in his correspondence. On his Facebook page he announced in Hebrew the establishment of a new organisation called 'the Christian Aramaic Organization in Israel'.[22] In addition, he promotes the learning of Aramaic, with the hope of reviving it as a daily language for Eastern Christians in Israel. He promotes a school which teaches Aramaic to children in his village, and also through the Maronite Church. In Haifa, his brother teaches Aramaic to the Maronite community. I visited the church in July 2014 and attended an Aramaic class, where I met the brother's daughter, a 10-year-old girl who can communicate in Aramaic. It seems that the horrors of 'ISIS' in Iraq and Syria were a turning point for people like Hallol, in their feeling of alienation from the Muslim 'Other'.

Further, it seems that the Aramaic movement in Israel, while still insignificant, relies on the Maronite community in Haifa and a few other villages close to the border with Lebanon. Consequently, one could also understand it as an extension of the Phoenician/Aramaic movement in Lebanon, as an expression of Lebanese local nationalism (discussed briefly in Chapter 1), and intellectually not separate from it. Meeting some Aramaic sympathisers among the Maronites in Haifa in summer 2014, I couldn't help but notice the contradictions in their discourse, the most obvious of which regards the physical and national territory of the Aramaic nation and its contours. At the same time, however, their discourse can be characterised by hostility to anything Arab and Muslim. One of the historian-theoreticians that inspires this group in Israel is Dr Henri Budrus Kifa, who is from Beirut, but with family roots in Orfa, Turkey. Kifa calls for a Greater Syrian Aramaic nation and for the revival of the Aramaic language, in opposition to anything Arab and Muslim. His lectures and articles are circulated on the social media,[23] and seem to alienate not only the Arabs, but also the Assyrian community in Iraq and Syria, for whom Aramaic never ceased to exist as a language of communication for thousands of years, and therefore it is a language which does not need revivification. These communities do also oppose a vision of a standardised Aramaic, which is different from their Syriac.[24]

Hallol was joined by Gabriel Naddaf, a priest from the Greek Orthodox Church in Nazareth. He called the Greek Orthodox community in Nazareth to change their status to 'Aramean' at the ministry of the interior, according to *Bokra* (2014a), a local media centre for Arabs in Israel. In response, the former head of the Greek Orthodox Council, Azmi Hakim, was swift to ask the Council to expel Naddaf from the Church (*Bokra* 2014b). Other community leaders condemned Naddaf as well. On my two visits to Nazareth since then, people refused to discuss this topic with me, even friends, which I took as an indication of how upsetting this decision of the ministry is to the people in Nazareth, as it touches the fabric of their communal life at its core.

Note that the decision to create an Aramean identity that was separate from Arab, in autumn 2014, coincided with the new bill proposing to turn Israel into a Jewish state. A sub-branch of this bill asks for omitting Arabic as an official language in Israel (*The Times of Israel*, 26 August 2014).[25] The bill did not pass and Netanyahu announced early elections for March 2015, as mentioned earlier. It remains to be seen whether the bill will be revived in the future with the new government.

This chapter discussed the difficult position of the Arabic language from the point of view of what I would describe as 'the volatile conditions' of

Arab citizenship in Israel. Azmi Bishara's political career is a good example of the limits of citizenship for the Arabs in Israel. His attempt at redefining the contours of 'the seamline' ultimately failed. The chapter also discussed the meaning of 'official' languages, the role of language academies, the language arrangement in bilingual schools, and lastly the new imagined nationality of 'Aramean' and its genealogical connection to Aramaic. This new identity is in line with the state's continuous attempts to fracture the Palestinian community in Israel, but at the same time it is drawing inspiration from the fragmentation of Arab communities in surrounding states such as Syria, Lebanon and Iraq. The next chapter will look at the status of Arabic through the language choice of three native speakers of Arabic who write in Hebrew.

Notes

1. Available at <http://www.adalah.org/en> (last accessed 7 November 2014).
2. Available at <http://civilsociety.haifa.ac.il/orgDet.asp?lang=eng&orgid=203> (last accessed 7 November 2014).
3. Available at <http://www.arabhra.org/> (last accessed 7 November 2014).
4. Available at <http://www.ilam-center.org/en/> (last accessed 7 November 2014).
5. Available at <http://mada-research.org/> (last accessed 7 November 2014).
6. Available at <http://english.dohainstitute.org/portal> (last accessed 12 November 2015).
7. Available at <http://english.dohainstitute.org/content/5a4156bf-ba64-4408-be64-5a0c753b7c71> (last accessed 19 July 2015).
8. Available at <https://www.dohainstitute.edu.qa/AR/About/DohaInstitute/Pages/Default.aspx> (last accessed 19 July 2015).
9. Available at <https://www.dohainstitute.edu.qa/AR/About/DohaInstitute/Pages/Message_from_Azmi_Bishara.aspx> (last accessed 19 July 2015).
10. <http://hebrew-academy.org.il/%D7%93%D7%A3-%D7%94%D7%91%D7%99%D7%AA-%D7%96%D7%9E%D7%A0%D7%99/> (last accessed 25 May 2016).
11. Available at <http://www.arabicac.com/> (last accessed 25 May 2016).
12. Available at <http://www.arabicac.com/?mod=articles&ID=130> (last accessed 18 December 2015).
13. Available at <http://www.arabicac.com/Public/main/history/english1.pdf> (last accessed 12 November 2015).

14. Available at <http://www.arabicac.com/Public/main/history/english1.pdf> p. 2 (last accessed 27 December 2015).
15. Available at <http://www.qsm.ac.il/Main.aspx?did=120&pid=4203> (last accessed 27 December 2015).
16. Available at <http://www.qsm.ac.il/ArbLanguage/About.aspx> (last accessed 7 July 2015).
17. Available at <http://www.qsm.ac.il/main.aspx?did=120&pid=4203> (last accessed 7 July 2015).
18. The Eastern Churches in Israel belong to the Greek Orthodox, Greek Catholic, Maronite, Syriac Catholic, and Orthodox Aramaic communities, with the Greek Orthodox being the largest. The number of Christians in Israel is estimated at 120,000, about 9 per cent of the total Arab population in Israel, which is roughly 20 per cent of Israeli population (Central Bureau of Statistics), <http://www1.cbs.gov.il/reader/shnaton/text_search_eng_new.html?CYear=2015&Vol=66&input=christians> (last accessed 18 December 2015).
19. Available at <http://www.i24news.tv/en/news/israel/society/46718-141010-birth-of-a-new-nationality-causes-tension-between-muslims-christians-in-israel> (last accessed 14 July 2015).
20. Available at <http://www.i24news.tv/en/tv/replay/interview#/interview/387241 3167001> (last accessed 14 July 2015).
21. Available at <http://www.i24news.tv/en/news/israel/society/46718-141010-birth-of-a-new-nationality-causes-tension-between-muslims-christians-in-israel> (last accessed 14 July 2015).
22. Available at <https://www.facebook.com/shadi.risho?fref=ts> (last accessed 14 July 2015).
23. For example, <http://www.bing.com/videos/search?q=%D9%87%D9%86%D8%B1%D9%8A+%D9%83%D9%8A%D9%81%D8%A7&FORM=VIRE3#view=detail&mid=F2D638815A02D3B00CF2F2D638815A02D3B00CF2> (last accessed 21 September 2015).
24. Available at <https://www.facebook.com/Ashuor.ashoraea/posts/3234993077 83614> (last accessed 21 September 2015).
25. Available at <http://www.timesofisrael.com/israeli-lawmakers-push-hebrew-only-bill/> (last accessed 9 December 2015).

5

Autobiography and Language Choice

David Crystal (2014) states that a language dies when its last speaker dies. There is little danger of this for Arabic, numerically speaking, but can Arabic die out in historic Palestine? What could bring about its demise? In Israel proper, the marginalisation of Arabic from the landscape goes hand in hand with the marginalisation of the Arab population in Israel. Open talks of 'transferring the remainder of the Arabs' are so far limited to right-wing groups and ministers such as Avigdor Lieberman, the minister of foreign affairs in autumn 2014, and defence minister in spring 2016. But, in polite company, most Israeli Jews decline to state their preferences, even though polls demonstrate that most Jews would have preferred Israeli Arabs to leave Israel after the establishment of the State of Palestine in the West Bank and in the Gaza Strip (*The Jerusalem Post*, 2008).[1] Thus, a discussion of the language must be accompanied by a discussion of the atmosphere of anxiety for Israeli Arabs, whose demographic growth is a topic of open discussion in the Israeli press and in the Knesset (see, for example, *The Guardian*, 2014).[2]

It seems that the permissible discourse regarding the status of the 1.7 million Palestinians within Israel's 1948–67 borders is becoming wider and wider. For example, since 2009, Netanyahu's government has passed about fifty laws that curtail the civil rights of Arabs in Israel (*Al-Jazeera*),[3] thus demonstrating a preference for resolving the seeming contradiction between being Jewish and being democratic, in a manner which favours the first. I emphasise the word 'seeming' as most democracies do have an ethnic component to them, in the words of Eric Hobsbawm (2008). The Israeli Knesset has also been proposing bills regarding the national service and the meaning of citizenship, mostly targeted towards the Arabs in Israel. For example, there was a proposal for national service in the state, which Arab parties in the Knesset protested against (see, for example, Ravid 2012). Embedded in this proposal is a further attempt to disintegrate the cohesion of the unity of Arabs in Israel. Netanyahu met with Christian leaders in the Arab community, in a gesture to indicate that this law is meant in order to separate the Christians from Muslims, but not without internal controversies within the 'Israeli Arab' communities (see for example, Naddaf 2014a and 2014b, on social media, the Greek Orthodox priest from Nazareth, mentioned in the previous chapter, who endorses this plan). The de facto result of a success of recruiting Christians for the national service is the creation of two tiers of citizenship for Arabs: non-service and thus undeserving of full rights (Muslims) and service groups which already include the Druze, the Bedouin and the Christians.

Since at least the signing of the Oslo Accords in 1993, Israeli leaders have been discussing the demographic threat of Israeli Arabs and the fear that Israel will not maintain a numerical majority (see Pappé 2014). Currently, it seems that the Netanyahu government is being innovative in resolving the demographic 'threat' to Israel, which was even on the table for Bill Clinton during the Oslo talks. Clinton comments in his book (2005) that he wouldn't allow a situation where Jews are not a majority on their land. Where does that lead us?

It should be noted that Israel does not live in isolation from its geographic context, as most Ashkenazi Jews would prefer to see it as a European oasis in a barbaric sea of Muslim Arabs. Since 2003, Iraq and Syria have disintegrated, Egypt has changed its regime, Lebanon has remained as destabilised as ever, while Jordan is becoming more and more nervous about the influx of refugees mainly from Syria, and about ISIS at its doors. Israel seems to have been immune to all of this. Government is strong, but has shown its limitations since at least 1967 with the continuous Palestinian 'disturbance' of 'order' in Israel. The descent into sectarian wars in Iraq and Syria has furthered the feeling that Muslims are inherently violent, as well as the hostility against minority groups. We hear every day of the plight of minorities in Iraq and in

Syria. This climate fuels a discourse which separates 'the Arabs inside Israel' into sects not necessarily with a common national goal, but with competing demands from the state.

In this context, does Arabic mean the same if you are an Arab Jew, meaning a Mizrachi Jew, or if you are Muslim, or Christian? Aiding me in this are the two memoirs of Sasson Somekh, an Arab Jew (2007, 2012a), the autobiographical novel of Anton Shammas (1989), a Christian Arab from Galilee, as well as the numerous articles and novels by Sayed Kashua, a Muslim from the Triangle.

I study the writing of Sasson Somekh, Anton Shammas and Sayed Kashua through the lens of their personal biographies, their background and their language choice (see also Y. Suleiman 2013 for a fruitful discussion of these authors' productions). The language choices of these authors help us understand the asymmetrical relationship between Israelis and Arabs, as well as the global linguistic homogenisation and perhaps the effects of collective traumas on the individual. The chapter concludes with a section on the 'Arab Jew', and the challenges of maintaining both constructs of this identity in Israel, in the case of the documentary of the 'Ethnic Devil' broadcast on Israeli television in summer 2013, and the case of the sociologist and poet, Sami Chetrit, an Arab Jew who does not speak Arabic.

Sasson Somekh

Sasson Somekh is a Jewish professor of Arabic at Tel-Aviv University. He was born in Baghdad to an established family there, and moved to Israel in his late teens as part of the mass exodus of this ancient community in Iraq. Upon arriving in Israel he had to learn Hebrew, like all immigrants to Israel. Steadily, Hebrew started taking over more and more domains of his life, until it prevailed over Arabic. Today, he is a member of the Hebrew language academy, as well as the Arabic language academy. Somekh, in addition, studied Arabic literature at Oxford University with the renowned Egyptian scholar, Mahmoud Al-Badawi, thus joining a cadre of influential scholars of Arabic trained by Al-Badawi, such as Roger Allen at the University of Pennsylvania. What distinguishes Somekh's career from others is the fact that Arabic was the main language of his expression until his move to Israel. He is the 'outsider' from within, an Arab Jew, who no longer fits in an Arab context, but at the same time, someone whose linguistic identity is no longer common for younger generations of Jews coming from Arab countries. Somekh's command of Arabic thought and Arabic literature is admirable. He fondly looks back on his relationship with Al-Badawi as a student and states that the Israeli-Arab conflict did not influence their relationship. This remark, while positive, is still a testimony of how the relationship of Arab-Jews with other Arabs became problematic after the Nakba, and particularly after 1967 (Somekh 2012a). Somekh also did not change his name upon arriving in Israel, as many Jews did. While his name is already Hebrew, it still carries the reverberations of Hebrew in an Arab context, and it indicates his Arab origins. In other words, he did not attempt to choose a name which is less ethnically marked. His command of Arabic is native and natural still, after decades of 'de-Arabisation', and in contrast to the next generations of Iraqi Jews who never learned Arabic. Yehouda Shenhav, a second generation Iraqi, and a professor of sociology also at Tel-Aviv University had to learn Arabic at an older age, a decision he made in identification with his Arab roots. He related to me in summer 2014 that since his spoken Arabic is 'Palestinian', his mother was not pleased at the fact that it is not 'Iraqi' like hers and the rest of his ancestors.

Somekh's life project portrays a remarkable love and admiration for the Arabic language, its literary heritage and intricate genres and styles. He is no less enthusiastic in his appreciation of Arabic production, old and modern alike. His fascination with the modern Arabic novel found its expression in his deep friendship with Najuib Mahfouz, as mentioned earlier. The result of this meeting of minds is a remarkable introduction to Mahfouz's literature to the non-expert Hebrew reader. In it, Somekh chronicles some of their meetings, and Mahfouz, the humanist, emerges out of these depictions. Somekh identifies strongly with Mahfouz's survival after an attempt on his life due to his perceived un-Islamic writing, in the late eighties. While Mahfouz was not physically harmed, Somekh is convinced that the attempt managed to silence the writer, as his writing slowed down significantly after the attempt (Somekh 2012b). Somekh also shares with the reader Mahfouz's (and other writers') dilemmas and stances in regard to the Arabic diglossia (see also Somekh 1991). Further, Somekh tackles the question of the impossibility of a viable Jewish literature on Arab land in modern times. He states that in the twentieth century, the literary environment in Iraq and, to a lesser extent, Egypt and Palestine was more inclusive of Jewish writers than other countries. However, as the century unfolded pronounced national movements in these places meant that the space for Jews to write in Arabic shrank significantly (Somekh 1994). The cost for Iraqi Jewish writers was first the avoidance of any political writing, before their writing in Arabic disappeared completely, with the exception of Samir Naqqash (1937–2004), and Yitzhak Bar-Moshe (1927–), who still wrote in Arabic (Somekh 1994: 193). Recently, Somekh co-edited a volume of the essays of Jacqueline Shohet Kahanoff, an Egyptian Jewish essayist, who after moving to Israel, started to publish in the Hebrew press. As a Jew, she never felt at home in Arabic while in Egypt, nor in Hebrew in Israel (Starr and Somekh 2011: xiv), and yet she promoted a romantic idea of a Levantine culture which is inclusive of all differences (ethnic, religious and so on). Today, this author is forgotten, just as her inclusive project is. Starr and Somekh's collection (2011) is an attempt at 'a memory for forget-fulness', to use Darwish's (2013) expression, in regard to Palestinian memory.

Lastly, I met Somekh in Ramat Aviv, on the campus of Tel-Aviv University in the summer of 2014. Somekh spoke in Iraqi Arabic throughout the meeting and topics discussed varied from reminiscences of his life in Baghdad, his involvement in literature in the Arab world, his deep friendship with Najuib Mahfouz, his mentors in Baghdad, some of whom are part of the Arab intelligentsia, and the impact of the educated Baghdadi Jews on Palestinian education in Israel. One of the ironies which did not escape me at the meeting is the fact that Somekh's physical world revolved for decades around Northern Tel-Aviv, the site of a ruined Arab village, Sheikh Mou'nis, with its abandoned mosque, reminiscent of a time, not too long ago, when the place used to speak Arabic.

Anton Shammas

Born shortly after the Nakba in an Upper Galilee Christian village bordering Lebanon, Shammas moved to Haifa as a child with his family where he received an education in a bilingual school, and started writing poetry in both languages as early as in the 1960s. He has also been engaged in translating to and from both languages works such as the poetry of Mahmoud Darwish and the novels of Emile Habibi (1922–96). But he became known in literary circles after publishing a widely acclaimed autobiographical novel, *Arabesques* (1984/9), in the Hebrew language. Claimed as one of the best novels of the year in 1984 by the *New York Review of Books*,[4] the novel was a huge success in Israeli literary circles and it was soon translated into English and many other languages. It has not yet been translated into Arabic and the lack of interest in doing so is perhaps an indication of the minimal dialogue among the various languages of the Middle East, including Hebrew (though one of Shammas's friends explained to me that Shammas himself refuses for his novel to be translated into Arabic during his lifetime). Shammas continues to translate between Arabic and Hebrew, even as he moved his residence to the United States, without seemingly having a problem in switching between both languages.

Further, Shammas's Christian Catholic identity dominates his novel, and the minute details of the daily rituals of this very small and pious village. It is a definite Christian experience in the larger discourse of dispossession, and a national aspiration which does not manifest itself other than in the want to live as a respected citizen of the state of Israel. But, unlike Kashua, who chronicles his life in his novels and articles and focuses on the 'here and now' in the state of Israel, and on how to fit in, Shammas brings the past into the present in his novel, as it keeps switching the character's lives in different times and different places. One could also argue that the Nakba trauma is the lynchpin on which the events of the novel rest in their movement backwards (through various techniques of flashbacks and free associations of the narrator) and forwards through relating these events to the present and, by implication, the future.

Lastly, Shammas's justification for choosing to write in Hebrew is articulated as:

> What I am trying to do – mulishly, it seems – is to un-Jew the Hebrew language, to make it more Israeli and less Jewish, thus bringing it back to its Semitic origins, to its place. This is a parallel to what I think the state should be. As English is the language of those who speak it, so is Hebrew; and so the state should be the state of those who live in it, not of those who play with its destiny with a remote control in hand. (Kimmerling 2008: 223)

As it will become clearer in the next section, while, both Shammas's and Kashua's projects aim at bridging the gap of citizenship and understanding between both peoples, they both arrive at it from different points. Kashua in his constant quest for 'fitting in' and 'passing' as an Ashkenazi in West Jerusalem, and Shammas through asserting his Christian identity within a Palestinian collective identity, within Israel.

Sayed Kashua

When he came of age in the 1980s, his family enrolled him in a Jewish school in Jerusalem, where he had to switch to Hebrew as a literary language. From that moment on, Hebrew became the language of his academic and public life. He enrolled at the Hebrew University, but did not graduate with a degree, instead, he turned to journalism in the 1990s, his formative intellectual years. Most of his novels and short articles are about the desire to fit in, in the Ashkenazi Israeli society. He is also most known for his television sitcom 'Arab Labour' (2007–), about an Arab protagonist who desires to live his life just like an Ashkenazi Jew. In autumn 2014, Kashua wrote an article in *Ha'aretz* on his decision to leave the country and not come back, as life had become impossible for him during the summer of 2014 (Kashua 2014). Kashua has been described as the Arab Palestinian Shalom Aleichem (1859–1916), who excelled in his depiction of nineteenth-century shtetl life in Europe and who is known for his wry humour (interview with Zuhair Bahloul, 12 August 2013).

Kashua was born in Tira, in the Triangle, to a middle-class family – a dispossessed family a generation earlier, due to the Nakba. His grandmother, having lost the right to cultivate her piece of land, like thousands of dispossessed Palestinians after the Nakba, had to become a wage earner in Israeli farms near her village. She raised her children and was able to send Kashua's father to the Hebrew University for his education. His father, in turn, tried to give Kashua a chance for education by sending him to a Jewish school where he was the only Arab student. Most of his writing was produced while he was living in Jerusalem.

Kashua's sitcom is a success among a certain stratum of Israeli society, namely, the urban Ashkenazi Jews, who generally have a higher socio-economic status and a higher education than the rest of the Israeli society. The Arab characters constantly switch between Hebrew and Arabic, while the Jewish characters speak only in Hebrew, but sometimes flavoured with a few Arabic idioms. The sitcom tells the story of an Arab man, Amjad, and his family, neighbours and friends, and his constant quest to be accepted in the Ashkenazi circles he moves in. The sitcom is not popular among Arabs. I asked a few people as to why, and the answer was that the character does not represent their quests, even in exaggeration. Lastly, the programme was broadcast at peak Hebrew viewing time. At first, the producers wanted the language to be 80 per cent Hebrew and 20 per cent Arabic, but Kashua refused this arrangement and they ended up adding more Arabic such as when Amjad speaks with his wife, parents and the car mechanic (Bleboim and Bernstein 2013: 51), but with a clear hegemony of Hebrew. The cast of the series are supposed to mirror the reality of Arabic use in Israel (Bleboim and Bernstein 2013: 50). Lastly, about 2.5 million people in Israel viewed this series (Bleboim and Bernstein 2013: 52).

As mentioned above, Kashua's novels as well as his articles and television sitcom revolve around an Arab protagonist trying to join Ashkenazi circles in Israel by adopting the language, accent and mannerisms. For instance, his novel *Second Person Singular* (2010) is about an Arab lawyer who tries hard to fit in with the Ashkenazim. He is married to a social worker who is also Arab (just like Kashua himself, who is married to an Arab social worker). At the end of the novel the protagonist suspects that his wife is having an affair with another Arab, like him, a Muslim from a village, who has been living as a Jew in Jerusalem for many years. His self-hate and his contempt for his own identity and that of the lover, magnifies the insult and the humiliation of his wife cheating on him. And he wonders if his wife's lover is more educated than he is, and better-read, otherwise why would his wife fall in love with such a person? The themes which Kashua weaves in this novel, and in all his writing, seem to be taken from his life and his personal struggles. His articles in *Ha'aretz* revolve around himself and his family and their daily world in Jerusalem, and now in the United States (see, for example, Kashua 2014, and Kashua and Keret 2014). As mentioned earlier, he is widely read among the upper and leftist strata of Jewish society in Israel, but in order to be recognised as a writer in Israel, does he have to write about himself, and in Hebrew? In other words, as someone occupying a 'subaltern'[5] position in a society, what choices does he have as a writer in Hebrew for a Jewish audience, other than writing about himself? Does he have choices? bell hooks (1989), the well-known African American writer, points out the trap in self-reporting. It was expected of her to write about herself, even when she was writing for an academic audience. The same expectation does not hold for the more dominant strata of society in hooks' case, being white, and preferably male does not build an expectation that the writer will disclose biographic information about himself.

I invited Kashua to Michigan State University in autumn 2014 to give a talk in Arabic to the Arabic students and a second talk in English to a general audience (29 September 2014). He mentioned during both talks that his village did not have a single library when he was growing up. Moreover, while his father emphasised the importance of reading, he never provided his children with books, other than one by Lenin with a picture of the author's severe face on the cover, which deterred the young Kashua from reading it. Kashua mentioned that his father was a member of the Communist Party in those days. Needless to say, it was this party which nurtured democratic values along with nationalistic aspirations among 'Israeli Arabs' back then (because it was a legitimate party with representation in the Knesset from both the Jewish and the Arab population). Ironically Kashua's first encounter with a library was through his Hebrew school in Jerusalem. He was fascinated by it and ended up reading most of the world's greatest literature through translations into Hebrew in this library. The first book he read was *Catcher in the Rye*, and it had an enormous impact on him. In other words, Hebrew represented intellectualism, world-class literature and enlightenment to the young Kashua. There was no similar representation in Arabic. Thus, in Kashua's context, Hebrew functioned as a central language and Arabic as a peripheral one, whereas Arabic is considered a 'supercentral' language in other contexts outside of Israel (see de Swaan 2001).

Furthermore, Kashua makes no reference to any Arab author who influenced him. When asked about this during his talk to the Arabic students at Michigan State University (29 September 2014), he said that he found Al-Mutanabbī (915–65), the emblematic poet of human pride, hard to read, for example, but that he read some contemporary Arabic literature, such as the novels of Najuib Mahfouz, through the Hebrew translations. Kashua spoke to the students in very rich and beautiful Palestinian Arabic and he commented that it was the first time he had been invited to an Arabic programme, rather than a Hebrew one, at a university setting in the US. An audience member who admired his Arabic asked him whether he would consider writing in Arabic and his response was: (1) that he made the language shift once, when he moved to the Jewish school and that it was hard enough back then, and he would not want to go through it again, and (2) it is about marketability of books written in Arabic in Israel. He gives an example of another Israeli Palestinian author, a friend of his, Alaa Hlehel, who is from a village in Northern Galilee, and who resides now in Akka. Hlehel writes in Arabic, but it is very difficult for him to find a publisher as there is not a strong market for his books in Israel, and there is no market for his books 'coming from Israel' for distribution in the Arab world. In fact, Hlehel had to self-publish his latest novel, *Au Revoir Akka* (2014), which tells the history of Akka through the eyes of its ruthless ruler, Ahmad Pasha Al-Jazzar, during the Napoleonic campaign in Palestine. The novel is available in select bookshops in Arab towns, as well as in Hlehel's mother's house, as his Facebook page indicates.[6]

Hlehel's situation, in contrast to Kashua's perhaps, is indicative of the following: (1) a general crisis of the Arabic language marketability these days, considering what is going on the Arab world, and (2) a specific marketability problem within Israel. These points could also be indicative of the lack of prestige of the Arabic language for Arab youth in general. It is more 'cool' to read and write in other languages, especially English and French, in the Arab world, and in Hebrew for Israeli Arabs, in addition to English in some circles (see C. Suleiman 2016). In addition, there seems to be a lack of interest in translating Hlehel to Hebrew. The Israeli public, in general, does not respect the Arabic language and its intellectual life (aside from reading some canonical works in Arabic, such as Mahmoud Darwish, Ghassan Kanafani (1936–72) and Najuib Mahfouz (1911–2006)). In that regard, Shouleh Vatanabadi (2013) makes reference to a larger Middle East phenomenon. Vatanabadi (2013) observes that Middle Eastern societies (Arabic, Persian, Turkish and, I would add, Hebrew), get to know each other through the medium of translating into English and rarely through translation of one of these languages to another, which is an indication to her as to how Eurocentric Middle Eastern societies still are. In other words, post-colonial societies, in their hierarchisation of languages, have not fully broken the mould of colonialism.

On the subject of translatability between Hebrew and Arabic, Shenhav (2012) problematises the issue further, by arguing the impossibility of a translation when the power relations between Palestinians and Israelis are in their current state. For example, 90 per cent of Palestinians in Israeli know Hebrew, while only 3 per cent of the Jews in Israel know Arabic (Shenhav 2012: 164). Moreover, only 2 per cent of Arabic works translated to Hebrew have attracted the attention of critics (Shenhav 2012: 167). However, even the simplest acts of translation are problematic. For example, how does one translate place names when they have all been changed to Hebrew, and yet it is the Arabic names which convey the history of the places and the Palestinians and their dispossession? How does one translate the word 'Nakba' into Hebrew, when the Israeli public is still in denial of the Nakba? (Shenhav 2012: 172–3, see also Jamal and Bsoul 2014.)

Lastly, while Kashua is Muslim by confession, there is no trace of Islamic tradition in any of his writing. His literary and journalistic projects could be considered as secular and aiming at full integration and citizenship in the state of Israel. His novel and his articles are futuristic (see, for example, his correspondence with the Israeli Jewish author and friend, Etgar Keret, in *The New Yorker*, 2014), but the Nakba is never tackled directly in his writing. In other words, his writings are more focused on the consequences of the Nakba and the establishment of the state of Israel, but not on the story of the Nakba itself. Some traces of the Nakba can be found in his public lectures, however. For example, in the public lecture he gave at Michigan State University in September 2014, he mentioned to the audience the fact that his family lost its land when the state of Israel was established. This is in contrast to Shammas, whose autobiographical novel revolves around the Christian daily activities of his village – and also, to some extent, in contrast to Somekh's memoir of Baghdad (2007), where, while fully integrated in the intellectual and literary life of the Baghdad of the 1940s, Somekh's Jewish identity is very central to these activities.

Juxtaposition of Somekh, Shammas and Kashua: When Someone Gives Up a Language, is it Considered a Loss? And by Whom?

The irony in the positioning of the Palestinian Arabs in relation to Mizrachim in Israel did not escape the pen of Sayed Kashua (2009) who wrote a short story for *Ha'aretz* about 'The Kidnapped from Baghdad'. In it, Kashua was invited to give a talk about his literary work at a British university. Upon arriving there, he discovers that the conference is about Iraqi Jewish literature, and that, as a writer in Hebrew from Israel, he was mistaken to be of Iraqi Jewish origins, rather than Palestinian Israeli. He opts for going along with this mix-up by giving a paper and pretending he is an Iraqi Jewish writer. One of the characters portrayed in the story *does* indeed resemble the profile of Sasson Somekh, who most likely would have been invited to such an event as well.

The three authors have been recognised for their works with prestigious awards: Somekh with the Israel Prize in 2005, in recognition for his work in bringing Arabic literature to the attention of Hebrew readers, Shammas received awards from the US, such as the Whiting Award in 1991 for his (1984) autobiographic novel, and Kashua won a number of awards such as the Prime Minister's Award for literature in 2004, in Israel. The three authors: Somekh, Shammas and Kashua, who represent three generations of Hebrew users, are likely to have had very different paths towards Hebrew. Somekh had to learn Hebrew as an adult in the 1950s, Shammas did so as a result of the bilingual environment he experienced in his youth, as his family moved to the mixed city of Haifa of the 1960s.[7] Kashua's Hebrew emerges through his protagonist, an Arab Palestinian male yearning to fit into Ashkenazi social circles. His protagonist's Hebrew is impeccable, and is always working at perfecting it and removing any traces of Arabic (see Bleboim and Bernstein 2013).

Somekh, however, does not express any concern for the influence of his Hebrew in his writing; however, in his memoir (2007), he envies the Ashkenazim whose Hebrew is more natural and 'native' because some of the Tel-Avivi colleagues grew up speaking it. On the other hand, he takes pride in how his knowledge of Arabic has helped him understand the intricacies of Hebrew.

As already mentioned, Kashua's first encounter with world literature was through the medium of Hebrew. Nowhere in his writing, is there any reference to Arabic literature with its rich history and tradition. Generally, it seems that he reads what an educated Hebrew speaker reads. He even makes reference to this in his novel *Second Person Singular* (2010), in that the protagonist, a young and successful lawyer, used to visit a second-hand bookshop in Jerusalem and buy books there to fill the gap, which he was ashamed of, between his literary knowledge and that of his Jewish colleagues. His protagonist never thought about his own literature and about the need to familiarise himself with literature in Arabic. In other words, Hebrew symbolises to Kashua (through his protagonist) access to the global community, and to education. Kashua's articles in *Ha'aretz*, after the summer of 2014, lament an Israel that he dreams of, that is no longer there – an Israel that includes him (see Kashua 2014). A significant part of fitting in, for Kashua and his protagonist, has been mastering the Hebrew language. In one of Kashua's recent articles, in which he is considering not going back to live in Israel after his year teaching Hebrew writing at the University of Illinois, he describes the anguish he is putting his young daughter through, as she may have to abandon the Hebrew language for English. One cannot help but ask what happened to her Arabic as a mother tongue. In comparison, such explicit discourse about the role of Hebrew in his education is absent from the work of Shammas.

In contrast, the formative years of Somekh were spent speaking Arabic in Baghdad, the affluent and confident Baghdad of the 1930s and 1940s – a Baghdad which also imposed itself on the scene of the Arab intellectual Naḥḍa which was taking place at the time of his youth. He wrote in Arabic then, and met some of the most important poets of Arabic literature at that time, as well as being taught by some of the best-known intellectuals in the Arab world. Later, after joining the Hebrew language academy and after investment in Hebrew in Israel, he went back to Arabic through his doctoral studies, and then through his career as a scholar of Arabic at Tel-Aviv University. In other words, Somekh grew up in the cosmopolitan Baghdad of the 1940s, where Arabic was the dominant language of all aspects of life, including the literary and intellectual. Shammas, on the other hand, grew up in Haifa in the 1950s and went to an integrated school for Arabs and Jews. Haifa, then, as now, was considered a tolerant city, where both Arabs and Jews live together, and in spite of the fact that it was difficult to find books in Israel, people were still able to obtain publications from the Arab world. Shammas also studied Arabic and English literature at the Hebrew University of Jerusalem. As for Kashua, he grew up at a time where the global influence of Arabic was perhaps waning, as the last decades of the twentieth century witnessed a significant dwindling in the number and quality of publications in Arabic (see Suleiman and Lucas 2012). Due to his particular education in the Jewish school in Jerusalem, he also was prevented from experiencing the depth of the Arabic language literary and intellectual heritage, a literature which Somekh (1991: 3) describes as 'impressive, indeed stunning, not only for its fecundity but also for its variety and originality'.

The three authors' works are translated to English, but not Arabic – except for an attempt at translating Kashua's first novel, *Dancing Arabs* (2002), but without his authorisation or approval, and in fact Kashua mocked the high Arabic used in the translation and commented that he didn't recognise the novel as his, after reading only a few pages of it (Kashua, lecture at Michigan State University, 29 September 2014). However, the point is that as much as both languages should be translating from each other, it is through English that the works of these authors have become more widely known.

In Somekh's second memoir, *Life after Baghdad* (Somekh 2012a: 29), he entitles one of his chapters: 'Lovers of Arabic in the first Hebrew city' and he wonders about one of his friends, David Semah, who became a professor of Arabic at Haifa University:

> Who in the Holy Land needed an Arab writer or poet in the Jewish state? And where would he publish his poems now? And who would read them? He had not yet sufficiently mastered the Hebrew language in order to try and write in it; even when he did learn Hebrew properly over the course of time, David (Semah) avoided using the language for his literary endeavors and limited his Hebrew writing to academic articles, as he became a professor at Haifa University in subsequent years. (Somekh 2012a: 31)

Somekh can be considered a rarity in his zeal to translate from Arabic to Hebrew. He states: 'the subject of mutual translation ... possessed me like a spirit for many years' (Somekh 2012a: 35). One of the ironies of his identity is that he used to edit the poetry of Mahmoud Darwish in Arabic, when Darwish was a young poet and still living in Israel (Somekh, personal correspondence, 12 June 2014). Later Somekh also translated some of Darwish's poems into Hebrew. He rarely translated from Hebrew to Arabic, with the exception of the work of Yehouda Amichai (1924–2000). The Palestinian poet, Rashid Hussein (1936–77), however, did translate some of the poetry and prose of Haim Nehman Bialik (1873–1934) into Arabic (Hussein 1966). Around that time, Ghassan Kanafani also wrote, in Arabic, a pioneer work of anthology of Hebrew literature (Kanafani 1968/2013).

Interestingly, Somekh states that people 'who knew Arabic had a difficult time learning Hebrew. A real cultural shock' (Somekh 2012a: 95). For example, when he saw the word 'mamale' written on a billboard for the first time, he could not understand what it was: 'this cannot be a Semitic word I announced loudly, on a poster, and someone said yes, it is in Yiddish, ya ima' (Somekh 2012a: 185), but, he concludes: 'and so, little by little, language melted into language, landscape into landscape, and culture into culture' (Somekh 2012a: 186).

There is more than one way we can establish differences between the three authors. What ties them together is the fact that the three write in Hebrew, even though their mother tongue is Arabic. The three of them also aspire to a just and democratic society in Israel, but understandably with different commitments to Zionism. Somekh, naturally, became fully integrated into Jewish society in Tel-Aviv. Being Jewish enabled him to be part of the Zionist project and in fact his knowledge of Arabic helped him integrate with the Israeli academia as an Arabic literature scholar. This by itself was the window for Somekh to participate in the nation-building in Israel, as he was, for example, one of the founders of the Arabic department at Tel-Aviv University. In other words, by entering the academic world he became an integral part of the building of academic and intellectual life in the early years of the state of Israel. However, he was able to move in different national circles at the same time. He was a respected member of the Arabic intelligentsia in Israel, having forged personal relations with people such as Mahmoud Darwish and Emile Habibi. In his remarkable career, he was even able to break the boundaries and forge a lifelong friendship with Najuib Mahfouz in Egypt, after the Camp David agreement between Israel and Egypt in 1977, which allowed for diplomatic relations between both countries. At the same time, he was at the heart of the intellectual scene of the Hebrew language as he was from early on a member of the Hebrew language academy. However, it is not surprising that he personally insisted that the Arabic department at Tel-Aviv University should teach its classes in Hebrew.

Being part of the national project through a capacity in Arabic, as in Somekh's case, is not unheard of. This might have been the only way someone with his background could integrate in the state of Israel. Yehouda Shenhav, a generation younger than Somekh, discusses in the introduction to his book, *the Arab Jew* (2006), how his father's knowledge of Arabic, while a liability as Arab Jews where not fully 'Jewish' in the eyes of the establishment and therefore the state needed to 'de-Arabise' them and turn them into full Jews, was also an asset, as he was asked to work for the Israeli intelligence services. Shenhav rightly expresses his own discomfort when he met one of his father's old colleagues, who wanted to talk about this period of Shenhav's father's life (Shenhav 2006). Naturally, neither Shammas nor Kashua would unequivocally support the Zionist project of the Jewish primacy in the land, but they both aspire for acceptance by the Jewish majority.

Another point of difference between the three is generational, with Somekh being the oldest and belonging to the generation which was dispossessed of its Iraqi land. His collective identity was altered as the Jewish community of Iraq moved to Israel. He soon started learning Hebrew and aspired to belong to the majority in Israel. Shammas is of the second generation, coming of age after the establishment of the state of Israel: his community was dispossessed during his parents' time. Kashua is a third-generation Palestinian. The three of them in many ways inhabit different spaces in Israel society, not only because of the generational gap, but also because of the state of the society at their respective times. Somekh was able to be part of the Jewish nationalism in Israel. Shammas as a second generation Palestinian aspired for integration and more meaningful citizenship in the state of Israel. And lastly, Kashua, as a third-generation dispossessed Palestinian, whose family made it to the middle class in the new economy of the state of Israel, is representing a young generation of Palestinians who have become part of the Israeli economic and cultural scene in Israel through their education in the Hebrew language, and ironically, through Hebrew, they are able to depict themselves as global citizens. In other words, they are citizens of the world because of the cultural and material capital they were able to accumulate in the neo-liberal atmosphere in Israel which has prevailed since the 1990s. As we are inevitably discussing class, Somekh comes from the urban intellectual class of the Baghdad of the first half of the twentieth century. His lifestyle and aspirations were those of a bourgeoisie Iraqi of his time, with a leaning towards socialism, if not communism, as was the case in his social milieu in

Iraq back then. But, upon arriving in Israel, his vision, while Jewish national-istic, was also secular (as it was in Iraq), which enabled him to forge a dialogue with the remaining Arab intellectuals of the state of Israel. On the other hand, both Shammas and Kashua belong to the rural classes of Palestine. The educa-tion system during the British Mandate and in the state of Israel allowed both Shammas and Kashua's parents' generation to receive an education as the level of literacy increased, and they became part of what Hunaida Ghanim calls the intellectual life of the 'rural town' (Ghanim 2009: 35). In her excellent book, *Reinventing the Nation: Palestinian Intellectuals in Israel*, Ghanim classi-fies the educated of the rural towns as primarily males, who moved to mixed towns of Arabs and Jews, such as Haifa or Jerusalem, and became part of the Arab elite as a result of their education in Israeli institutes. Ghanim refers to them as 'patriarchal' as they took their village values with them when they moved to the city. Following Azmi Bishara, she attributes the difficulties of the Palestinian collective in Israel to the fact that the urban centres and their intellectual life disappeared after the Nakba. Instead, a new society emerged, rural in essence, but socially mobile as a result of education and internal dispossession, and at times, internal dislocation as well. Ghanim even puts Mahmoud Darwish and Emile Habibi in this category.

As mentioned earlier, the works of Shammas and Kashua are not trans-lated to Arabic, and generally not read by Arabs. Their choice of language signals to Arabic speakers that perhaps they are not the target audience. In Shammas's case, while he was celebrated in Hebrew circles, some Hebrew speakers felt uneasy about a Palestinian expressing himself in the national language of the Jews. As time passed, these reservations diminished, as we see in Kashua's case, but for Kashua, while his language choice is not attacked per se, he received death threats from some Jewish extremists, as a result of his writing, during the difficult summer of 2014 (Kashua 2014). In spring 2013, I interviewed students from the faculty of humanities at the University of Alexandria, in Egypt, about their own language choices, and when I told them the life story of Shammas and his language choice, they called him a traitor. These students, while having a very sophisticated understanding of language choices, perceived of Hebrew as the national language of the Jews in Israel and argued that as a dispossessed Palestinian Shammas should not betray his nationalism and his collective grievance by trespassing into the

Jewish culture through language choice (see C. Suleiman 2016). Note that Mahmoud Darwish was fluent in Hebrew and he also read widely in Hebrew; however, his language choice in his poetry and various articles and essays was always Arabic. Also, the interviews he gave to the Hebrew media, were in Arabic. He would even sometimes accept the questions in Hebrew by his Jewish interlocutors, but respond in Arabic. However, the Old Testament and Jewish religious-literary tradition and mythology are all important sources, among others, for the imagery and associations in Darwish's poetry.

Further, Shammas was involved in a controversy in 1985 regarding the nature of the state of Israel. It started when he published an article on 13 September, 'A New Year for the Jews', in the Hebrew *Kol Ha'ir*. In it, he expressed hopes for a better Israel in future, an Israel which does not exclude him in anything, and which has a place for his collective identity and national symbols. In other words, he was redefining what 'Israeli' means by fully including his national affiliation in the project of 'Israeli nation-building'. He was fiercely attacked by Jewish writers, among them, Sammy Mikhail, the Iraqi Jewish writer who had decided to write in Hebrew and abandon his mother tongue, Arabic. He was also attacked by the 'leftist' and 'liberal' writer, Abraham B. Yehoshua. Yehoshua is one of the best-known Israeli novelists, and he won several recognitions, including the prestigious Israel Prize in 1995 (interestingly, the Palestinian Israeli writer, Emile Habibi, accepted it too in 1992). Yehoshua harshly asked Shammas to move his residence a few miles to the West Bank, so that he could reside in an Arab territory. He compared the Jewishness of Israel to the Frenchness of France. At that Shammas responded that 'Jewish' may not necessarily equal 'Israeli'. Needless to say, by asking to be included fully as a citizen, Shammas was pointing out the tensions and contradictions of Israeli democracy: that it is Jewish and democratic at the same time (see Kimmerling 2008: 222–6, for a full discussion of the controversy). Shammas ended his dream of 'eye-level' citizenship by deciding to leave the country and to reside in the United States.

Almost thirty years later, Sayed Kashua had to face a similar controversy. It started in summer 2014, when Israel was attacking Gaza and Kashua was expressing his discomfort through the platform of the Hebrew press. He was shocked by the hostile reactions of readers and started worrying about his and his family's safety in Jerusalem, where he resides. He decided to leave the country earlier than he had initially planned (to spend it in a Midwestern American college town teaching Hebrew writing, as a visiting writer), and was contemplating leaving the country for good (Kashua 2014). He saw that his dream of an Israel which included him (similarly to Shammas) was unachievable under the circumstances. The reactions to his decisions varied, but one Jewish writer in *Ha'aretz*, Zvi Bar'el, stands out in his courage by articulating the hypocrisy of the Jewish left, in his article 'Arab Elite, You're Israel's Fig Leaf: Don't Run Away. We on the superficial left need you. Just stop protesting against the Gaza war and forget about the Nakba, O.K.?' (Bar'el 2014). Kashua continued to write for *Ha'aretz* from the US, as well as for the American media. His correspondence with his Jewish writer friend, Etgar Keret, which was published in two parts in *The New Yorker*, stands out in its poignant tone of despair. It seems from reading these exchanges that Kashua has lost all hope for 'fitting in' in his beloved home (see Kashua and Keret 2014). Kashua ended up deciding to spend another year with his family on the quiet Midwestern campus.

One must not forget that one of the intellectual ancestors of both Shammas and Kashua is Emile Habibi, the prolific Palestinian writer and Journalist who belongs to Somekh's generation. He was a member of the Israel Communist Party and a member of the Knesset as well, and the editor of *Al-Ittiḥād*, the Arabic communist newspaper. In his writing, Habibi was trying to depict the absurdity of the Palestinian life in Israel after the Nakba (see, for example, Habibi 1985). Habibi was also fluent in Hebrew, but always wrote in Arabic. His Arabic writing demonstrates an admirable command of Arabic literary styles from different time periods. The mixing of 'high' styles with his Palestinian local idiom makes him a compelling writer, respected in the Arab world as well. Habibi accepted the Israel Prize in 1992 after Yeshayahu Leibowitz, the Jewish philosopher, rejected it. The contrast between the two did not escape Habibi's readers, and he was heavily criticised for accepting the prize. Moreover, a prominent Egyptian writer described to me in spring 2013 the cold reception Habibi received at the book festival in Cairo at the time, when Egyptian writers refused to speak to him. This is reminiscent of how the Egyptian students reacted when I told them about Anton Shammas. Habibi was a member of the Communist Party in Palestine, which consisted of Jewish and Arab members. This party accepted the UN Partition Plan in 1947, and in 1948 recognised the establishment of the state of Israel. In addition, in the 1950s Habibi argued through the platform of *Al-Ittiḥād* newspaper for the necessity of the Zionist project in Palestine and the legitimacy of Israel. He also preached for coexistence with the Jews as early as the 1950s (Manaʿa 2015).

Habibi, while not writing in Hebrew, does allude to the language choice as an integral part of the Palestinian identity in Israel and its post-traumatic coping mechanism. In his widely acclaimed *The Secret Life of Saeed: The Pessoptimist* (translated to Hebrew by Anton Shammas), he does make several references to language. For example, in one scene in the story, the protagonist is walking in Haifa and a Jewish man stops him to ask the time. The protagonist hesitates as to what language he should choose to answer the man. If he chose Arabic, then he would immediately be giving away his identity as an Arab in the early times of Israel and its military rule over its Arab citizens, and as a result he might get harassed. If he answered in Hebrew, his accent might give away his identity (just like in the later novels of Kashua and in his sitcom, *Arab Labour*, where the protagonist Amjad makes so much effort to perfect his accent in Hebrew, so that it sounds Ashkenazi). Habibi's protagonist chooses to answer in German, as he happens to know the word for 'eight' in German. At this point, he finds that the man speaks German as well, as he is a German Jew.

To sum up, it seems that Shammas and Kashua, committed writers to the 'Israeli' equal citizenship status for Arabs, have found out the impossibility of this dream (thirty years apart from each other). Having paid a heavy price, which includes not having their work translated into Arabic, and not being recognised by the Arab literary-intellectual milieu, both seem to have arrived at a moment of despair regarding their project which tries to correct historic injustices, heal and move on. Neither Sammy Mikhail nor Sasson Somekh, however, have had to take such a drastic step. They have given up on their Arabic and to a great extent they have given up on their Arab-Islamic civilisational heritage. In return, however, they have found a respectable place for themselves in the state of Israel. Their education and their writing have allowed them to enter the Ashkenazi elite institutions, which include Tel-Aviv University and the Hebrew Academy for Language in the case of Somekh, and many awards and recognitions in Israel and outside it, in the case of Sammy Mikhail. Their Jewish identity enabled both to enter the public arenas of Israel that were not open for Shammas and Kashua.

Lastly, the 'subaltern' position which Kashua speaks from is somewhat shared by Shammas, but not fully. Shammas's voice entered the Israeli hegemonic space, but at the expense of writing a personal account, an autobiography, about his family and growing up in the northern Christian village of Fassuta. However, being older than Kashua, Shammas is preoccupied by the Nakba and its aftermath, which are somewhat absent from Kashua's narrative. As a result, Shammas problematises the Israeli democratic process more forcefully than Kashua. Needless to say, the Israeli public sphere has very limited spaces for both of their voices. Both of them currently live in the US and express dismay at the current political atmosphere in Israel. In contrast, Somekh's voice is still within the structural narrative of Zionism. His career flourished in Israel and he still resides there. The 'seamline zone' (Eyal 2006) seems to have moved to include the Arab Jew, in the case of Somekh, but to exclude both Shammas and Kashua. The literary projects of both these authors were a point of hope for more inclusion, but ultimately they were disappointed.

The Arab Jew

It is agreed that the Zionist movement in Europe, while having several competing strands, evolved into a political movement aspiring to build a Jewish state in Israel, with Hebrew as its language. The new Jews in this movement were the European Ashkenazi immigrants to Palestine, shedding centuries of diasporic submission to foreign nations and reinventing themselves from the ashes of the past in the new land. Many scholars consider Zionism to be one of the last European colonial movements of the nineteenth century (see Pappé 2006). Bringing Jews from Arab countries to Israel began in the 1950s. Many scholars agree that the Sephardi Jews came to Israel as a result of a need to replace the Arab workforce, and because after the Zionist leadership failed to bring more Jews from Europe or to mobilise the American Jews to move to Israel, they had to resort to the Jewish masses of the Middle East. Those masses were seen by the Ashkenazi elite as coming from a 'non-European, other, underdeveloped backward world', (Chetrit 2013: 17). Up until the 1980s they were referred to as 'Eidot Ha-Mizrach', in order to avoid the term

'Sephardi', which refers to specific religious rites. It literally meant 'the eth-nicities of the East'. Chetrit and others note that the term meant to sug-gest the negative stereotypes mentioned above. However, after some political organising on the part of these groups, they themselves as a group designated the term 'Mizrachi' to themselves (Chetrit 2013: 18). Mizrachim constitute Jewish communities from 'North Africa, from Morocco to Egypt, to the Jews of Lebanon, Syria, Turkey, Iraq and Kurdistan, to the Jews of Iran and Afghanistan, the Caucasus and Uzbekistan, to the Jews of Yemen and Aden' (Chetrit 2013: 18). Chetrit also notes that the term 'ethnicities' came to refer only to Eastern Jews, and not European Jews. Jews who also lived in Palestine before the creation of Israel were subsumed under this category, as they were outside of the Zionist project in the first place. The intention of the state institutions was to 'Ashkenise' these groups and fully assimilate them by dis-avowing their Middle Eastern roots. The desire for the disavowal existed on both sides. Mizrachi Jews also were excluded from the 'nation-building' of the post-colonial Arab states, because these states emphasised Arab nationalism and started to conceive of the Jews as alien elements in society who support the Zionist movement in Palestine (see Kimmerling 2001, Chetrit 2013). Chetrit goes further than Kimmerling when he compares the Ashkenazi atti-tude towards the Mizrachi to that of the Orientalist racism of Europe, dis-cussed by Edward Said (1978).

In other words, the Orientalist outlook came to dominate all aspects of life in Israel: academic, media, society, jobs and place of living. It is a reminder of Said's poignant outlook towards Orientalism:

> My contention is that without examining Orientalism as a discourse one cannot possibly understand the enormously systematic discipline by which European culture was able to manage and even produce the Orient politi-cally, sociologically, militarily, ideologically, scientifically, and imaginatively during the post-Enlightenment period. Moreover, so authoritative a posi-tion did Orientalism have that I believe no one writing, thinking, or acting on the Orient could do so without taking account of the limitations on thought and action imposed by Orientalism. (Said 1978: 3)

Because of the large number of the Mizrachim, the Ashkenazi establish-ment was discussing their 'ethnic threat' in terms of a fear that the Jewish state would be 'Levantinised' (Kimmerling 2001: 96), and in terms of 'Shed Eidati', 'the ethnic devil' (Kimmerling 2001: 106), thus discursively delegitimising any calls for social justice on the part of the Mizrachim as a group. Nonetheless, it is estimated today that 300,000 Moroccan Jews and about 100,000 Iraqi Jews in Israel have some knowledge of Arabic. But the numbers are progressively dwindling (Bleboim and Bernstein: 2013: 50).

In the spring and summer of 2013, Amnon Levi, a well-known Israeli broadcaster of Mizrachi origins, created a four-episode documentary on the 'ethnic devil', in Israel.[8] The series caused much debate about the legitimacy of these documentaries. The detractors accused Levi of stirring communal conflicts in Israel (see, for example, Michael Handelzalts in *Ha'aretz*, 16 August 2013), while defenders of the topic felt that the discussion was long overdue. One of the interviewees, a well-known sociologist at Tel-Aviv University, Yehouda Shenhav, whom I cited earlier in connection with Sasson Somekh, advised Amnon Levi to go to the 'periphery' and meet Mizrachim there. By 'periphery' he meant what Israeli institutions call 'development towns', which are situated away from the metropolitan centre in Tel-Aviv. These towns include Ashdod and Ashkelon to the south of Tel-Aviv, Beersheba in the Negev Desert and Bet She'an in the Jordan Valley, among others. Shenhav argues in the documentary that the Mizrachi Jews were deliberately separated by the authorities at the start of their immigration to Israel. Once these immigrants arrived, they were put in 'temporary trailers', 'Ma'barot', and then moved to these towns. This was their rite of initiation in Israel. Today, and as Levi's documentary series shows, there is little interaction between Mizrachi and Ashkenazi Jews. Interviewing Mizrachim from different generations, it became clear to Levi that Mizrachim live a separate life, in a world of poverty, unemployment and under-development. Some of the youth he interviewed even thought that the Ashkenazim speak a different language from their own. Those who succeeded and were able to build careers (Shenhav, for example, as well as Levi himself) felt in the series that they have done so by integrating fully in the Ashkenazi world and adopting the Ashkenazi mannerism and accent through their higher education in Israeli universities. But this came with a high emotional cost, as they became estranged sometimes from their families and their immediate communities. Levi came from a family of Syrian immigrants and he confesses that all of his life he aspired to be an Ashkenazi.

His brother commented in the documentary that he wished to have lighter skin than he has. The desire for lighter skin was heard many times in the series from various interviewees. Moreover, all of the interviewees who 'made it' into the Ashkenazi world spoke with an Ashkenazi accent during the series. This is reminiscent of Kashua's protagonist who aspires to pass as non-Arab. Kashua discusses light skin as an asset which helped his protagonist pass as Jewish, as well as the Ashkenazi accent (Kashua 2010).

The statistics are even more disturbing. First there was difficulty in acquiring any straightforward statistics as the Israeli Bureau of Statistics does not give out statistical data on third-generation Israelis. The picture which emerged from the statistical investigation, which had to be carried out without relying on official records, pointed to a triangle of 'Mizrachi', 'periphery' and 'poverty'. The three always went together. For example of the 5,000 people in the faculties of various academic institutions in Israel, only 9 per cent are Mizrachi and only 1 per cent are Mizrachi women. Of every four students at university level, only one is Mizrachi. In other words, while the Mizrachi could very well be the majority, numerically speaking (in the 1950s they already constituted more than half of the Jewish population, see Chetrit 2013: 3), to all intents and purposes, they are treated as a minority group within Israel. Yehouda Shenhav, in the first episode of the series, admits that he speaks Arabic, which he learned as an adult in order to reconnect to his Arabic roots, with an Ashkenazi accent.

However, what is absent from Amnon Levi's (2013) series *The Ethnic Devil* is any desire by the interviewees to learn Arabic (except for Shenhav). Many of them are the first generation not to speak Arabic as a mother tongue (including Levi himself). The desire of most of the interviewees is for the Mizrachim to be recognised as fully equal to the Ashkenazi, in terms of rights and opportunities for better education and better jobs. Further, there was no single reference to the plight of the Palestinians living in Israel who hold Israeli citizenship. The two projects seemed disconnected. I interviewed Levi on 27 August 2014 in regard to this series and he insisted that the Palestinian-Israelis are not absent from it. This series is simply about the Mizrachi Jews and their lack of equal opportunities, and nothing else. When I asked Levi why the word 'identity' does not appear in any of the discussions in this series, he also insisted that the series is not about 'identity' but simply about a request for 'equal opportunities', and a more fair society. But he admitted that many 'Israeli Arabs' wrote to him and said that he is speaking of their strife and grievances as well.

Some Mizrachim, however, do make that connection to a 'mother' civilisation which is based in the Islamic world and the Arabic language. In general, they also connect their plight to that of the Palestinians and their aspiration for self-determination, as well as to the aspiration of fuller and more meaningful citizenship for the Palestinians in Israel. In this regard, Ella Shohat (1988), herself of Iraqi-Jewish roots, states:

> The Zionist denial of the Arab-Moslem and Palestinian East, then, has its corollary the denial of Jewish 'Mizrachim' (the 'Eastern Ones') who, like the Palestinians, by more subtle and less obviously brutal mechanism, have also been stripped of the right of self-representation. Within Israel and on the stage of world opinion, the hegemonic voice of Israel has almost invariably been of European Jews, the Ashkenazim, while the Sephardi voice has been largely muffled or silenced.
>
> Filtered out by a Euro-Centric grid, Zionist discourse presents culture as the monopoly of the West, denuding the people of Asia and Africa, including Jewish people, of all cultural expression. The rich culture of Jews from Arab and Moslem countries is scarcely studied in Israelis schools and academic institutions. (Shohat 1988: 140, 153, cited in Chetrit 2013: 41–2)

Sami Chetrit is one of the few who share Shohat's sentiments in stating the fluid connection between the identity of 'Arab' Jews and the rest of the Arab world, the Palestinian collective included, and juxtaposing it with the Ashkenazi European Jewish identity of the forefathers of the Zionist movement, particularly East European Jews from Poland, Russia and German territories. Chetrit who is in his fifties, was born in Morocco and moved with his family as a child to the 'peripheral' town of Ashdod (Chetrit 2015). Like most of his cohorts, he lost the connection to Arabic and Morocco. He describes the despair of his parents' generation at their cultural dispossession as they were trying to make a new life for themselves and their children in Israel. For instance, his uncle, who held an important job in Morocco and was educated, was reduced in Ashdod to a poor under-employed man selling mint at the market. Sami, the boy, would pretend not to notice his uncle, for fear of embarrassing him in the market. However, it was this uncle who kept the sounds of Arabic alive for Chetrit, as he insisted on telling him stories from the past in Moroccan Arabic. Chetrit's poem (2007) below is making the distinction between the Palestinian Arab Jew in him, as opposed to the Ashkenazi (Polish) Jewish other, who is seen as disempowering both the Palestinian and the Arab Jew, though in different ways, by erasing the Palestinian, physically and metaphorically, but by erasing the Arab in the Arab Jew, physically, linguistically and metaphorically. Chetrit's poem is dedicated to Mahmoud Darwish.

> From 'Mural without a Wall: A Poem to Mahmoud Darwish'
> Sami Chetrit (2007), my own translation
> 'The Arab died. The Arab died'
> Let the new Jew live
> Register
> I was born Jewish out of the heart of your Arab death in me
> And thus, we danced the 'Hora' dance
> Myself and this Pole
> The Pole is touching my grandpa's beard
> And pointing to my dark skin and singing
> 'I am from here, from here I came, and this is my home'
> As for myself, I was filled with a new Jewish pride
> But for you: 'get out of here'
> And you refused to leave my eyes
> Those eyes looking towards the Western horizon
> You became the enemy who looks at me every morning in the mirror,
>   forever
> And myself, I spit and curse
> And I kill you one time after another
> So that I am reborn
> A renewed Jew
> But don't mistake me, I am not here
> In order to displace you

What is remarkable for Chetrit, who knows very little Arabic, is that while writing and reading his poetry in Hebrew, he maintains an Arabic accent

(Chetrit 2007, 2015), unlike Shenhav, whose Arabic sounds Ashkenazi, in his own words (Levi 2013, part 1).[9] Further, just as noted earlier by Vatanabadi (2013), translation between the two languages remains minimal. Chetrit's poetry is not known in Arabic, even though it was translated into many languages, including English.

To sum up, this chapter started with a bleak picture of the political stifling of the Arabic language in Israel, only to end up with a rather complex view in regard to the survival of Arabic in Israel. Through the lens of the linguistic choices of three writers, Arabic emerges as the abandoned language of these Arabic natives. A closer look reveals a Hebrew choice, where these authors are read, discussed and recognised in Israel and internationally, but not among Arab authors (except for Somekh's academic work in English). All three writers, while coming from three different generations, also come from different spheres for Arabic: as the language of intellectual life of Iraq of the 1940s for Somekh, as a language used in everyday life in the mixed and tolerant city of Haifa, and at the same time, as the language of expression at the tail end of the Arab Naḥda while Shammas was growing up (but still it was the time of the military rule over the Arab population of Israel), and lastly, as a language which lost its cachet among a certain stratum of 'Palestinian-Israelis' – today, a stratum which aspires for integration and for social mobility in the state of Israel. I also started the chapter by stating the religious affiliation of these three authors, which does not seem to be a factor in their language choice, as the three represent the three major religions. However, the ethnic division between Arab and Jew seems to have contributed to Somekh's thriving in Israeli, while Shammas and Kashua, about thirty years apart, feel betrayed and unable to continue to try to integrate and bring the two peoples together through their writing. The three authors have had to deal with their position in 'the seamline' between what is an Arab and what is a Jew, in a state which relies on the dichotomy between Arab and Jew for its very existence, and the margins for inclusion in the hegemonic space seems more elastic in the case of Somekh, than it is for Shammas and Kashua. As Eyal (2006) argues, those margins are fluid and unstable, and in a constant state of flux, yet there is more rigidity in regard to the category of 'Israeli Arab' than there is for the 'Arab Jew'. Nonetheless, Levi's *The Ethnic Devil* (2013) demonstrates the persistence of the integration 'problem' of Mizrachi Jews, in spite of the fact that some of them have succeeded/survived by assimilating into the Ashkenazi community, such as the cases of Levi himself, Somekh, Shenhav, and others.

To conclude, what I have tried to show in this chapter is that Somekh, Shammas and Kashua are demonstrating asymmetries that exist in their language choices. One asymmetry that is clearly apparent is that between Hebrew and Arabic in Israel. This reflects the broader political relationship between Arabs and Jews, and in that I am simply confirming literature that already exists in this regard.

Also, in the case of these authors, both Arabic and Hebrew often encounter each other through the global hegemony of English. This has parallels throughout the Middle East and its languages, and is a reflection of the much larger global dynamic of English being the 'hypercentral' language which devours the space of the others in the galactic space of languages, to use de Swaan's (2001) metaphor.

Lastly, it seems that language choice remains a choice of the author. Somekh, Shammas and Kashua's language choices are not solely determined by global forces, or even the political local dynamics between the two nations, as language choice cannot merely be a function of sociological factors such as generation, education, class and geographic location. While the global, local and sociological factors are important, in the end, it is up to the author to choose what they deem worthy of being marketed, read or written, as an expression of their identity. The three come from traumatised communities, albeit under different but interrelated circumstances, and this chapter has shown how the three deal with the language displacement in both convergent and divergent ways, and at the same time as a result of personal choices each is making. For Chetrit, who is a generation younger than Somekh, the Arabic language is lost and therefore he has no choice in regard to writing. His poetry is in Hebrew, and while it is translated into English, it is not translated to Arabic, and predictably, he is not known to Arabic readers.

Notes

1. Available at <http://www.jpost.com/Israel/Poll-Israelis-favor-Arab-transfer-to-Palestine> (last accessed 9 December 2015).
2. Available at <http://www.theguardian.com/world/2014/mar/25/transfer-arab-israeli-citizens-palestinian-state> (last accessed 9 December 2015).

3. Available at <http://www.aljazeera.com/news/middleeast/2014/12/are-not-citizens-with-equal-rights-201412214135428310.html> (last accessed 11 November 2014).

4. Available at <https://en.wikipedia.org/wiki/Anton_Shammas> (last accessed 1 September 2016).

5. I use 'subaltern' as in Gayatri Spivak (2010) to refer to voices in society that are not permitted to be part of the Israeli cultural and political narrative.

6. Available at <https://www.facebook.com/search/top/?q=ala%20hlehel> (last accessed 29 November 2014).

7. See Wikipedia, available at <https://en.wikipedia.org/wiki/Anton_Shammas> (last accessed 19 June 2016).

8. Available at <https://www.youtube.com/watch?v=ZFH0RF-_O10> (last accessed 23 June 2015).

9. Available at <https://www.youtube.com/watch?v=HAi-mFrpeqQ> (last accessed 25 June 2015).

6

Arabic in Jordan and Palestine

I will be discussing here the interface between Palestinian and Jordanian nationalism and the effect of globalisation on both. The two sides of the River Jordan have been in constant intensive communication since antiquity, with the Jordanian towns providing a contrast with the nomadic lifestyle, and with agricultural villages scattered along the mountain range facing the Jordan River (Salibi 1993). Further, the topography of both Jordan and Palestine has resulted in similar lifestyles, and population movement across the river. On both sides of the river, the fertile Jordan Valley is an ideal site for agricultural produce all year round. The valley borders a series of mountains on each side, opening up to the vast Arabian deserts in the east, and to the Mediterranean Sea to the west. Moreover, both Palestine and Jordan were stops on important ancient trading routes between Africa, Arabia and Asia Minor. Many ancient peoples came and went, taking their place in history, and making their mark on the stones, as both places were considered to be part of Bar Al-Sham, or the 'Land of Sham' in Arab historiography. During Ottoman times, the Jordanian Sanjaks reported to the Vilayet of Damascus, while their Palestinian counterparts reported to the Vilayet of Beirut (except for the independent Jerusalem Mutasarrifiyya 'province'). Naturally, modern history allowed for the creation of economic and cultural centres on the Mediterranean coast, in for example Akka, Haifa and Yaffa, and to some extent in Jerusalem and Nablus on the west side of the Jordan River and

Valley, but less so on the east side of the Jordan. Economic development in the nineteenth century (and even since the seventeenth century, as Eugene Rogan (2009) would argue) also allowed Palestinian towns to develop centres for learning, as well as an active press, facilitating the emergence of a middle class which was dependent on a modern world economy. In Jordan, the towns were smaller, and economic development was generally less tied to the global markets. Lastly, Bedouin pastoral life was also present on both sides of the river up until the time of the modern state, when people were encouraged to settle in one place, thus bringing to an end centuries of nomadic life for some of these tribes (see Figure 6.1).

In the aftermath of the disintegration of the Ottoman Empire after World War I, new political entities emerged, including Transjordan with Emir Abdullah as its leader. During the British Mandate, Jordan was ruled indirectly through the Hashemites, while Palestine was ruled directly from Britain, and between the two world wars, while Palestinians were resisting British colonialism on the one hand, and Zionism on the other, Emir Abdullah was consolidating his power in Jordan by incorporating different groups into his regime. Among these were the merchant classes of Palestinian, Syrian and Jordanian origin, the different tribes, as well as the religious minority of Christians and the ethnic minority of Circassians. He also chose Amman as the capital, over the more politically and economically established town of Salt, to the west and towards the Jordan Valley. In 1948, the population of Jordan doubled overnight, as a result of the Palestinian exodus, and because the West Bank and East Jerusalem were brought under Jordanian control. Palestinians were given Jordanian citizenship, under the flag of the Hashemite Jordanian Kingdom. The west bank of the river, which includes Jenin and the plains surrounding it, Nablus and its environs, East Jerusalem, and the city of Hebron to its south, were called the West Bank (of the River Jordan), as a reference to Jordan being a united country on both sides of the river. Amman became a commercial and political centre at the expense of Jerusalem and Nablus, and many Palestinian families moved to Amman as a result. The Jordanian regime held the banner of Arabism, but with an emphasis on Jordan. King Hussein (1952–99) himself, and in contrast to Jamal Abd Al-Nasser in Egypt or the Ba'thists in Syria and Iraq, held the belief that Arab countries should unite not politically as one country, but economically and

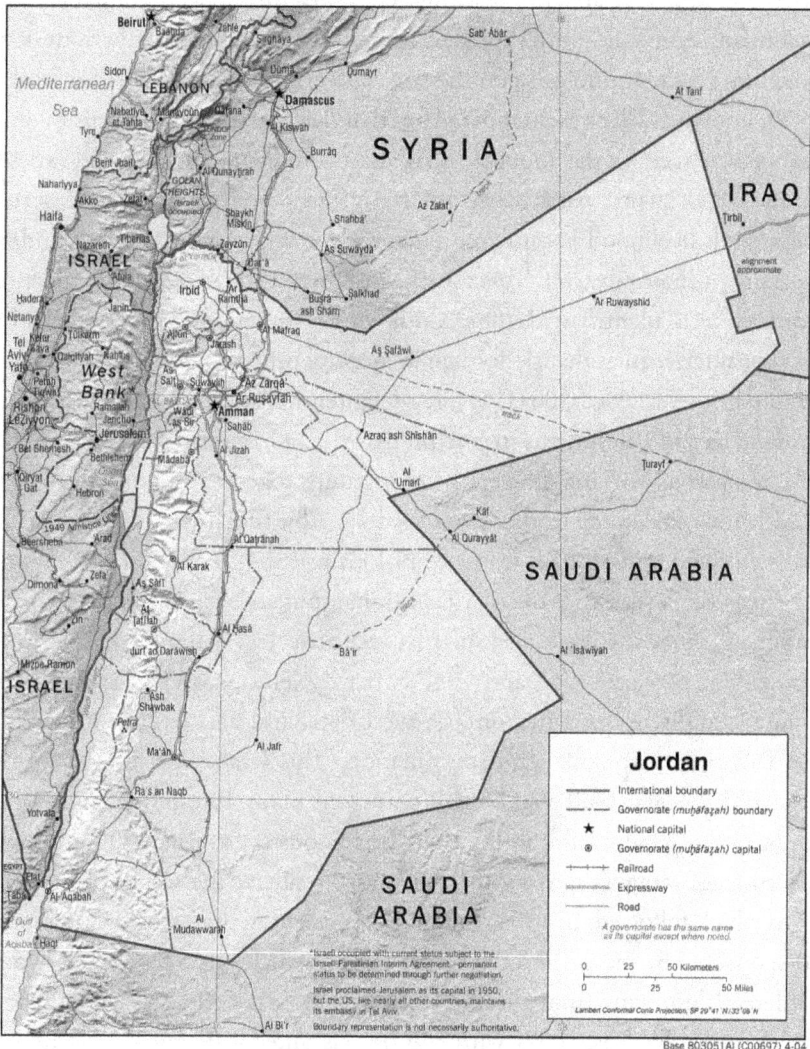

Figure 6.1 Map of Jordan, June 2016. (*Perry-Castañeda Map Collection*, University of Texas Library Online)[1]

culturally, as a loose coalition under Arab government *à la* European style (Hussein 1962).

In 1967, Jordan lost its west bank and East Jerusalem to Israel. At that time, the PLO was emerging as a representative of the Palestinian struggle under the leadership of the young charismatic Yasser Arafat. Arafat and other Palestinian/Arab nationalist fighter groups threatened to destabilise the Jordanian regime, if not to topple it. King Hussein had to react with military power and he sent out tanks on the streets to crush the fighters in September 1970, known as Black September. After that date, it became apparent that the regime was seeking the support of the East Jordanian tribes, at the expense of the Palestinians, particularly in the military and in the public sector. Palestinian livelihood became more dependent on the private sector and on working in the Arab Gulf. This was the time when the state-building institutions began to identify with the Bedouin life in Jordan as an example of what was considered an authentic Jordanian identity prior to the Palestinian move to Jordan (see Massad 2001). While social tensions were mounting between Jordanians and Palestinians in Jordan, many people influential in the politics of Jordan were working to keep the two groups together and to find ways to absorb the tension, as in the case of Adnan Abu Odeh, an advisor to King Hussein, who himself hails from the Nablus region (Abu Odeh 1999).

In 1988, a year after the first Palestinian intifada against the Israeli occupation of the West Bank and in the Gaza Strip (the latter under Egyptian occupation between 1948 and 1967, when Israel took over), King Hussein announced disengagement from the West Bank and East Jerusalem, to allow the Palestinians to seek self-determination. This was overshadowed by the events of the first Gulf War, which witnessed many Palestinians moving to Jordan from Kuwait after losing their livelihoods there. The 1990s also witnessed Iraqi refugees moving to Jordan as a result of the war and the sanctions which followed. In 1991, Jordan participated in the Madrid Conference co-sponsored by the US and the Soviet Union, which called for a 'New World Order'. Palestinians from the West Bank and Gaza Strip also participated, which initiated direct talks with the Israelis and facilitated the signing of the Oslo Accords in 1993 between the PLO and the Israeli government for future peace negotiations. In 1994, Jordan signed Ha-'Araba Accords with Israel, thus normalising relations, in a similar way to Egypt's Camp David Accords in 1978. Jordanian public opinion was against this agreement, which prompted the regime to issue a series of oppressive press laws in order to curtail the opposition to the accords (Lucas 2005).

In Jordan, the past two decades have witnessed a move towards a more neo-liberal economy, with more emphasis on consumerism. This neo-liberalism has resulted in more economic inequality, but has at the same time resulted in spectacular urban development in Amman. The protests of the disgruntled in the aftermath of the Arab Spring were kept under control and out of the hearing of the new business classes and foreign investors (Schwedler 2012). Neo-liberal reforms touched on the economic structure, as well as the military, but escaped the realm of political reforms (Baylouny 2008, see also Yom 2014). In other words, the regime was able to co-opt the new business classes, without having to undergo a process of political reforms for the masses. These business classes became interested in keeping the political status quo and in blocking any political change that could hurt their economic interests (Muasher 2011), which have, in effect, created a consumer society in Jordan. In such a system there is less emphasis on the ethnic origin (Palestinian versus Jordanian), and more emphasis on economic gain, as the new class consists of both groups. At the same time, nationalism does not die easily. Jordan is still divided across the two ethnic national groups and parliamentary and public discourse platforms have witnessed the ethnic tensions between both. Suggestions for stripping Palestinians of their Jordanian citizenship are voiced, and politicians generally use this issue to rally people around them. At the same time, economic development in the north of the country is much stronger than it is in the south, which receives fewer resources and less attention from Amman. This has led to unrest in cities such as Maʿān on several occasions (Abu Odeh 1999, Lucas 2005, Schwedler 2012).

Since the Palestinian National Authority's (PA) return to the West Bank and the Gaza Strip in 1996, it has launched several attempts at liberalising the economy in Palestine, despite Israel's ultimate control over the West Bank and the Gaza Strip. According to Khalidi and Samour (2011: 8):

> Today, with the palpable failure of armed struggle, the PA is offering the Palestinian people in the West Bank a program predicated upon delivering growth and prosperity without any strategy for resistance or challenge to the parameters of occupation. The program is inspired by a model of neo-liberal governance increasingly widespread in the region, indeed in neocolonial states around the world, but which socially, culturally, and politically remains an alien creation of the Washington-based international financial institutions. (2011: 8)

Khalidi and Samour add that 'such developments have no doubt given credence to the statehood-or-bust narrative, creating something akin to an "economic-peace bubble" emanating from Ramallah' (2011: 8). This growth has become a national goal 'in and of itself' (Khalidi and Samour 2011: 10), and has caused rising rates of poverty in the West Bank. It has also been an important component of normalising political and economic relations with Israel, allowing Palestinian workers to work in Israel, but of course, after security clearances. Thus:

> The PA neoliberal growth strategy *is based on*, and will be furthered by *its security coordination with Israel*, domestic policing and effective containment of internal political opponents. (Khalidi and Samour 2011: 15, emphasis added)

One cannot but notice the mirror image of both political entities, the Palestinian and the Jordanian with their emphasis on a neo-liberal economy, which resulted in furthering the economic inequality in both cases, combined with the securitisation of the social and the political apparatus in Palestine, as compared to the militarisation of the political system in Jordan. At the same time, public discourse is still nationalistic in both places, emphasising the unity of Jordan in one, and the struggle against Israel's occupation in the other. However, one casualty of the neo-liberal stance in Palestine might be its educational curricula. A study of school textbooks notes the decontextualisation and depoliticisation of Palestinian culture and identity (Khatib 2012).

Amal Jamal (2005: 122) comments that 'the brief Palestinian experience with self-rule shows that the PA is following other post-colonial states by overinflating its administrative machine'. This mechanism is meant to co-opt opposition, as well as reward consent. There has been overinflation in regard to the 'magic' job of consultant to the PA, and its administrative apparatus (Jamal 2005: 129). This and other mismanagement techniques have caused a commentator to argue that:

> The PA's corruption, by now almost universally recognized, and financial mismanagement of donor funds flow from the mentality of a guerilla organization that continues to prevail, when the leadership cannot be questioned and operates in secrecy and without accountability. Hence, the PA's

parallel budgets, one public and one covert, the latter containing hundreds of millions of dollars of public money distributed to buy loyalty to the regime. (Jamal 2005: 130)

The dominant leaders who returned with Arafat were eager to establish power bases in regard to every aspect of state-building institutions. This resulted in what Jamal calls a 'neopatrimonializing' political system (2005: 132) with the middle class of the Palestinian secular elite turning to the NGO sector to protect their status and power (Jamal 2005: 144). They have also become the main defenders of democracy in the West Bank and Gaza (Jamal 2005: 145). Jamal concludes:

> In the last three decades the Palestinian political elite has experienced a continuous process of fragmentation that has led to constant competition between different belief systems, a lack of shared ethos, and reciprocal distrust and suspicion. This fragmentation, and in particular the increased circulation of elites, their internal disunity, and their competition for power, has been viewed as a major source for growing authoritarianism in the Palestinian political system. Furthermore, the competition for power between elites has been assumed to be a major source of instability that has been disrupting the routinization of Palestinian politics into commonly accepted procedural patterns, leading to self-defeating patterns of behavior by various political actors, a major waste of public resources, and a lack of a common strategy of struggle to achieve national goals. (2005: 167)

Thus, it seems that the fragmentation of the Palestinian political elite is in line with political convictions, as well as in line with the proximity to the economic resources of the PA and its neo-liberal orientation. In this way, Palestinian politics is similar to the politics of Jordan, where neo-liberal class interests are able to cut through the political division between Jordanian and Palestinian, which has dominated Jordanian politics since 1970. This is not to say that the ethnic division has diminished and is no longer significant in Jordan. To the contrary, the neo-liberal economy has allowed a reorganisation of the political elites in Jordan in ways that sometimes cross through the ethnic divisions.

To sum up, while Jordanian and Palestinian histories have been tied together since antiquity, in the age of nationalism since the twentieth century, both Jordanians and Palestinians have forged for themselves historic narratives that are separate from each other, and often juxtaposed, particularly in the case of Jordanian nationalism which seems to have turned the Palestinian into the ethnic 'Other'. At the same time, Jordanians of varied backgrounds of sedentary/Bedouin, Muslim/Christian, Northerner/Southerner, and Arab/ Circassian (in Amman) have been perceived as one hegemonic group constituting the East Jordanians. Some of these historiographic tensions are apparent in academic scholarship on Jordan and on Arabic. The next two sections address some of these tensions.

'Can the Subaltern Speak?'[2] The Andrew Shryock-Joseph Massad Debate

I would like to highlight an exchange in the leading Middle East Studies journal, *International Journal of Middle East Studies* in 2007 between Joseph Massad, a professor of Middle East politics at the University of Columbia and a protégé of Edward Said, and Andrew Shryock, a professor of anthropology at the University of Michigan. Shryock (2006) reviewed Massad's book (2001) on the state institutional building in the early decades of Jordan, and its effect on the development of the Jordanian nation-building throughout the twentieth century. Massad deconstructs the notion of a Jordanian nation and discusses the particularities of Jordan, compared to other post-colonial political systems. In the shadow of British hegemony, and with a ruling monarchy from Hejaz, the regime was able to stabilise the state despite regional upheavals. Massad also shows how the regime managed the two main interest groups of the Palestinians and the East Bankers, by choosing to build the state symbols on the East Jordanian Bedouin tradition, imagined or real. Shryock describes the book as an impressive 'Palestinian Jordanian commentary', on 'the making of national identity in Jordan' (2006: 478), thus alluding to Massad's ethnicity as a Palestinian with Jordanian citizenship. Shryock adds that in the book, 'Massad is alert to the legal apparatus that underlies Jordanian identity; his historical analysis of it is careful and insightful. On matters of Jordanian identification, however, there is much he cannot see' (2006: 478).

Massad takes this as a statement on a seemingly myopic view of Jordan, as a result of being Palestinian (2007: 161). He quickly points to the long-established Western gaze and its presumption at impartiality, and he states 'in line with standard Western colonial views of native scholars, Shryock reminds us that a Western scholar, like himself, has little to learn from the limited analysis of a native scholar'. Shryock responds in the same issue by rejecting Massad's attempt 'to recast my [Shryock's] observations as a grand struggle between exemplary Orientalist and exemplary Other. It is a powerful motif; it is also a fantasy (2007: 163)'. But, is it a complete fantasy?

When Shryock (1997) views his own identity in relation to his subject of study, the Jordanian tribal oral history, he compares himself to Smadar Lavie (1990) who studied the Bedouin tribes in Sinai and problematised her identity as a Yemeni Israeli-Jew, and Lila Abu-Lughod (1993), who studied Bedouin tribes in Egypt and also problematised her Palestinian-American identity in relation to the women she was studying. Shryock describes his identity as peripheral. He notes:

> This sense of being on the periphery was real for me in obvious ways. I am neither a Palestinian American, nor an Arab Israeli Jew, nor a Muslim, not even a 'halfie' of any advantageous sort. When I arrived in Jordan, I had no 'natural' ties to the tribal community I intended to study, only 'political' ones – American, guest, client, financial resource, Orientalist, future patron, potential spy – and my hosts sought vigorously, and with genuine concern, to 'naturalize' me. I was taught to speak the Balgawi dialect; I was schooled in Bedouin manners and customs; I was even grafted, always a bit playfully, onto 'Abbadi and 'Adwani lineages. No one, however, mistook me for part of the local world. I was constantly slipping in and out of that world, and it was precisely this slippage, which increased alongside all efforts to incorporate me, that made me interesting, problematic, appealing, troublesome, and forever in need of instruction. (Shryock: 1997: 4)

Shryock's account of ethnography is a combination of his 'oblique commentary on the already formed notions of history, nationality, kinship and religion I brought with me to the field', but at the same time, 'it is also an intellectual argument steeped in the odd and utterly personal experience of "objectivity" that my marginal positon in tribal society made possible' (Shryock 1997: 5).

In many ways, the clash between Shryock's (1997) and Massad's (2001) projects seems inevitable: one recording the tribal mores of a society in Jordan in transition and facing the effects of, first, modernisation and, second, glo-balisation. Massad, however, is critiquing Jordan's reliance on these very tribal mores in its state symbols and in the distribution of resources. In addition, it would be hard to imagine a Palestinian-Jordanian scholar having the same access to the tribal society as an American would, particularly in the pre-neo-liberal times of Jordan. These ethnic boundaries were real for Massad, regard-less of his status as a scholar. In the eyes of Shryock's informants, Massad is a Palestinian and therefore he may not have the luxury of access to the Bedouin communities of Jordan, the way Shryock might.

But, perhaps the answer to the above-mentioned dilemmas of the 'pol-itics of location' (bell hooks 1989: 35) of insider versus outsider, is to be found in more recent research in, for example, the linguistic anthropology of Yazan Doughan (2010, 2014). Doughan finds the dialects of Jordan, as 'enregistering' urbanity versus Urduni (Jordanian) identity, which implies 'authentic Jordanian' of East Banker origins (Doughan 2010: 38). Doughan's most recent research (2014) is an ethnographic account of the economically underprivileged classes in East Amman, who mostly hailed originally from the tribes of northern Jordan. Their account of who they are is in stark con-trast to the virtuoso images of the tribes of the 1990s described by Shryock. In the aftermath of the Arab Spring, young people from these groups have challenged the national norm of tribal mores, and even expressed outright contempt for it. Doughan's ready access to these groups is perhaps an indica-tion of the process of globalisation in Jordan, which has created an underclass of both Palestinian and Jordanian origins alike, thus to some extent breaking the dichotomous national divide of Palestinian versus Jordanian into one that is rather rich versus poor. In that sense, Doughan himself, as a Palestinian Jordanian does not seem to have trouble accessing these groups. In other words, the neo-liberal age of the twenty-first century has created yet another new division, which may or may not overlap with the earlier regime-focused divisions of Jordanian versus Palestinian. Shryock and Massad had to deal primarily with the ethnic division when they were doing their research in the 1990s, and whether the researcher is a member of one of these two groups, or a total outsider, seemed to be detrimental to gaining access to the groups. For Doughan, on the other hand, the insider/outsider division seems to be eco-nomic rather than ethnic. Further, and no less important, is the Arab Spring

and its effect on the youth culture in Jordan. While Jordan remained relatively immune to the upheavals everywhere in the region, the regime exerted
an effort to crush any protest at the beginning of the Arab Spring. The pro-
testers were young and they demanded more meaningful political participation and more economic equality (just like the rest of the youth of the Arab
world). At that particular historic moment, some Palestinian and Jordanian
young people found closeness, and the ethnic divide seemed less important
(see, for example, the Jordanian English language blogazine, *Black Iris*, edited
by Naseem Tarawneh (2016), a young East Jordanian.

One last issue researchers generally neglect to discuss is the fact that the
borders between Arab countries may be open for the Western researcher who
has more freedom to travel than is the case for the researcher of Middle East
origins. For Doughan and Massad for example, it was impossible to cross the
River Jordan for research purposes before 1994. And even after that, when
Jordan and Israel signed a peace treaty, it is still generally hard for a Jordanian
citizen to freely do research across the river. An American researcher, however,
can choose to do research on either side of the river, in addition to being able
to travel anywhere in the Middle East, provided that personal safety is not an
issue.

The (Re)Production of Knowledge on Arabic

It is possible that the study of the contemporary dialects of Greater Syria
can be traced as far back as the work of the German Orientalist, Gotthelf
Bergsträsser, in the early twentieth century (Bergsträsser 1915), who was travelling in the region at a very tumultuous time in Middle Eastern history, and
at the moment of transition to the domination of the great powers, which
resulted in the dividing of the area of Greater Syria into the modern states
that we know today. For Bergsträsser this was part of a long tradition of
studying the Middle East in Germany and other European countries. For
example, Arabic had been studied and taught in various Scandinavian universities since the seventeenth century (Palva 1992). In this regard, Heikki Palva,
from the University of Helsinki, and an heir to this rich tradition of Arabic
scholarship, has travelled in Jordan and in Israel/Palestine since the 1960s to
record the dialects of the region. His work varies from the dialects of Lower
Galilee (1969) to the dialects of Salt and Karak in Jordan (2008), to the

dialect of the Jordanian tribe of Bani Saxar (1980), to a study of the features of Jordanian dialects and where they stand in the dichotomy of Bedouin/sedentary dialects of Arabic (1992). Palva's impressive record of research in Jordan and Israel/Palestine is a testimony to: (1) the long Nordic (European) tradition of studying Arabic, (2) a strict sense of methodology derived from the positivism of his time, (3) an advantageous position regarding the politics of location. In this regard, bell hooks (1989) discusses the relative ease of movement across borders, and access to the people under study, for a total outsider. In fact, Palva comments on his informants in Lower Galilee when he did his study, that they were welcoming, amiable and very generous and friendly with him. He was travelling between Tiberias (to his Jewish friends, Palva 1969: 6) and to the Arab villages of the Galilee, with no apparent difficulty, at a time when the Arab informants themselves were under military rule in Israel. He was even allowed by his informants to tape his conversations on a portable tape recorder (Palva 1969: 18). Palva comments that 'I felt myself cordially welcome, and *where no suspicion was felt as to the purpose of my activities*' (1969: 17, emphasis added). The data was collected in 1961, and in 1963, as a returning researcher to the same villages in 1959 and 1960 (Palva 1969: 17). It is well documented (Pappé 1994) that his informants needed to report regularly to the military governor of their district in order to get work permits and to gain permission to move out of their locality to the next one. In other words, for Palva's informants to agree to be taped must have been a huge risk on their part. One could assume that the informants and the families Palva visited had to be approved by the military governor. But, we must be thankful for the accessibility which Palva enjoyed, in region that was otherwise very difficult to study, and where being a total outsider helped enormously.

The next systematic attempt at studying the dialects of Jordan is perhaps Abdel-Jawad's extensive study of the language variation in Amman (1981). He emphasised the distinction among urban, rural 'fallāḥīn' and Bedouin phonological variation in allophones such as the glottal stop 'ʔ', 'k', 'q' and 'g'. These particular phonological features may have been the most studied in regard to the Ammani dialect (Al-Wer and Herin 2011). Researchers are interested in these social markers which have also become markers of national identity between Jordanian (Bedouin) and Palestinian (Y. Suleiman 1999), thus becoming a second and third order index to ethnic or national variation (by indexing lifestyle (urban-rural/Bedouin) and ethnic origin (Palestinian/Jordanian), Doughan 2010).

Enam Al-Wer and Bruno Herin (2011) ask why both varieties of '?' and 'g' still exist in Ammani speech (the 'k' variable is disappearing as it is stigmatised because it indicates rural Palestinian), even with the same speaker sometimes: the glottal stop '?' is associated with urbanity, Palestinianness and femininity, while 'g' is associated with Bedouin life, Jordanianness and masculinity. The answer lies in what they identify as a Ammani dialect emerging from the language contact between Palestinians (mostly from the city of Nablus) and Jordanians (mostly from Salt), as both localities, in A-Wer and Herin's analysis, constitute the core of Amman's inhabitants since it became the new capital of Jordan. Moreover, the Palestinians changed localities as a result of their dispossession in 1948 and in 1967 (see also Al-Wer 2007). Al-Wer identifies other features emerging from the contact between both dialects, such as the vowel raising as well as syntactic changes (Al-Wer 2002a, 2002b, 2012). Her research, while immersed in traditional sociolinguistics, and taking into consideration variables such as education or gender (see Al-Wer 2002b and 1999, respectively), can be considered as the most extensive in regard to the Arabic of Amman, both synchronically and diachronically, as her research spreads over at least two decades. Doughan (2010) complements this extensive research by demonstrating the complex web of relations his speakers identify in their usage of some of the above-mentioned variables. They showed remarkable awareness of the social message according to the variable used, and when one code-switches even from one sentence to another. In other words, terms such as 'crossing' (Rampton 2006) may fall short of explaining the full range of these variables and when they are used.

On the Palestinian side, conducting research is more difficult. The only known recent research in Gaza is William Cotter's (2013). He was able to enter Gaza through Egypt for four weeks in May 2013 (Cotter and Horesh 2015: 462). His collaboration with Uri Horesh, who studies the Palestinian dialects in Israel, particularly the Yaffa dialect, yielded a rare instance of comparing Yaffa's dialect between Yaffa refugees in Gaza and Yaffa residents of today, thus shedding the light on how the different political circumstances have resulted in different contact languages and dialects for Yaffa speakers, whether it is the intra-Palestinian dialects in Gaza or the bilingualism with Hebrew in Yaffa (Cotter and Horesh 2015). Both researchers have registered a language change in process in both localities but with different social and linguistic forces.

Further, as mentioned earlier, the 1990s opened doors for contact and collaboration between Palestinians and Israelis as a result of the relative openness of Israeli society, due to their history as a modern state, and also a result of the Oslo Accords creating an opportunity for dialogue and collaboration. One of the benefits of this is a rare linguistic collaboration between Israeli and Palestinian academics, resulting in valuable research on Bethlehem and its environs. This research was led by Bernard Spolsky from Bar-Ilan University and facilitated by funding from the Netherland-Israel Research Programme, with Dutch researchers on the team as well (Spolsky et al. 2000: 5). The researchers found a linguistic landscape in transition, due to the demographic fluidity of the area. Christians have been emigrating from the town since the nineteenth century, but more so during the second half of the twentieth century. While Muslims have been migrating to the town from the surrounding villages. Thus, the rural features of Palestinian dialects are present, along with urban features such as those of nearby Jerusalem.

As for multilingualism, the researchers found that while Arabic is the dominant language, many other languages co-exist due to the heavy tourism in the city, and also as a result of schooling. Bethlehemites generally have functional literacy in Arabic, in addition to one or two more languages, such as English, French, Italian, Hebrew and others. Missionary schools are very old in Bethlehem and they emphasise European languages, sometimes at the expense of Arabic, which is not treated as the most prestigious of these languages. Most Christians go to these schools. Muslims, on the other hand, mostly go to state schools, where English is compulsory but is not taught well. The difference in education between Christians and Muslims results in differential attitudes towards Arabic and its fuṣḥā mode for both groups. Regarding Hebrew, the researchers found that gender is a significant factor, as many men work in Israel and therefore have some knowledge of Hebrew, as compared to women. Unfortunately, later political developments made further such collaboration impossible.

It may be too early for the effect of the recent globalisation or migration (often forced in the case of the Middle East) to be studied in the Jordanian or Palestinian contexts. For example, research on Jordan is still emphasising the national dichotomy between Palestinian and Jordanian, and not seemingly paying attention to the influx of Palestinians from Kuwait and Iraq in 1990, Iraqis since 1990, and Syrians since the Arab Spring in 2011, on the inter-dialectal and intra-dialectal interactions in Arabic in Jordan. Research also generally seems not to consider the effect of the new (neo-liberal, urban and business-oriented) classes on the language and on the discourse of how people view themselves, with the exception of Doughan's (2014) work on the economically disadvantaged Jordanians in East Amman. Palestinians living in East Amman or in refugee camps are also generally not studied.

To sum up, the scholarship on Jordanian Arabic is conducted: (1) in juxtaposition to Palestinian Arabic, at the expense of intra-Jordanian and intra-Palestinian dialect differences (sometimes vast in themselves), and at the expense of Arabic inter-dialectal and intra-dialectal interactions, thus keeping up with the national discourse of Jordanian versus Palestinian, (2) the scholarship while using nuances in sociolinguistic research of leading universities in Britain or in the US, does not seem to examine how diverse a city like Amman has become, as a result of the influx of refugees for at least two decades now, and last, (3) in keeping with the national discourse of East Bankers versus West Bankers, regardless of religious affiliation, the research does not examine religion as a variable. A city like Amman has always had different Christian denominations, in addition to Sunni Islam. On the other hand, many Iraqi residents of the city are Shiite. This last point is also true in regard to the anthologies and dictionaries being published by Palestinians from both sides of the river. These anthologies emphasise the Palestinian and Arab character of Palestinian Arabic. In comparison, Arabic inside Israel presents researchers with a different set of questions. As discussed extensively in Chapter 2, scholarship conducted on this group seems to be tied to the project of nation-building in Israel, and the place of the Palestinian Israelis in it as a subordinate minority. This research, as a result, reflects the status of Arabic as a minority language. It also seems to emphasise the binary divisions of sedentary/Bedouin and Muslim/Christian. As Saʿdi (2014) has shown us, reproducing these divisions were part of Israel's policy in regard to the surveillance methods of the state and its Arab minority.

However, the national division in Jordan may have reflected a tendency towards also examining language within those lines.

The commodification of Arabic in today's Amman, as part of the neo-liberal economy of the city, can be noticed in, for example, shop signs in the glitzy malls of West Amman. For instance, Figure 6.2 represents the Linguistic Landscaping of West Amman's malls.

One could notice that while Arabic appears first, it is actually a transliteration of the English names for American and European chain stores (except for the sign indicating the direction to the East Court of the mall). Figure 6.3 is yet another example, with names that are even harder to pronounce when written in Arabic, such as the sign for the British store, Mothercare.

Further, chains such as Burger King or Starbucks can also be seen in Amman. Arabic seems to take primacy with its big letters for both (Figures 6.4 and 6.5).

As for the historic downtown of Amman, the author noticed new signs in summer 2014 in both Arabic (for the locals as well as Arab visitors), and English directed at English-speaking tourists. Both languages explain historic landmarks such as the traditional Gold Market, as in Figures 6.6 and 6.7.

However, it is still delightful to see the bookstalls in Arabic in central Amman (see Figure 6.8), a familiar scene in other Arab cities such as Cairo, Rabat and others, but unfortunately not in Jerusalem or Ramallah. Books in Arabic are confined to the less than a handful of bookshops in each of these two cities. The books on display at these stalls give an idea of the impressive variety of books Jordanians read in Arabic: translations of well-known novels such as those of Paulo Coelho, books from the Arab Nahḍa such as those of Abd Al-Rahman Al-Kawakibi, history books, books on Islam, poetry, bestseller novels in Arabic from all over the Arab world, biographies of people such as Malcolm X, Anwar Sadat and others, how to speak English, Kalila wa Dimna from the Middle Ages, and many others. These books are relatively inexpensive and within the reach of most Jordanians. The owner of one of these stalls told me in summer 2014 that the book buyers are from all walks of life and from different economic backgrounds.

As for Ramallah, which became the commercial and cultural hub of Palestinians in the West Bank, road signs are in both Arabic and English, but with Arabic above English, and with English being a transliteration of

Figure 6.2 An upmarket mall in Amman, summer 2014. (Photo: author)

Arabic, even when the name of the street is 'the Main Street', it is still written in English transliteration. See, for example, the signs in Figure 6.9.

Further, the commodification of Arabic in Ramallah is less noticeable than in Amman, as the national struggle is still the most conspicuous aspect of Palestinian public life. For example, in the main commercial area

Figure 6.3 An upmarket mall in Amman, summer 2014. (Photo: author)

Figure 6.4 Burger King sign on a major road in Amman, summer 2005. (Photo: author)

of Ramallah, posters of national figures, such as Marwan Al-Barghouti who has been in Israeli prisons since the year 2000, can fill the entire front of a building, with a quote from Al-Barghouti which translates as 'if the price of the freedom of my people is my loss of freedom, I am willing to pay the price' (see Figure 6.10).

But is Arabic threatened in Jordan? In 2015, King Abdullah II issued a law for the protection of the Arabic language.[3] The law requires the Arabic language to be correct and not contain linguistic or syntactic mistakes, in public signs, announcements and so on. The law states that all signs in public places must be in Arabic; other languages may be added, as long as Arabic is in larger letters and more conspicuous. It also states that all non-Arabic films must be translated to Arabic. Item 5 of the law states that all names of institutions must be written in Arabic, as well as diplomas and certificates. Item 6 states that all names of streets, neighbourhoods and public squares must be in Arabic, except for foreign names, as well as all institutions which include

Figure 6.5 Starbucks in an affluent Amman neighbourhood, summer 2005. (Photo: author)

Figure 6.6 Central Amman, summer 2014. (Photo: author)

Figure 6.7 Central Amman, summer 2014. (Photo: author)

the commercial, industrial, scientific – their signs must be in Arabic, too. Also, all teachers, including those in higher education, must teach in Arabic. Lastly, item 16 calls for the Academy of the Arabic Language in Jordan to form a committee in collaboration with other ministries in order to guarantee the execution of the law. Anyone who violates the law may be fined between 1,000 and 3,000 Jordanian Dinars.

The Jordan Academy of Arabic was established in 1976 by a royal decree, as a continuation of an earlier body which was established at the beginning of the state in 1924 by Emir Abdullah, and called 'the Academy of Science'.[4] The vision of the academy is stated simply as 'the Arabic language is the identity of the nation, the foundation of its unity, the container of its culture and the method of communication among its sons. The mission is to spread the Arabic language in all aspects of life'.[5] One cannot but compare this with the goals of the Arabic Language Academy in Israel, cited in Chapter 4, with its emphasis on Hebrew as well. The official website of the Academy in Jordan lists its achievements as Arabising higher education, Arabising new words, publishing an anthology of public life in Jordan, the revivification of the Arab-Muslim heritage, and examining the weakness of the language among its native speakers.[6]

Figure 6.8 A bookstall in central Amman, summer 2014. (Photo: author)

Figure 6.9 Road signs in Ramallah, summer 2015. (Photo: author)

Figure 6.10 A busy commercial street in Ramallah, summer 2015. (Photo: author)

However, Samih Ma'āytah, a former minister of information, who also was the head of the Jordan Press Foundation (parent to *Al-Rai* and the *Jordan Times*, two official newspapers in Jordan, one in Arabic and one in English) when I visited his office at *Al-Rai* newspaper on 23 June 2014, is not concerned about the status of Arabic and its competition with English in Jordan. He emphasises that the English influence is relatively new in Jordan, and is only felt in certain strata of society who belong to the consumerist class. It is 'exhibitionist', or 'Isti'rāḍiyyah' and faddish and is not deeply entrenched in the linguistic practices of Jordanian society. In fact, the Arabic of Jordanian society is correct and close to fuṣḥā, as Jordanian Arabic is a language of Al-Badia, in spite of its regional variation. He also added that Arabic is secure and safe and appreciated by Muslims and Christians alike.

Lastly, in the West Bank and under the auspices of the PA, one cannot but notice a growing interest in documenting Palestinian Arabic. An example is the dictionary of Abdullatif Al-Barghouti (2001) of Colloquial Palestinian Arabic. Al-Barghouti states that Palestinian Arabic is a 'daughter' of fuṣḥā, and not a second language in its own right (Al-Barghouti 2001: 7). He also adds that the lexical resources of Palestinian Arabic are mainly from fuṣḥā, but with a small number of words from foreign languages such as Persian, English, French, Turkish and Italian (Al-Barghouti 2001: 21). Note the absence of Hebrew as a language which Palestinian Arabic borrows from. Geographically speaking, Al-Barghouti defines Palestinian Arabic as the language of the Palestinian people who originated from historic Palestine. A quick look at the dictionary though, gives the impression that the dictionary pays more attention to the rural Palestinian usages of the West Bank. Further, the dictionary does not list Aramaic as a source for Palestinian Arabic, at least historically, but it does mention sometimes the Aramaic origin, at the entry of some words. This is in contrast to Shehadeh's (2014b) and Bassal's (2012) attention to Aramaic in relation to Palestinian Arabic. One of the reasons for this difference is the academic training of Shehadeh and Bassal; other differences might be ideological. In other words, the public discourse in the West Bank is to resist the Israeli occupation, while the public discourse of the Arabs inside Israel is generally to find common denominators between Arabs and Jews.

Another example of Palestinian Arabic and its preservation is the anthology of the towns and villages of Palestine by Amneh Abu Hajar (2003) published in Jordan. Abu Hajar states in her introduction to the two volumes that it is an individual effort on her part, in order to record the names of places in Palestine before they succumb to forgetfulness. The anthology covers all of historic Palestine and it does mention the Roman, Greek, Canaanite, Syriac or biblical old names of some of the places, but not systematically, and certainly not the Hebrew origins, for obvious reasons.

To sum up, this chapter started with the historic interaction of people from both sides of the River Jordan, and how this developed in an age of nationalism into two distinct nationalities: Palestinian and Jordanian. This binary, while encouraged by the Jordanian regime, particularly after the events of 1970, has an echo in the production of knowledge about Jordanian versus Palestinian nationalism and also about Jordanian versus Palestinian Arabic. The scholarship, while important, seems to overlook other factors in the equation such as the economic factors and movement across borders, as a result of political unrest. It also seems not to pay enough attention to how diverse the city of Amman has become. Lastly, with one exception, the linguistic research does not generally seem to address the new class reconfiguration, as a result of the neo-liberal economy of cities such as Amman. But, as mentioned above, these changes may be too recent to be documented and analysed. Lastly, another dimension of this scholarship is the ease with which Western scholars can move across borders, which is not the case for the indigenous scholars, even when they are affiliated with European or American universities. This has direct implications on the scope of the research and on the questions that can or cannot be asked. As for research on Palestinian Arabic in the West Bank and Gaza by Palestinian scholars, this seems to be confined to anthologies and dictionaries of Palestinian Arabic. An exception is the research done on Bethlehem in the 1990s. This may be directly related to the increasing difficulty of moving from one location to another for Palestinians.

Notes

1. Available at <*www.lib.utexas.edu/maps/*> (last accessed 2 June 2016).
2. Gayatri Chakravorty Spivak, [1989] 2010.
3. Available at <http://www.majma.org.jo/index.php/2015-07-14-08-30-44.html> (last accessed 5 November 2015).

4. Available at <http://www.majma.org.jo/index.php/2008-12-21-07-49-01.html> (last accessed 5 November 2015).

5. Available at <http://www.majma.org.jo/index.php/mission.html> (last accessed 5 November 2015).

6. Available at <http://www.majma.org.jo/> (last accessed 1 November 2015).

Conclusion

Arabic in Israel is a subject which has not been given due attention. Arabic became a minority language overnight in 1948, as a result of the Palestinian exodus that year. However, perhaps as a gesture to the international community and to indicate that Israel was founded on democratic principles, Arabic continued to be an official language along with Hebrew, as it was under the British Mandate in Palestine between the two World Wars, but this time with the primacy of Hebrew. Earlier, English was also an official language, but under Israel this was no longer the case, even though English continues to have a strong presence in Israel in public and private life. In October 2015, the Israeli Knesset, with a majority of right-wing parties, passed a bill in its first reading making Arabic compulsory in Jewish schools from the age of six. This bill followed another bill less than a year earlier, which was not passed, calling for omitting Arabic as an official language in Israel. That bill was reiterating the two principles most Israeli parties support: that Israel is Jewish and democratic at the same time. It called for passing a law re-emphasising the Jewishness of the state, and the fact that Hebrew is its national language. In both cases, language is at the centre of a national debate which touches the core principles of the state's identity and how it sees itself: in the first case, as an exclusively Jewish state, in spite of a substantive Arab minority, and in the second case, the demand for making Arabic learning compulsory in Jewish schools is a move that can ironically unite right-wing parties along with the leftists and the Arab parties in the government, thus proving that Arabic is 'in the fray', to echo the title of one of the renowned scholar Yasir Suleiman's books on Arabic (Y. Suleiman 2013).

To solve the many seeming contradictions of Israel defining itself as Jewish and having Arabic as an official language (albeit as a minority language), this book delves into the tensions and contradictions of the Arabic presence in Israel, discussing them from the following vantage points: the historic context of Arabic in Israel, the attempts at minoritising, Orientalising and securitising the language, the Linguistic Landscape of Arabic in Israel, the effect of globalisation, modernisation and citizenship status on the status of Arabic, Hebrew as a language choice of (semi) autobiographical productions of three Israeli authors, native speakers of Arabic, and lastly, a brief comparison with the status of Arabic in both Jordan and Palestine (West Bank and Gaza Strip) where Arabic is the official language.

As the discussion unfolds, it becomes clear to the reader that the volatile and complex situation of Arabic is tied to the status of the Palestinians who have been fighting for their self-determination as a nation for most of the past century, and of Hebrew, a relative newcomer to everyday spoken language in the Middle East serving as an emblem of the success of the Zionist movement in building a home for the Jews in Palestine, thus becoming the central language (de Swaan 2001) for a peripheral Arabic in Israel. While Arabic speakers (whether Israeli Arab or Mizrachi Jews) occupy the grey area of the fluid and permeable contours of the seamline of Israeli national identity, Arabic became susceptible to the full forces of the Israeli-Arab conflict. Is diglossia a sufficient, or even relevant, concept for such a discussion? Not really. What about concepts such as 'superdiversity', 'crossing', 'enregisterment', 'first, second and perhaps, third order indexicality', and others? Such concepts seem to abandon the positivism of past research, in favour of an examination of the hybridity of the late modernity notions of language and of identity. This research hopes to open up the dialogue about Arabic so that it bypasses discussion of the dichotomous nature of its usage, and moves more into analysing the forces of Arabic today, and how citizenship status and history might affect it. Should we still analyse Arabic through its diglossic exceptionalism? This is obviously a case study of Arabic in one country and one political context. Arabic is an official language in all of the twenty-two countries of the

Arab League, in addition to a few others. These countries have complex societies and many of them have experienced population movement for different reasons. How does that affect the use of Arabic? How does the new world economic order, combined with relatively easy internet access, affect these societies and their language use? And how does political identity influence language? What is the status of Arabic in all of these societies, considering that the societies in these countries are built on the principle of the nation-state, and that these societies have witnessed recent political upheavals in varying degrees of intensity? Any nation-state is exclusionary by definition. And with that exclusion comes language privileges, or lack thereof. The unfolding of the story of Arabic in Israel hopefully helps the reader in identifying some of the problems and challenges that other countries may have been dealing with.

Chapter 1 of the book discussed the Arab Nahḍa, and its yearning for a definition of the modern state. Palestine was part of these intellectual debates about 'what is an Arab?' and 'what is Arabic?' These trends can manifest themselves in today's fractured political frameworks of Palestine, Jordan and the politics of the Israeli Arabs. For the latter group, while not physically becoming refugees (though many of them experienced internal dispossession), they had to deal with the competing forces of the Israeli nation-state and its ideas of language.

Chapter 2 discussed the notions of Orientalising, minoritising and securitising the Arabs and the Arabic of Israel. It first demonstrates how the academic departments dealing with Arabic and other Semitic languages borrowed many ideas from European Orientalism of their time, mainly German Orientalism, and these ideas consequently offered scope for analysing the 'Arab' and 'Arabic'. The chapter also identified three generations of scholars of Arabic and the differences and similarities among them. While each generation provided continuity with its predecessors, it was still a product of its intellectual times (academic, political and other). In addition, in the new language reconfiguration, Hebrew prevailed at the expense of Arabic. The status of Arabic cannot be separated from the status of its speakers: the indigenous minority of Israel. But, at the same time, it was the language of a feared enemy, hence, all the attempts at securitizing the teaching of Arabic in Jewish schools. This mirrors the treatment of the Israeli Arabs as a citizenship category, which is not Jewish, in a Jewish state. This special category of citizenship and identity makes it hard for the Israeli Arabs to be fully absorbed in the state institutions, as their 'Israeliness' may be described as 'hollow' (Jamal 2007). The chapter incudes fieldwork conducted with media personalities and students. They all express concern at the eroding of the presence of Arabic in public spaces and their personal struggle in keeping Arabic relevant to all aspects of life for the Arabs in Israel.

Chapter 3 discussed the LL for Arabic. It provided examples from public signage (both official and also commercial) from Nazareth, Haifa, Tel-Aviv, Jerusalem and Ras Al-Naqoura on the border with Lebanon. It also follows the signage between the two major gates of the Old City of Jerusalem. The Old City signage tells a story of two peoples living separate lives while sharing a very confined space. Lastly, the LL analysis provides a glimpse of how Arabic is marginalised in Israel and the forces (legal and other) which ensure its subordination to Hebrew, if not its outright invisibility.

Chapter 4 discussed the forces of modernisation which affected Israeli Arab society in the aftermath of the Nakba in 1948. From what remained of Palestinian society, Azmi Bishara emerged as the Arab nationalist voice among the fractured politics. The rise and fall of his project is a testimony to the precariousness of being an Arab in Israel. In the 1990s, when Israel as a whole became more open to self-criticism/analysis, Bishara tried to promote a political project which included the Arabs in a more meaningful citizenship in Israel. He had to leave the country as his project proved impossible to carry out. The chapter also discussed the influences of globalisation on Israeli societies (both Arab and Jewish), what Hebrew means to Israelis and how the state-supported institutions provide the tools to strengthen the Hebrew language. The opposite is generally not true for Arabic. Lastly, the chapter ended with a discussion of the new official identity of Aramean and attempts at reviving Aramaic in some Arab Christian circles. This is further evidence of the fractured politics of Israeli Arabs and the challenges they face internally in regard to their identity as one community. On the other hand, it is proof that Israel is not isolated from other events in the Middle East, in spite of its impermeable borders, a Middle East in which the negotiations of ideas about identities beyond the Arab or the Islamic have had deadly repercussions as of late.

Chapter 5 discusses the Hebrew language choice of three writers from three generations, who confess to three religious faiths. The question asked:

what role, if any, does religion play in their language choice? It seems that Judaism was able to keep Sasson Somekh under the umbrella of the state Zionism. On the other hand, not being Jewish, for Shammas and for Kashua alike, seems to have played a role in both of their decisions to leave the country (thirty years apart). Not to be Jewish seems to allow the Israeli Arab citizen some negotiation space, in regard to their place in Israeli politics and society. But that space for a possibility of equal citizenship has shrunk for both authors, a testimony to the unsustainability of such a dream. The chapter ended with a discussion of the status of the Mizrachi Jews and attempts at challenging the space the state and its institutions have allocated for them.

Chapter 6 discussed the situation of Arabic in Jordan and in Palestine (focusing on the West Bank), at first through the nation-building projects in both places and the effects of globalisation on national projects. Arabic seems to have been more commodified in advertisements at, for example, malls in Amman, in comparison to the shopping streets of Ramallah. In addition, the language research in Jordan seems to focus on the national division between 'Jordanian' and 'Palestinian'. However, Jordan, and Amman in particular, has witnessed some significant demographic changes lately due to the wars and unrest in the surrounding countries. The changes are perhaps still too recent for any research project to include them.

One recurrent theme throughout the chapters is the mobility (or lack of) that any researcher has to deal with. In the early state of Israel, mobility was very difficult for the Israeli Arabs even inside the Green Line. That changed after 1966, but it is still very difficult for a research project to be conducted simultaneously on different Palestinian communities. It might be easier for a foreign researcher to move across borders and communities, but mobility is not only state-enforced. For example, theoretically speaking, a Jordanian researcher can conduct research in Israel, and vice versa, but this type of mobility is still non-existent for many other political and social reasons. So, while many Arab communities were forced to relocate in the Middle East, as of late, natural movement of researchers across state borders has yet to be seen. This by itself affects the scope of the research and limits its conclusions.

I also hope that during this journey of Arabic in Israel, the reader will become convinced that if we confine ourselves to the popular model of 'diglossia' and 'code-switching', we miss out on very complex social, historic, and political phenomena which make Arabic into what it is today. Rather, a model which is flexible in its tools, and which may use a variety of data may be able to answer some questions more successfully. Further, while not incorporating post-structuralist analytical tools such as 'superdiversity', 'crossing', 'translingualism', and so on, I hope to have at least succeeded in opening up the discussion for including Arabic into debates about language, human and social mobility, history, political systems and globalisation. Lastly, while the Palestinians lost their inheritance of the land, which has resulted in a century of political conflict, the Arabs' inheritance of the Arabic language in Israel, while much less visible as a conflict, does not lack the same political intensity.

Bibliography

Abdel-Jawad, Hassan (1981), *Lexical and Phonological Variation in Spoken Arabic in Amman*. A Dissertation in Linguistics, Philadelphia: University of Pennsylvania.

Abdo, Nahla and Nira Yuval-Davis (1995), 'Palestine, Israel and the Zionist Settler Society', in Daiva Stasiulis and Nira Yuval-Davis (eds) *Unsettling Settler Societies*, London: Sage Publications, pp. 291–332.

ʿAbduh, Mohammad (1963), *Muthakkarāt Al-Imam Muhammad ʿAbduh* [in Arabic; The Memoir of the Imam Mohammad Abduh], Cairo: Dar al-Talal.

Abu Amr, Adnan (2015), 'How the IDF Goes Undercover among Palestinians', in *Al-Monitor: The Pulse of the Middle East*, 15 October 2015, available at <http://www.al-monitor.com/pulse/originals/2015/10/palestine-gaza-israel-soldiers-mistaravim-civilians-disguise.html> (last accessed 21 October 2015).

Abu Hajar, Amneh (2003), *Anthology of the Palestinian Towns and Villages* [in Arabic], 2 vols, Amman: Dar Usama.

Abu-Lughod, Lila (1993), *Writing Women's Worlds*, Berkeley: University of California Press.

Abu Odeh, Adnan (1999), *Jordanians, Palestinians and the Hashemite Kingdom in the Middle East Peace Process*, Washington, DC: United States Institute of Peace.

Agha, Asif (2007), *Language and Social Structure*, Cambridge: Cambridge University Press.

Al-Barghouthi, Abdullatif (2001), *Al-Qāmūs Al-Arabi Al-Shaʿbī Al-Falasṭīnī: Al-Lahja Al-Falasṭīniyya Al-Dārija* [in Arabic; Dictionary of Colloquial Palestinian Arabic]. Al-Bira, Palestine: Jamʿiyyat Inʿāsh Al-Usra (Association for Family Revivification).

Albirini, Abdulkafi (2016), *Modern Arabic Sociolinguistics: Diglossia, Variation, Codeswitching, Attitudes and Identity*, London: Routledge.

Al-Haj, Majid (1995), *Education, Empowerment and Control: The Case of the Arabs in Israel*, Albany: State University of New York Press.

Al-Ḥuṣri, Sati' (1985), *Fī al-lugha wa-l-adab wa'alāqatihimā bi-al-qawimyya* [in Arabic; About Language and Literature and their Relation to Nationalism], Beirut: Markaz Dirāsāt Al-Wiḥda al-'arabiyya.

Al-Jazeera (2014a), 'Yidi'ot: Qānūn Li-Isqāṭ Al-Āthān Bi-Israel', 'A Bill to Silence Āthān in Israel', 29 October 2014, available at <http://www.aljazeera.net/news/press tour/2014/10/29/إسرائيل-بـ-الأذان-لإسكات-قانون-يديعوت/> (last accessed 16 November 2015).

Al-Jazeera (2014b), 'Wāqi' Filisṭīniyyī 48 Dākhil Al-Mujtama' Al-Israeli', 'The reality of the 48 Palestinians in Israeli society', 10 November 2014, available at <http://bcove.me/wfzclf9t> (last accessed 11 November 2014).

'Alosh, Ibrahim (2007), 'Wathīqat Haifa ... Da'wa li-Asrala Marfūḍa Israīliyyan' [in Arabic; 'Haifa Document: A call for an Israelisation Rejected by Israel'], *Al-Jazeera*, 24 May 2007, available at <http://www.aljazeera.net/knowledgegate /opinions/2007/5/24/إسرائيليا-مرفوضة-لأسرلة-دعوة-حيفا-وثيقة/> (last accessed 2 July 2015).

Al-Quds Al-Arabi, 'Qadiyyat Mahmoud Darwish Al-Kubrā: Naṣ Rajā' Al-Naqqāsh' [in Arabic; 'The great case of Mahmoud Darwish: Text of Rajā' Al-Naqqāsh'], available at <http://www.alquds.co.uk/?p=250993, 16 November 2014> (last accessed 16 November 2014).

Al-Sakakini, Khalil (1925), *Muṭāla' āt fī Al-Lugha Wa Al-Adab*, ['Readings in Language and Literature'], Jerusalem: Maṭba'at Madrasat Al-Aytām Al-Islāmiyyah (The Islamic Orphanage School Publishing House).

Al-Sakakini, Khalil (1982), *Kathā Anā Yā Dunyā: Muthakkarāt Khalil Al-Sakakini*, [in Arabic; 'Such Am I, O World: A Memoir of Khalil Al-Sakakini'], 2nd edn, Beirut: Al-Ittiḥād Al-'ām li-l-Kuttāb wa-l-Ṣaḥafiyyīn Al-Filisṭīniyyīn, 'The Union of Palestinian Writers and Journalists'.

Al-Shanti, Issam Mohammad (1967), *Khalil Al-Sakakini Al-Lughawi*, ['Khalil Al-Sakakini, the Linguist'], Cairo: Ma'had Al-Buḥūth Wa Al-Dirāsāt Al-Arabiyya (Institute of Arabic Research).

Al-Wer, Enam (1999), 'Why do Different Variables Behave Differently?', in Yasir Suleiman (ed.), *Language and Society in the Middle East and North Africa*, London: Curzon Press, pp. 38–57.

Al-Wer, Enam (2002a), 'Jordanian and Palestinian Dialects in Contact: Vowel Raising in Amman', in Mari Jones and Edith Esch (eds), *Language Change: The Interplay of Internal, External and Extra-Linguistic Factors*, Berlin: Mouton de Gruyter, pp. 63–79.

Al-Wer, Enam (2002b), 'Education as Speaker Variable', in Aliya Rouchdy (ed.), *Language Contact and Language Conflict in Arabic: Variation on a Sociolinguistic Theme*, London: Routledge, pp. 41–53.

Al-Wer, Enam (2007), 'The Formation of the Dialect of Amman: From Chaos to Order', in Catherine Miller, Enam Al-Wer, Dominique Caubet and Janet Watson (eds), *Arabic in the City: Issues in Dialect Contact and Language Variation*, London: Routledge.

Al-Wer, Enam (2012), 'Yod-dropping in b-imperfect Verb Forms in Amman', in Froud, Karen and Reem Khamis-Dakwar (eds), *Perspectives on Arabic Linguistics XXVI: Papers from the Annual Symposium of Arabic Linguistics*, New York: John Benjamins, pp. 29–43.

Al-Wer, Enam and Bruno Herin (2011), 'The Lifecycle of Qaf in Jordan', in *Langage et Société*, no. 138, pp. 59–76.

ʿAmara, Mohammad (1968), *Al-Aʿmāl Al-kāmila li-Jamal Al-Din Al-Afghani,* [in Arabic; 'The Complete Works of Jamal Al-Din Al-Afghani'] vol. 1, Cairo: Al-Muʾassasa Al-Miṣriyya li-l-taʾlīf wa-l-Nashr.

Amara, Mohammad (2013), 'Mawqiʿ Al-Lugha Al-ʿArabiyya fī Wathāʾiq Al-Taṣawwurāt Al- Mustaqbaliyyaʾ, [in Arabic; 'The Status of Arabic in the Future Vision Documents']. Dirāsāt (the Arab Center for Law and Policy) Yearbook 2013, vol. 6: 112–21. Nazareth: Dirāsāt Center.

Amara, Mohammad and Sufian Kabaha (1996), *Zehut Chatsuya: Chaluka Politit Veheshtakfuyut Chevratiyot Bekfar Chatsuy* [in Hebrew; 'Divided Identity: A Study of Political Division and Social Reflections in a Split Village'], Givat Haviva, Israel: Institute for Peace Studies.

Amara, Mohammad and Abd Al-Rahman Marʿi (2002), *Language Education Policy: The Arab Minority in Israel*, London: Kluwer Academic Publishing.

Arlozorof, Mirav (2015), 'Bennett Doʿeg la-Yladim Ha-ʿAravim', [in Hebrew; 'Bennet is Concerned for the Arab Children'], *Ha'aretz*, 9 June 2015, available at <http://www.haaretz.co.il/tmr/1.2655639> (last accessed 7 July 2015).

Bale, Jeffrey (2011), 'Language Education and Imperialism: The Case of Title VI and Arabic, 1958–1991', *Journal for Critical Education Policy Studies*, vol. 9, no. 1, pp. 376–409.

Bale, Jeffrey (2014), 'Heritage Language Education and the 'National Interest', *Review of Research in Education*, vol. 38, pp. 166–88.

Bar'el, Zvi (2014), 'Arab Elite, You're Israel's Fig Leaf: Don't Run Away, We on the Superficial Left Need you. Just Stop Protesting against the Gaza War and Forget about the Nakba, O.K.?', *Ha'aretz*, 7 July 2015, available at <http://www.haaretz.com/opinion/.premium-1.606719> (last accessed 8 July 2015).

Bar-On, Dan (2006), *Tell your Life Story: Creating Dialogue among Jews and Germans, Israelis and Palestinians*, Budapest: Central European University Press.

Bassal, Ibrahim (2008), 'Kufur-Yasif Dialect: A Morphophonemic Description', in *Lingua-Culture Contextual Studies in Ethnic Conflicts of the World*, vol. 8, Osaka: Osaka University, pp. 85–99.

Bassal, Ibrahim (2012), 'Hebrew and Aramaic Substrata in Spoken Palestinian Arabic', in *Mediterranean Language Review*, vol. 19, pp. 85–104.

Bassal, Ibrahim (2015), 'Hebrew and Aramaic Elements in the Israeli Vernacular Christian-Arabic and in the Written Christian Arabic of Palestine, Syria and Lebanon', In *The Levantine Review*, vol. 4, no. 1, pp. 77–106.

Bassiouney, Reem, (2015), *Language and Identity in Modern Egypt*, Edinburgh: Edinburgh University Press.

Bauman, Zigmunt (1987), *Legislators and Interpreters*, Cambridge: Polity Press.

Baylouny, Anne Marie (2008), 'Militarizing Welfare: neo-liberalism and Jordanian Policy', *Middle East Journal*, vol. 62, no. 2, pp. 277–303.

Bekerman, Zvi (2016), *The Promise of Integrated Multicultural and Bilingual Education: Inclusive Palestinian-Arab and Jewish Schools in Israel*, Oxford: Oxford University Press.

Ben-Rafael, Eliezer, Elana Shohamy, Muhammad Amara and Nira Trumper-Hecht (2006), 'Linguistic Landscape as Symbolic Construction of the Public Space: The Case of Israel', in *International Journal of Multilingualism*, 3 (1), pp. 7–31.

Ben-Rafael Eliezer and Miriam Ben-Rafael (2010), 'Diaspora and Returning Diaspora: French-Hebrew and Vice-Versa', in Elana Shohamy, Eliezer Ben-Rafael, and Monica Barni (eds), *Linguistic Landscape in the City*, Bristol: Multilingual Matters, pp. 326–43.

Bergsträsser, Gotthelf (1915), *Sprachtlas Von Syrien Und Palästina*: 42 Taflen Nebst 1 Übersichtskarte Und Erläuterndem Text Von Dr. G. Bergsträsser, Leipzig: J. C. Hinrichs.

Bishara, Azmi (1993), 'On the Question of the Palestinian Minority in Israel', *Theory and Criticism*, 3, pp. 7–20.

Bishara, Azmi (1997), 'Min Jadaliyyat al-Wujūd ilā Jadaliyyat al-Jawhar', [in Arabic; 'From the Dialectic of Existentialism to the Dialectic of Substance'], *Al-Karmel* 53, pp. 11–35.

Bishara, Azmi (2003), *The Arabs in Israel*, New York: Interlink Publishing Group.

Bishara, Azmi (2004), 'The Arabs in Israel 2004: The Status of the Arab Minority in the Jewish State', in Elie Rekhess and Sarah Ozacky-Lazar (eds), *The Status of the Arab Minority in the Jewish Nation State*, Tel-Aviv: Adenuaer Program for Jewish-Arab Co-operation, pp. 95–111.

Black Iris, ed. Naseem Tarawneh, available at <https://www.facebook.com/the blackiris/> (last accessed 3 June 2016).

Blanc, Haim (1953), *Studies in North Palestinian Arabic: Linguistic Inquires among the Druzes of Western Galilee and Mt. Carmel*, Jerusalem: Israeli Oriental Society No. 4.

Blanc, Haim (1964), *Communal Dialects in Baghdad*, Boston: Harvard University Press.

Blau, Joshua (1966), *A Grammar of Christian Arabic: based Mainly on South Palestinian Texts from the First Millennium*, Leuven: Catholic University of Louvain.

Bleboim, Rivka and Marc Bernstein (2013), 'Huwiyya (Zihut) Ve-Chavayat Ha-'Ivrit Bi-Sidrat Ha-Tilivizia "Avodah 'Aravit"', [in Hebrew; 'Identity and the Experience of Hebrew in the Television Series "Arab Labour"'], *Israel Studies in Language and Society*, 6 (2), pp. 49–70.

Blommaert, Jan (2005), 'Situating Language Rights: English and Swahili in Tanzania revisited', *Journal of Sociolinguistics* 9/3, 390–417.

Blommaert, Jan (2013), *Ethnography, Superdiversity and Linguistic Landscapes: Chronicles of Complexity*, Bristol: Multilingual Matters.

Blommaert, Jan and Piia Varis (2015), 'Enoughness, Accent and Light Communities: Essays on Contemporary Identities', in *Tilburg Papers in Culture Studies: Paper 139*, the Netherlands: Tilburg University, available at <https://www .tilburguniversity.edu/research/institutes-and-research-groups/babylon/tpcs/> (last accessed 6 November 2015).

Bokra (2014a), 'Al-Kāhin Jibrael Naddaf Yad'ū Al-Masīḥiyyīn lil-Tawwajuh li-Wazārat Al-Dākhiliyya wa-Taghyīr Al-Qawmiyya min 'Arabi ilā Ārāmi', [in Arabic; 'The priest Jibrael Naddaf Calls for the Christians to go to the Ministry of Interior and Change their Nationality from Arab to Aramaic'], 16 September 2014, available at <http://www.bokra.net/Article-1268313> (last accessed 16 November 2014).

Bokra (2014b), 'Qadiyyat Al-Qawmiyya Al-Ārāmiyya Maskhara, wa Sa'aṭlub Majlis al-Ṭā'ifa bi-Ṭard Ghayr Al-'Arab', [in Arabic; 'Dr Azmi Hakim: the case of Aramaic nationality is a joke, and I will ask the (Orthodox) Church Council to expel non-Arabs'], 21 October 2014, available at <http://www.bokra.net /Article-1272573> (last accessed 16 November 2014).

Boudon, R. (1990), *La Place du désordre. Critique sociale du jugement*, Paris: Les Éditions de Minuit.

Bourdieu, Pierre (1993), *The Field of Cultural Production: Essays on Art and Literature*, New York: Columbia University Press.

Brosh-Vaitz, Shoshan (2005), 'On the State of Literacy in Israel: Background Paper Prepared for the Education for All Global Monitoring Report 2006, Literacy for Life', UNESCO, 2006/ED/EFA/MRT/PI/17 (last accessed 25 May 2016).

Butler, Judith (2012), "'What Shall We Do without Exile?' Said and Darwish Address the Future", Alif: Journal of Comparative Politics, vol. 32, pp. 1–7.

Butts, Aaron (ed.), forthcoming, *Studies in Semitic Language Contact*, Leiden: Brill.

Canagarajah, Suresh (2015), *Translingual Practice: Global Englishes and Cosmopolitan Relations*, London: Routledge.

Chetrit, Sami (2007), 'Mural without a Wall: A Poem for Mahmoud Darwish', available at <https://www.youtube.com/watch?v=FhXhTtixnno> (last accessed 24 June 2015).

Chetrit, Sami (2013), *Intra-Jewish Conflict in Israel: White Jews, Black Jews*, New York: Routledge.

Chetrit, Sami (2015), lecture at Michigan State University, 24 March, available at <https://www.youtube.com/watch?v=Q9AeUynHZrI> (last accessed 24 June 2015).

Clinton, Bill (2005), *My Life*, New York: Vintage Press.

Cobban, Helena (1992) [1984], *The Palestinian Liberation Organization: People, Power and politics*, Cambridge: Cambridge University Press.

Cohen, Hillel (2004), *Tzava Hatslalim: Falastinim Bishirut Hatzuynut* [in Hebrew; 'Army of Shadows: Palestinians in the Service of Zionism'], Jerusalem: Hemed.

Cotter, William (2013), *Dialect Contact and Change in Gaza City*, MA thesis, University of Essex.

Cotter, William and Uri Horesh (2015), 'Social Integration and Dialect Divergence in Coastal Palestine', *Journal of Sociolinguistics*, vol. 19, issue 4, pp. 460–83.

Coupland, Nikolas (2003), 'Introduction: Sociolinguistics and Globalization', *Journal of Sociolinguistics*, 7 (4), pp. 465–72.

Crystal, David (2014), *Language Death* (repr.), Cambridge: Cambridge University Press.

Darwish, Mahmoud (2013), *Memory for Forgetfulness: August, Beirut, 1982*, trans. Ibrahim Muhawi, Berkeley: University of California Press.

De Swaan, Abram (2001), *Words of the World: The Global Language System*, Cambridge, MA: Polity Press.

Doughan, Yazan (2010), 'Imaginaries of Space and Language: The Production of Jordanian Locality', A Master's thesis in Anthropology at the University of Chicago.

Doughan, Yazan (2014), 'Speaking to Authority, Speaking with Authority: Forms of Public Criticism in Jordan's Protest Movement', a paper presented at the 113 American Anthropological Association Annual Meeting, November, Washington, DC.

Eid, Jawdat (2003), *Nashāz*, [in Arabic; 'Disharmony'], Nazareth: Al-Bashir Publisher.

Estren, Daniel (2015), 'Netanyahu Fights for Right-wing Vote as Israelis Go to the Polls', *The Huffington Post*, 17 March 2015, available at <http://www.huffingtonpost.com/2015/03/17/israel-election-netanyahu_n_6884652.html> (last accessed 15 September 2015).

'Etser, Oranit (2009), 'Sa'ar: Shnat Ha-Limudim Ha-Ba'a-Shnat Ha-'Ivrit' [in Hebrew; 'Sa'ar: Next Year's Academic Year is the Year of the Hebrew'], Channel 7, 30 December 2009, available at <http://www.inn.co.il/News/News.aspx/198503> (last accessed 27 May 2015).

Eyal, Gil (2006), *The Disenchantment of the Orient*, Palo Alto, CA: Stanford University Press.

Feghali, Michel (1928), *Syntaxe des parlers arabes actuels du Liban*, Paris: Bibliothèque de l'École des Langues Orientales vivantes 9.

Ferguson, Charles (1959), 'Diglossia', *Word* 15, pp. 325–40.

Ferguson, Charles (1991), 'Diglossia Revisited', *Southwest Journal of Linguistics* 10(1), pp. 214–34.

Filc, Dani (2010), *The Political Right in Israel*, New York: Routledge.

First, Anat and Eli Avraham (2009), *American in JeruSALEm: Globalization, National Identity, and Israeli Advertising*, Lanham, MD: Lexington Books.

Fishman, Joshua (ed.) (1974), *Advances in Language Planning*, The Hague: Mouton.

Foucault, Michel (1977), *Discipline and Punish*, Harmondsworth: Penguin Press.

Foucault, Michel (1982), *The Archaeology of Knowledge*, New York: Vintage Press.

Fraser, Nancy (2003), 'From Discipline to Flexibilization? Rereading Foucault in the Shadow of Globalization', *Constellations* 10 (2), pp. 160–71.

Geva-Kleinberger, Aharon (2000), 'Al-Lahjāt Al-'Arabiyya Li-Yahūd Al-Jalīl fī Al-Niṣf Al-Awwal min Al-Qarn Al-'Ishrīn', [in Arabic; 'The Arabic Dialects of the Jews in Galilee in the First half of the Twentieth Century'], in Abderrahim Youssi, Fouzia Benjelloun, Mohamed Dahbi and Zakia Iraqui-Sinaceur (eds), *Aspects of the Dialects of Arabic Today: Proceedings of the 4th Conference of the International Arabic Dialectology Association (AIDA), Marrakesh, April 1–4, 2000*, Rabat: Amapatrail, pp. 473–80.

Ghanem, As'ad (2001), *The Palestinian-Arab Minority in Israel 1948–2000: A Political Study*, Albany: State University of New York Press.

Ghanim, Hunaida (2009), *Reinventing the Nation: Palestinian Intellectuals in Israel* [in Hebrew], Jerusalem: The Hebrew University Magnes Press.

Goffman, Erving (1981), *Forms of Talk*, Philadelphia: University of Pennsylvania Press.

Goitein, Shlomo Dov (1964), *Jews and Arabs: Their Contact Through the Ages*, New York: Schoken Books.

Goitein, Shlomo Dov (1979), 'David Hartwig (Zvi) Baneth', in Joshua Blau, S. Piner, M. Kister and S. Shaked (eds), *Studio Orientalia Memoriae D. H. Baneth Dedicata*, Jerusalem: The Hebrew University Magnes Press, pp. 1–5.

Gorter, Durk (2006), 'Introduction: The Study of Linguistic Landscape as a New Approach to Multilingualism', *International Journal of Multilingualism*, 3 (1), pp. 1–6.

Gorter, Durk, Heiko Marten and Luk Van Mensel (eds) (2012), *Minority Languages in the Linguistic Landscape*, New York: Palgrave Macmillan.

Griffith, Sidney (1992), *Theodore Abu Qurrah: The Intellectual Profile of an Arab Christian Writer of the First Abbasid Century*, Tel-Aviv: Tel-Aviv University Press.

The Guardian (2014), 'Plan to Transfer Arab-Israelis to new Palestinian State Seeks Legal Approval', available at <http://www.theguardian.com/world/2014/mar/25/transfer-arab-israeli-citizens-palestinian-state> (last accessed 9 December 2015).

Habibi, Emile (1985), *The Secret Life of Saeed, the Pesoptimist*, trans. Salma Khadra Jayyusi and Trevor LeGassick, London: Zed.

Ḥadidi, Subḥi (2008), 'Rūḥī Al-Khalidi: Munāḍil Siyāsi wa Mu'arrikh Rā'id', 'Rouhi Al-Khalidi: Political Activist and Pioneer Historian', in *Al-Jazeera*, 23 May 2008, available at <http://www.aljazeera.net/news/arabic/2008/5/23/روحي-الخالدي-مناضل-سياسي-ومؤرخ-رائد> (last accessed 16 May 2008).

Halliday, Fred (2009), 'The Modernity of the Arabs', in *International Journal of Middle East Studies* (41), pp. 16–18.

Handelzalts, Michael (2013), 'Word Play, the (Ethnic) Devil is in the Details: How, When and Why did this Intricate and Painful Mizrachi-Ashkenazi Issue Take on such a Devilish Character?', *Ha'aretz*, 16 August 2013, available at <http://www.haaretz.com/weekend/pen-ultimate/.premium-1.541913> (last accessed 24 June 2015).

Hasso, Francis (2015), *Resistance, Repression and Gender Politics in Occupied Palestine and Jordan*, Syracuse: Syracuse University Press, Amazon Digital Services.

Hawker, Nancy (2013), *Palestinian-Israeli Conflict and Linguistic Processes*, London: Routledge.

Henken, Roni (2000), 'Tense-Switching in Narratives of Negev Bedouin Men and Women', in Abderrahim Youssi, Fauzia Benjelloun, Mohamed Dahbi and Zakia Iraqui-Sinaceur (eds), *Aspects of The Dialects of Arabic Today: Proceedings of the 4th Conference of the International Arabic Dialectology Association (AIDA), Marrakesh, April 1–4, 2000*, Rabat: Amapatrail, pp. 288–98.

Hennessey, Andrew (2011), *The Linguistic Integration of the Palestinian Refugees in Beirut: A Model for Analysis*, MA thesis: American University in Beirut.

Hlehel, Ala (2014), *Au Revoir Akka* [in Arabic], Acre, Israel: Kotob Qadita.

Hobsbawm, Eric (1996), 'Language, Culture and National Identity', in *Social Research*, vol. 63, no. 4, pp. 1065–80.

Hobsbawm, Eric (2008), *Globalisation, Democracy and Terrorism*, London: Abacus.

Hofman, John and Nadim Rouhana (1976), 'Young Arabs in Israel: Some Aspects of a Conflicted Social Identity', in *Journal of Social Psychology*, 99, pp. 75–86.

hooks, bell (1989), *Talking Back: Thinking Feminist, Thinking Black*, New York: Routledge.

Horesh, Uri (2014), *Phonological Outcomes of Language Contact in the Palestinian Dialects of Jaffa*, PhD thesis, University of Essex.

Horesh, Uri (2015), 'Structural Changes in Urban Palestinian Arabic Induced by Contact with Modern Hebrew', in Aaron Butts (ed.), *Studies in Semitic Language Contact*, Leiden: Brill, pp. 198–233.

Hovel, Revital (2012), 'Professors Fume over Dominance of English Language in Israeli Academia', *Ha'aretz*, 12 October 2012, available at <http://www.haaretz.com .proxy1.cl.msu.edu/news/israel/professors-fume-over-dominance-of-english -language-in-israeli-academia.premium-1.469547> (last accessed 7 July 2015).

Hudson Alan (2002), 'Outline of a Theory of Diglossia', *International Journal of the Sociology of Language* 157, pp. 1–48.

Hussein, (King of Jordan) (1962), *Uneasy Lies the Head*, London: William Heinemann.

Hussein, Rashid (1966), *Haim Nehman Bialik: A Selection of His Poetry and Prose* [in Arabic], Tel-Aviv: Dvir Publishing.

Ḥusayn, Ṭāha (1944), *Mustaqbal al-thaqāfa fī miṣr*, [in Arabic; 'The Future of Culture in Egypt'], Cairo: Matba'at al-Ma'ari.

Jamal, Amal (2005), *The Palestinian National Movement*, Bloomington: Indiana University Press.

Jamal, Amal (2006), 'The Arab Leadership in Israel: Ascendance and Fragmentation', *Journal of Palestine Studies*, vol. xxxv, no. 2, pp. 6–22.

Jamal, Amal (2007), 'Nationalizing States and the Constitution of "Hollow Citizenship": Israel and its Palestinian Citizens', in *Ethnopolitics*, 6, 4, pp. 471–93.

Jamal, Amal (2011), *Arab Minority Nationalism in Israel: The Politics of Indigeneity*, London: Routledge Studies in Middle East Politics.

Jamal, Amal and Samah Bsoul (2014), 'The Palestinian Nakba in the Israeli Public Sphere: Formations of denial and Responsibility', Nazareth, Israel: I'lam: Media Center for Arab Palestinians in Israel.

The Jerusalem Post (2008), 'Poll: Israelis Favor Arab Transfer to Palestine', available at <http://www.jpost.com/Israel/Poll-Israelis-favor-Arab-transfer-to-Palestine> 31 March 2008 (last accessed 9 December 2015).

The Jerusalem Post (2015), 'Ayelet Shaked Responding to Attacks: Everyone, Left, Right, Needs to Lower the Volume', available at <http://www.jpost.com/Israel-News/Politics-And-Diplomacy/Ayelet-Shaked-responding-to-attacks-Everyone-Left-Right-needs-to-lower-the-volume-438833> 15 December 2015 (last accessed 29 July 2016).

Jibreal, Rula (2014), 'Minority Life in Israel', *The New York Times*, (27 October 2014), available at <http://www.nytimes.com/2014/10/28/opinion/rula-jebreal-minority-life-in-israel.html?partner=rss&emc=rss> (last accessed 3 November 2014).

Kabaha, Mustafa (2007), *The Palestinian Press as Shaper of Public Opinion 1929–39: Writing Up a Storm*, London: Vallentine Mitchell.

Kampf, Zohar (1913), *Hebrew and the Israeli Media in the 21st Century*, a report submitted to the Centre for Sociolinguistics and Communication, University of Barcelona.

Kanafani, Ghassan (1968/2013), *In Zionist Literature* [in Arabic], Limassol: Rimal Publications.

Kashua, Sayed (2002), *Dancing Arabs* [in Hebrew], Jerusalem: Modan.

Kashua, Sayed (2009), 'The Kidnapped from Baghdad', *Ha'aretz*, 26 June 2009, available at <http://www.haaretz.co.il/hasite/spages/1095612.html> (last accessed 26 June 2009).

Kashua, Sayed (2010), *Second Person Singular* [in Hebrew], Jerusalem: Keter.

Kashua, Sayed (2014), 'Why Sayed Kashua is Leaving Israel and Never Coming Back', *Ha'aretz*, 5 August 2014, available at <http://www.haaretz.com/weekend/weekend/.premium-1.602869> (last accessed 3 November 2014). Also appeared in *The Guardian*, available at <http://www.theguardian.com/world/2014/jul/20/sayed-kashua-why-i-have-to-leave-israel> (last accessed 16 November 2014).

Kashua, Sayed and Etgar Keret (2014), 'Tell me a story with a happy ending', *The New Yorker*, 14 October 2014, available at <http://www.newyorker.com/books/page-turner/tell-story-happy-ending-exchange-etgar-keret-sayed-kashua> (last accessed 16 November 2014). Part 2, <http://www.newyorker.com/uncategorized /tell-story-happy-ending-exchange-etgar-keret-sayed-kashua-part-ii> (last accessed 16 November 2014).

Kassab, Elizabeth Suzanne (2010), *Contemporary Arab Thought: Cultural Critique in Comparative Perspective*, New York: Columbia University Press.

Katriel, Tamar (1986), *Talking Straight: 'Dugri' Speech in Israeli Sabra Culture*, Cambridge: Cambridge University Press.

Katriel, Tamar (2004), *Dialogic Moments: From Soul Talks to Talk Radio in Israeli Culture*, Detroit: Wayne State University Press.

Keay, John (2003), *Sowing the Wind: The Seeds of Conflict in the Middle East*, New York: W. W. Norton & Co.

Kershner, Isabel (2015), 'Deep Wounds and Lingering Questions after Israel's Bitter Race', *The New York Times*, 17 March 2015, available at <http://www.nytimes.com/2015/03/18/world/middleeast/netanyahu-israel-elections-arabs.html?_r=0> (last accessed 18 December 2015).

Khalidi, Raja and Sobhi Samour (2011), 'Neoliberalism as Liberation: The Statehood Program and the Remaking of the Palestinian National Movement', *Journal of Palestine Studies* vol. XI, No. 2, pp. 6–25.

Khalidi, Rashid (1997), *Palestinian Identity*, New York: Columbia University Press.

Khatib, Usama (2012), *Manāhij Al-Insāniyyāt Wal-'ulūm Al-Ijtimā'iyya fī Madāris Barṭa'a Al-Mashṭūra': Taḥawwulāt Al-Huwiyya Al-Waṭaniyya Al-Falasṭīniyya*, [in Arabic; 'Textbooks of Humanities and Social Sciences in the schools of the 'Split' Village of *Barṭa'a*: The Transformations of the Palestinian National Identity'], Master's Thesis in Contemporary Arab Studies, Palestine: Birzeit University.

Kimmerling, Baruch (2001), *The Invention and Decline of Israelness: State: Society and the Military*, Berkeley: University of California Press.

Kimmerling, Baruch (2008), *Clash of Identities: Explorations in Israeli and Palestinian Societies*, New York: Columbia University Press.

Krashen, Stephen (2003), *Explorations in Language Acquisition and Use*, Portsmouth, NH: Heinemann.

Krashen, Stephen (2004), *The Power of Reading*, Portsmouth, NH: Heinemann.

Kutscher, Eduard Yechezkel (1976), *Studies in Galilean Aramaic*, Ramat-Gan: Bar-Ilan University.

Kutscher, Eduard Yechezkel (1982), *A History of the Hebrew Language*, ed. Raphael Kutscher, Jerusalem: The Hebrew University Magnus Press.

Kymlicka, Will (2001), *Politics in the Vernacular: Nationalism, Multiculturalism and Citizenship*, Oxford: Oxford University Press.

Labov, William (1966), *The Social Stratification of English in New York City*, Washington, DC: Center for Applied Linguistics.

Laḥūd, Abdallah (1993), *Lubnan: ʿarabiyyu al-Wajh, ʿarabiyyu al-Lisān*, [in Arabic; 'Lebanon: Arab-Face and Arab-Tongue'], Beirut: Dar Al-ʿilm li-l-Malāyīn.

Latour, Bruno (1993), *We Have Never been Modern*, Cambridge, MA: Harvard University Press.

Lavie, Smadar (1990), *The Poetics of Military Occupation*, Berkeley: University of California Press.

Levi, Amnon (2013), *The Ethnic Devil*, available at <https://www.youtube.com /watch?v=ZFH0RF-_O10> (last accessed 25 June 2015).

Liebes, Tamar and Zohar Kampf (2010), '"Hello! This is Jerusalem Calling": The Revival of Spoken Hebrew on the Mandatory Radio (1936–1948)', *Journal of Israeli History: Politics, Society, Culture*, vol. 29, no. 2, September 2010: 137–58.

Liphshiz, Canaan (2008), 'Technion to Switch to English in Main MBA Program', *Haʾaretz*, 28 March 2008, available at <http://www.haaretz.com.proxy1.cl.msu .edu/print-edition/news/technion-to-switch-to-english-in-its-main-mba -program-1.242888> (last accessed 7 July 2015).

Lockman, Zachary (2004), *Contending Visions of the Middle East: The History and Politics of Orientalism*, Cambridge: Cambridge University Press.

Loller, Travis (2011), 'Two Muslim Men Kicked out of Flight Sue Airline', *The Huffington Post*, 19 December 2011, available at <http://www.huffingtonpost. com/2011/12/19/muslims-kicked-off-sue-airlines_n_1158815.html> (last accessed 6 December 2015).

Lucas, Russell (2005), *Institutions and the Politics of Survival in Jordan: Domestic Response to External Challenges, 1988–2001*, New York: State University of New York Press.

Lustick, Ian (1980), *Arabs in the Jewish State: Israel's Control of a National Minority*, Austin: University of Texas Press.

Maltz, Judy (2012), 'Study at the Hebrew U. – without Hebrew', *Haʾaretz*, 8 August 2012, available at <http://www.haaretz.com.proxy1.cl.msu.edu/news/features /study-at-hebrew-u-without-the-hebrew-1.456765> (last accessed 7 July 2015).

Manaʿa, Adel (2015), 'Forgetfulness and Oppression of Palestinian Historical Memory', paper presented at the International Conference on Dilemmas of Recognition in Asymmetric Conflicts, The School for Peace, Neve Shalom, Israel, 4–5 May 2015, available at <http://sfpeace.org/intl-conference-on -dilemmas-of-recognition-in-asymmetric-conflicts/> (last accessed 10 November 2015).

Marʿi, Abd Al-Rahman (2013), *Wallah Beseder: Diokan Lishoni shel Ha-ʿaravim Bi-Yisrael*, [in Hebrew; 'A Linguistic Diary of Arabs in Israel'], Jerusalem: Keter.

Marten, Heiko, Luk Van Mensel and Durk Gorter (2012), 'Studying Minority Languages in the Linguistic Landscape', in Gorter, Durk, Heiko Marten and Luk Van Mensel (eds), *Minority Languages in the Linguistic Landscape*, New York: Palgrave Macmillan, pp. 1–18.

Massad, Joseph (2001), *Colonial Effects: The Making of National Identity in Jordan*, New York: Columbia University Press.

Massad, Joseph (2006), 'Palestinians and the limits of racialized discourse', in *The Persistence of the Palestinian Question: Essays on Zionism and the Palestinians*, London and New York: Routledge, pp. 79–95.

Massad, Joseph (2007), 'A Reply to Andrew Shryock's Review of *Colonial Effects: The Making of National Identity in Jordan (IJMES* 38 [2006]: 478:79', in *International Journal of Middle East Studies*, 39, pp. 161–4.

May, Stephen (2005), 'Language Rights: Moving the Debate Forward', *Journal of Sociolinguistics* 9/3: 319–47.

Mendel, Yonatan (2014a), *Arabic Studies in Israeli-Jewish Society*, unpublished dissertation, University of Cambridge.

Mendel, Yonatan (2014b), *The Creation of Israeli Arabic: Political and Security Considerations in the Making of Arabic Language Studies in Israel*, New York: Palgrave Macmillan.

Mendel, Yonatan and Yasir Suleiman (2010), 'Language, Conflict and Security: Report of a Conference held at the Prince Alwaleed Bin Talal Centre of Islamic Studies', University of Cambridge 10–11 April 2010, available at <http://www.cis.cam.ac.uk/reports/post/41-language-conflict-and-security> (last accessed 29 September 2015).

Morag, Shlomo, Issachar Ben-Ami and Norman Stillman (eds) (1981), *Studies in Judaism and Islam*, Jerusalem: The Hebrew University Magnes Press.

Morris, Benny (1989), *The Birth of the Palestinian Refugee Problem: 1947–1949*, Cambridge: Cambridge University Press.

Muasher, Marwan (2011), 'A Decade of Struggling Reform Efforts in Jordan', *The Carnegie Papers*, Washington, DC: Carnegie Endowment for International Peace, May 2011.

Musa, Salama (1928), *Al-Yawm wa-Ghadan*, [in Arabic; 'Today and Tomorrow'], Cairo: Salama Musa li-l Nashr wal-Tawzīʿ.

Musa, Salama (1964), *Miṣr Aṣl Al-Ḥaḍāra*, [in Arabic; 'Egypt: The Founder of Civilization'], Cairo: Salama Musa li-l Nashr wal-Tawzīʿ.

Musallam, Akram (ed.) (2003), Yawmiyyāt Khalil Al-Sakakini: Al-Kitāb Al-Awwal, 1907–1912, [in Arabic; 'Diary of Khalil Al-Sakakini: The First Book, 1907–1912'], Ramallah: Khalil Al-Sakakini Center.

Naddaf, Gabriel (2014a), 'Nādī Aṣdiqā' Al-Ab Jibrael Naddaf', 'Friends of Jibrael Naddaf', <https://www.facebook.com/FFGNIL/> (last accessed 30 July 2016).

Naddaf, Gabriel (2014b), 'Facebook Page', available at <https://www.facebook.com/frgabrielnaddaf/> (last accessed 30 July 2016).

Neuman, Efrat and Jasmin Gueta (2014), 'Israel's Language War II: This Time it's Over English', Ha'aretz, 19 January 2014, available at <http://www.haaretz.com/business/.premium-1.569406> (last accessed 27 May 2015).

Palva, Heikki (1969), Lower Galilean Arabic: An Analytic of its Anaptyctic and Prothetic Vowels with Sample Texts, Helsinki: Studia Orientalia.

Palva, Heikki (1980), 'Characteristic of the Arabic Dialect of Bani Saxar tribe', in Orientalia Suecana, vol. XXIX, pp. 112–39.

Palva, Heikki (1992), 'Typological Problems in the Classification of Jordanian Dialects: Bedouin or Sedentary', in The Middle East Viewed from the North: Papers from the First Nordic Conference on Middle Eastern Studies, Uppsala 26–29, January 1989, ed. Bo Utas and Knut Vikør, Bergen: Nordic Society for Middle Eastern Studies, pp. 53–62.

Palva, Heikki (2008), 'Sedentary and Bedouin Dialects in Contact: Remarks on Karaki and Salti (Jordan)', in Journal of Arabic and Islamic Studies, vol. 8, pp. 53–70.

Pappé, Ilan (1994), The Making of the Arab-Israeli Conflict: 1947–1951, London: I. B. Tauris.

Pappé, Ilan (2006), The Ethnic Cleansing of Palestine, Oxford: Oneworld.

Pappé, Ilan (2014), The Idea of Israel: A History of Power and Knowledge, London: Verso.

Peled-Elhanan, Nurit, (2012), Palestine in Israeli School-Books: Ideology and Propaganda in Education, London: I. B. Tauris.

Piamenta, Moshe (1966), Studies in the Syntax of Palestinian Arabic: Simple Verb Forms in Subordinate and Main Clauses of Complex Sentences, Jerusalem: The Israel Oriental Society.

Piamenta, Moshe (1968), Speak Arabic: An Introduction to Eretz Yisraeli Arabic, Tel-Aviv: Maariv.

Piamenta, Moshe (1979), 'The Negev Bedouin Verbal Etiquette System and its Linguistic Description', in Studia Orientalia: Memoriae D. H. Baneth Dedicata, Jerusalem: The Hebrew University Magnes Press, pp. 125–73.

Piamenta, Moshe (1981), 'Selected Syntactic Phenomena of Jerusalem Arabic Narrative Style in 1900', in Shlomo Morag, Issachar Ben-Ami and Norman Stillman (eds), *Studies in Judaism and Islam*, Jerusalem: The Hebrew University Magnes Press, pp. 203–30.

Piamenta, Moshe (2000), *Jewish Life in Arabic Language and Jerusalem Arabic in Communal Perspective: A Lexico-Semantic Study*, Leiden: Brill.

The Political Committee [of Mapai] (24 January 1952), 'Protocol of the Meeting', *The Lavon Archive of the Histadrut in Tel-Aviv*, Files 2-026-1952-10.

Pores, Yoni (2015), 'Lo Rak Tsalav: Ha-Historia Ha-lo-Notzrit shel "Batay Ha-Sefer Ha-Notzrim"', 'Not Only a Cross: The Non-Christian History of the "Christian Schools"', in *Ha'aretz*, 8 December 2015, available at <http://www.haaretz.co.il /blogs/sadna/1.2794459> (last accessed 18 December 2015).

Prawer, Joshua (1981), 'Preface', in Shlomo Morag, Issachar Ben-Ami and Norman Stillman (eds), *Studies in Judaism and Islam*, Jerusalem: The Hebrew University Magnes Press, pp. 9–10.

Rabbath, Edmond (1962), 'The Common Origin of the Arabs', in Sylvia G. Haim (ed.), *Arab Nationalism: An Anthology*, Berkeley: University of California Press.

Rajuan, Maureen and Zvi Bekerman (2010), 'Inside and outside the Integrated Bilingual Palestinian-Jewish Schools in Israel: Teachers' Perceptions of Personal, Professional and Political Positioning', *Teaching and Teacher Education*, pp. 1–11.

Ram, Uri (2008), *The Globalization of Israel: MacWorld in Tel-Aviv and Jihad in Jerusalem*, New York: Routledge.

Rampton, Ben (2006), *Language in Late Modernity*, Cambridge: Cambridge University Press.

Rampton, Ben (2015), 'Post-panoptic Standard Language?', in *Working Papers in Urban Language and Literacies*, Paper 162, London: King's College, available at <https://www.academia.edu/13106780/WP162_Rampton_2015._Post-panoptic_ standard_language> (last accessed 6 November 2015).

Rampton, Ben, Jan Blommaert, Karel Arnaut and Massimiliano Spotti (2015), 'Superdiversity and Sociolinguistics', in Working Papers in *Urban Language and Literacies: Paper 152*, available at <http://www.lrc.columbia.edu/sites /lrc/files/Rampton%2C%20Blommaert%2C%20Arnaut%2C%20 Spotti%282015%29%20Superdiversity%20and%20sociolinguistics.pdf> (last accessed 6 November 2015).

Ravid, Barak (2012), 'Netanyahu: Israel soon to Require National Service for Israeli Arabs', in *Ha'aretz*, 29 April 2012, available at <http://www.haaretz.com

/israel-news/netanyahu-israel-soon-to-require-national-service-for-israeli
-arabs-1.427078> (last accessed 9 December 2015).

Ricoeur, Paul, (1990), *Time and Narrative, vol. 3*, trans. Kathleen Blamey and David
Pellauer, Chicago: University of Chicago Press.

Riḍa, Rashid (1934), *Al-Khilāfa Aw Al-Imāma Al-ʿUthmā*, [in Arabic; 'The Caliphate
or the Great Imamate'], Cairo: Maṭbaʿat Al-Manār bi-Miṣr (Al-Manār Press).

Rogan, Eugene (2009), *The Arabs: A History*, New York: Basic Books.

Romano-Hvid, Carmit (2015), 'Zionism and Bilingualism: Palestinian-Jewish
Bilingual Schools in Documentary Films', unpublished manuscript.

Rosenhouse, Judith (1984), *The Bedouin Arabic Dialects: General Problems and a Close
Analysis of North Israel Bedouin Dialects*, Wiesbaden: Otto Harrassowitz.

Rosenhouse, Judith (2008), 'Colloquial Arabic (in Israel): The Case of English
Loanwords in a Minority Language with Diglossia', In Judith Rosenhouse and
Rotem Kowner (eds) *Globally Speaking: Motives for Adopting English Vocabulary
in Other Languages*, Toronto: Multilingual Matters, pp. 145–63.

Rosenhouse, Judith (2009), 'Jerusalem Arabic', in Encyclopedia of Arabic Language
and Linguistics (*EALL*), 2, pp. 481–93. Managing Editors Online Edition: Lutz
Edzard and Rudolf de Jong, Brill Online Reference Work.

Rosenhouse, Judith (2011), 'Tacit (Implicit) Language Acquisition and Arabic
Dialects', in Durand Olivier, Angela Diana Langone and Guiliano Mion (eds),
Alf Lahja Wa-Lahja 'A Thousand Dialects': Proceedings of the 9th AIDA Conference,
Vienna: Institut fur Orientalistik der Universitat Wien, pp. 387–94.

Rosenhouse, Judith and Haya Fisherman (2008), 'Hebrew: Borrowing Ideology and
Pragmatic Aspects in a Modern(ised) Language', In Judith Rosenhouse and
Rotem Kowner (eds) *Globally Speaking: Motives for Adopting English Vocabulary
in Other Languages*, Toronto: Multilingual Matters, pp. 121–44.

Rosenhouse, Judith and Rotem Kowner (eds) (2008), *Globally Speaking: Motives for
Adopting English Vocabulary in Other Languages*, Toronto: Multilingual Matters.

Rouhana, Nadim (1997), *Palestinian Citizens in an Ethnic Jewish State: Identities in
Conflict*, New Haven: Yale University Press.

Saban, Ilan and Mohammad Amara (2002), 'The Status of Arabic in Israel: Reflections
on the Power of Law to produce Social Change', *Israel Law Review*, Hebrew
University Faculty of Law, vol. 36, no. 2, summer 2002, pp. 5–39.

Said, Edward (1978), *Orientalism*, New York: Pantheon Books.

Saʿdi, Ahmad (2014), *Thorough Surveillance: The Genesis of Israeli Policies of Population
Management, Surveillance and Political Control towards the Palestinian Minority*,
Manchester: Manchester University Press.

Salibi, Kamal (1993), *The Modern History of Jordan*, London: I. B. Tauris.

Schwedler, Jillian (2012), 'The Political Geography of Protest in neoliberal Jordan', *Middle East Critique*, 21: 3, pp. 259–70.

Shafir, Gershon and Yoel Peled (2002), *Being Israeli*, Cambridge: Cambridge University Press.

Shammas, Anton (1989), *Arabesques*, trans. Vivian Eden, New York: Harper & Row.

Shehadeh, Haseeb (1995), 'Børad and His Brothers in the Kufir-Yasif Dialect', in: *Dialectologia Arabica. A Collection of Articles in Honour of the Sixtieth Birthday of Professor Heikki Palva*, Studia Orientalia, ed. the Finnish Oriental Society, 75, Helsinki, pp. 229–38.

Shehadeh, Haseeb (2014a), 'On the Arabic in Israel', in *Al-Hasad* 4, pp. 188–222, Kfar Saba, Israel: Beit Berl College, Arab Academic Institute for Education.

Shehadeh, Haseeb (2014b), 'A View on the Phenomenon of the Extinction of Languages and the Future of Arabic Language', in *Al-Hasad* 4, pp. 103–28, Kfar Saba, Israel: Beit Berl College, Arab Academic Institute for Education.

Shenhav, Yehouda (2006), *The Arab Jews*, Stanford: Stanford University Press.

Shenhav, Yehouda (2012), 'Ha-Politika vi-Ha-Ti'ologia shel Ha-tirgum: Keitzad Mitargimim Nakba mi-'Aravit li-'Ivrit?', [in Hebrew; 'The Politics and Theology of Translation: How do you Translate Nakba from Arabic to Hebrew?', *Sotziologia Yisraelit, (Israeli Sociology)* (1), pp. 157–84.

Shohamy, Elana (2007), 'Reinterpreting Globalization in Multilingual Contexts', in *International Multilingual Research Journal*, 1(2), pp. 1–7.

Shohamy, Elana and Marwan Abu Ghazaleh-Mahajneh (2012), 'Linguistic Landscape as a Tool for Interpreting Language Vitality: Arabic as a Minority Language in Israel', in Durk Gorter, Heiko Marten and Luk Van Mensel (eds), *Minority Languages in the Linguistic Landscape*, New York: Palgrave Macmillan, pp. 89–108.

Shohamy, Elana, Eliezer Ben-Rafael and Monica Barni (eds) (2010), *Linguistic Landscape in the City*, Bristol: Multilingual Matters.

Shohat, Ella (1988), 'Sephardim in Israel: Zionism from the Point of View of its Jewish Victims', *Social Text*, 19–20 (fall), pp. 1–35.

Shohat, Ella (2013), 'The Sephardi-Moorish Atlantic: Between Orientalism and Occidentalism', in Evelyn Alsultany and Ella Shohat (eds), *Between the Middle East and America: The Cultural Politics of Diaspora*, Ann Arbor: University of Michigan Press, pp. 42–64.

Shryock, Andrew (1997), *Nationalism and the Genealogical Imagination: Oral History and Textual Authority in Tribal Jordan*, Berkeley: University of California Press.

Shryock, Andrew (2006), review of Joseph Massad, *Colonial Effects: The Making of National Identity in Jordan* (New York: Columbia University Press, 2001), in *International Journal of Middle East Studies*, 38, pp. 478–9.

Silverstein, Michael (1979), 'Language Structure and Linguistic Ideology', In Paul Clyne, William Hanks and Carol Hofbauer (eds), *The Elements: A Parasession on Linguistic Units and Levels*, Chicago: Chicago Linguistic Society, pp. 193–247.

Skop, Yarden (2014a), 'Jury out on whether Israeli Law Schools should Teach in English too', *Ha'aretz*, 6 March 2014, available at <http://www.haaretz.com.proxy1.cl.msu.edu/news/israel/1.578216> (last accessed 7 July 2015).

Skop, Yarden (2014b), 'English Law Studies in Israel Nipped in the Bud', *Ha'aretz*, 11 April 2014, available at <http://www.haaretz.com.proxy1.cl.msu.edu/news/israel/.premium-1.584935> (last accessed 7 July 2015).

Skutnabb-Kangas, Tove (2009), 'Multilingual Education for Global Justice: Issues, Approaches, Opportunities', Tove Skutnabb-Kangas, Robert Phillipson, Ajit K. Mohanty and Minati Panda (eds), *Social Justice through Multilingual Education*, Bristol: Multilingual Matters, pp. 19–35.

Skutnabb-Kangas, Tove and Robert Phillipson (eds) (1994), *Linguistic Human Rights: Overcoming Linguistic Discrimination*, Berlin: Mouton de Gruyter.

Smith, Charles (1996), *Palestine and the Arab-Israeli Conflict*, 3rd edn, New York: St. Martin's Press.

Smooha, Sammy (1989), *Arabs and Jews in Israel*, Boulder, CO: Westview Press.

Smooha, Sammy (2001), 'The Model of Ethnic Democracy', European Centre for Minority Issues, ECMI Working Papers # 13, p. 24.

Somekh, Sasson (1991), *Genre and Language in Modern Arabic Literature*, Wiesbaden: Otto Harrassowitz.

Somekh, Sasson (1994), 'Lost Voices: Jewish Authors in Modern Arabic Literature', in Hanna Wirth-Nesher (ed.), *What is Jewish Literature?* Philadelphia: The Jewish Publication Society, pp. 188–98.

Somekh, Sasson (2007), *Baghdad Yesterday: The Making of an Arab Jew*, Jerusalem: Ibis Publications.

Somekh, Sasson (2012a), *Life after Baghdad: Memoir of an Arab Jew in Israel*, trans. Tamar Cohen, Eastbourne: Sussex Academic Press.

Somekh, Sasson (2012b), *Naguib Mahfouz: Fiction, Encounters, translations* [in Hebrew], Jerusalem: Carmel Publications.

Spivak, Gayatri Chakravorty (1999), *A Critique of Post-Colonial Reason: Toward a History of a Vanishing Present*, Boston: Harvard University Press.

Spivak, Gayatri Chakravorty ([1989] 2010), '"Can the Subaltern Speak?" revised edition, from the "History" chapter of *Critique of Postcolonial Reason*', in Rosalind C. Morris (ed.) *Can the Subaltern Speak? Reflections on the History of an Idea*, New York: Columbia University Press, pp. 21–80.

Spolsky, Bernard (2004), *Language Policy*, Cambridge: Cambridge University Press.

Spolsky, Bernard (2014), *The Languages of the Jews: A Sociolinguistic History*, Cambridge: Cambridge University Press.

Spolsky, Bernard and Robert Cooper (1991), *The Languages of Jerusalem*, Oxford: Clarendon Press.

Spolsky, Bernard, and Elana Shohamy (1999), *The Languages of Israel: Policy, Ideology and Practice*, Clevedon: Multilingual Matters.

Spolsky, Bernard, Hanna Tushyeh, Muhammad Amara and Kees de Bot (with the assistance of Naseef Mu'allem, Judith Musleh and Wael Abdeen) (2000), *Languages in Bethlehem: The Sociolinguistic Transformation of a Palestinian Town*, Amsterdam: Royal Tropical institute.

Starr, Deborah and Sasson Somekh (eds) (2011), *Mongrels or Marvels: The Levantine Writings of Jacqueline Shohet Kahanoff*, Stanford: Stanford University Press.

Stasiulis, Daiva and Nira Yuval-Davis (eds) (1995), *Unsettling Settler Societies*, London: Sage Publications, pp. 291–332.

Stone, Chris (2014), 'Teaching Arabic in the US after 9/11', *Jadaliyya*, 11 April 2014, available at <http://www.jadaliyya.com/pages/index/17286/teaching-arabic-in -the-us-after-9-11n> (last accessed 29 September 2015).

Strickland, Patrick, 'We are not Citizens with Equal Rights: Controversial Jewish State Bill Follows a Series of Laws Targeting Israel's Arab Minority, Rights Groups Say', *Al-Jazeera*, 3 December 2014, available at <http://www.aljazeera.com/news /middleeast/2014/12/are-not-citizens-with-equal-rights-201412214135428310 .html> (last accessed 11 November 2014).

Suleiman, Camelia (2010), 'Contending Visions of Arabic Linguistics and their Historical Roots', *Middle East Critique*, vol. 19, no. 2, pp. 115–34.

Suleiman, Camelia (2011), *Language and Identity in the Israel-Palestine Conflict: The Politics of Self-Perception in the Middle East*, London: I. B. Tauris.

Suleiman, Camelia (2016), 'The Arabic Language ideology and Communication: An Image from Egypt', in Donal Carbaugh (ed.), *Handbook of Cross-Cultural Communication*, London: Taylor & Francis, pp. 42–54.

Suleiman, Camelia and Russell Lucas (2012), 'Debating Arabic on Al-Jazeera: Endangerment and Identity in Divergent Discourses', *The Middle East Journal of Culture and Communication* 5: 2, pp. 1–21.

Suleiman, Yasir (ed.) (1996), *Language and Identity in the Middle East and North Africa*, Oxford: Routledge.

Suleiman, Yasir (1999), 'Language and Political Conflict in the Middle East: A Study in Symbolic Sociolinguistics', in Yasir Suleiman (ed.), *Language and Society in the Middle East and North Africa: Studies in Variation and Identity*, London: Curzon Press, pp. 10–37.

Suleiman, Yasir (2003), *The Arabic Language and National Identity: A Study in Ideology*, Washington, DC: Georgetown University Press.

Suleiman, Yasir (2010), *Arabic, Self and Identity: A Study of Conflict and Displacement*, Oxford: Oxford University Press.

Suleiman, Yasir (2013), *Arabic in the Fray: Language Ideology and Cultural Politics*, Edinburgh: Edinburgh University Press.

Talmon, Rafi (2000), 'Preparation of the Northern Israeli Arabic Sprachatlas: A Report', in Abderrahim Youssi, Fauzia Benjelloun, Mohamed Dahbi and Zakia Iraqui-Sinaceur (eds), *Aspects of The Dialects of Arabic Today: Proceedings of the 4th Conference of the International Arabic Dialectology Association (AIDA), Marrakesh, 1–4 April, 2000*, Rabat: Amapatrail, pp. 68–80.

Tamari, Salim (2015), 'You are here! You were here: Chutzpa or Kharbata?', in *Jadaliyya*, 24 September 2015, available at <http://www.jadaliyya.com/pages/index/22754/you-are-here-you-were-here-chutzpah-or-kharbata> (last accessed 24 September 2015).

The Times of Israel (2014), 'Israeli Lawmakers Push Hebrew-Only Bill', available at <http://www.timesofisrael.com/israeli-lawmakers-push-hebrew-only-bill/> (last accessed 9 December 2015).

Trumper-Hecht, Nira (2010), 'Linguistic Landscape in Mixed Cities in Israel from the Perspective of "Walkers": The Case of Arabic', in Shohamy, Ben-Rafael and Barni, pp. 235–51.

Ṭuqan, Fadwa ([1987] 1991), *A Mountainous Journey: A Poets Autobiography*, trans. Olive Kenny, MN: Graywolf Press.

Urry, J. (2000), *Sociology beyond Societies: Mobilities for the 21st Century*, London: Routledge.

Vatanabadi, Shouleh (2013), 'The Uneven Bridge of Translation: Turkey in Between East and West', in Evelyn Alsultany and Ella Shohat (eds), *Between the Middle East and the Americas: The Cultural Politics of Diaspora*, Ann Arbor: University of Michigan Press, pp. 299–318.

Vertovec, Steven (2007), 'Super-diversity and its Implications', *Ethnic and Racial Studies* 30 (6), pp. 1024–54.

Vertovec, Steven (2010), 'Towards Post-Multiculturalism: Changing Communities, Contexts and Conditions of Diversity', *International Social Science Journal* 199, pp. 83–95.

Wahba, Kassem, Zeinab Taha and Liz England (eds) (2006), *Handbook for Arabic Teaching in the 21st Century*, Mahwah, NJ: Lawrence Erlbaum.

Weiss, Yfat (2014), *Nisiʿa vi-Nisiʿa Midoma: Leah Goldberg Bi-Girmanya 1930–1933*, [in Hebrew; 'A Journey and an Imagined Journey: Leah Goldberg in Germany 1930–1933'], Jerusalem: Mirkaz Zalman Shazar.

Wiley, Terrence (2014), Lecture given at Michigan State University, 'Consideration for Linguistic Landscape Analysis in the Midwest with a few Lessons Learned from the Southwest', available at <http://sites.cal.msu.edu/linguisticlandscapes /lecture-by-dr-wiley/> (last accessed 30 March 2015).

Yadid, Judd (2013), 'Word of the day/ Melhemet Hasafot-Sabra-rattling at the Technion', *Ha'aretz*, 1 August 2013, available at <http://www.haaretz.com .proxy1.cl.msu.edu/misc/article-print-page/.premium-1.539099?trailingPath=2 .169%2C2.216%2C2.221%2C2.487%2C> (last accessed 7 July 2015).

Yitzhaki, Dafna (2008), *Minority Languages and Language Policy: The Case of Arabic in Israel*, PhD dissertation, submitted to the English Department, Ramat Gan: Bar-Ilan University.

Yom, Sean (2014), 'Tribal Politics in Contemporary Jordan: The Case of the Hirak Movement', in *Middle East Journal*, vol. 68, pp. 229–47.

Youssi Abderrahim, Fouzia Benjelloun, Mohamed Dahbi and Zakia Iraqui-Sinaceur (eds) (2000), *Aspects of the Dialects of Arabic Today: Proceedings of the 4th Conference of the International Arabic Dialectology (AIDA), Marrakesh, April 1–4, 2000*, Rabat: Amapatrail.

Ziadeh, Nicola (1957), *Syria and Lebanon*, New York: Frederick Praeger.

Index

EU representative:
Easy Access System Europe
Mustamäe tee 50, 10621 Tallinn, Estonia
Gpsr.requests@easproject.com

www.ingramcontent.com/pod-product-compliance
Lightning Source LLC
Chambersburg PA
CBHW050351270326
41926CB00016B/3697